NOSTRADAMUS

JAMES LAVER

Nostradamus
or The Future Foretold

*Ca épouvante et énerve
l'imagination*
NAPOLEON III

GEORGE MANN · MAIDSTONE

James Laver
NOSTRADAMUS
or The Future Foretold

Copyright © James Laver 1942, 1952, 1973

First published in the United Kingdom by Collins, 1942
Substantially revised edition published by Penguin Books, 1952
Further revised edition published 1973

Reprinted 1978

ISBN 0 7041 0010 X

Printed in Great Britain by
Biddles Ltd, Guildford, Surrey
for George Mann Books, P.O. Box 22, Maidstone,
in the County of Kent

CONTENTS

PROLOGUE	7
1. *Nostradamus the Physician*	13
2. *Nostradamus the Prophet*	37
3. *The House of the Seven*	60
4. *The House of Bourbon*	90
5. *Nostradamus and the History of England*	117
6. *Nostradamus and the French Revolution*	138
7. *Nostradamus and Napoleon I*	165
8. *The Restoration that was and the Restoration that wasn't*	190
9. *To the End of the World*	218
EPILOGUE	242
APPENDIX	
The Prophecy of Olivarius and the 'Prophétie d'Orval'	253
BIBLIOGRAPHY	
Principal Early Editions of the Centuries; *List of Principal Commentators; Other Works Consulted*	262

Prologue

NOSTRADAMUS is a name, like so many others, which crops up from time to time in everybody's reading. He is usually spoken of, at least in references of the last hundred years or so, with a tinge of contempt – one more figure in the endless procession of charlatans which has wended its way through history, a man who might perhaps have deceived his contemporaries and enjoyed some credit in the ages of superstition but in these enlightened times recognizably a fraud and unworthy of the attention of serious men.

So he remained in my own mind, pigeon-holed with Cagliostro and Old Moore for some years, although during those years I must, sometime, have looked him up in the *Biographie Universelle* or a similar publication, for I knew that he was born at St Remy in Provence and spent most of his life at Salon. During a tour in the south of France I passed through both these places and, remembering their connexion with Nostradamus, made a mental note to glance at the astrologer's works if they should ever come my way.

A year later I was engaged in that most fascinating of all occupations of the hour of idleness, strolling along the *quais* in Paris and pausing from time to time to turn over the *bouquins* in the booksellers' stalls perched so precariously on the edge of the Seine. In one of these, somewhere on the Quai St Michel, on the south bank of the river, I came across a somewhat battered little book bound in frayed yellow leather. It was Bareste's edition of Nostradamus.

'*Combien, Madame?*'

The proprietress of the stall glanced from me to the book and back again. Obviously price was a matter which depended as much upon the look of the prospective purchaser as on the appearance of the wares. Neither in this instance was in 'mint condition': no *jeunesse dorée*, no 'top edges gilt'. Calculations of lightning rapidity went on in the brain beneath that screwed back hair and after barely a second, the sibyl spoke.

'*Quinze francs, monsieur.*'

With my prize in my pocket, for the volume is a small one, I made my way along the *quai*, past the Louvre and the Pont Neuf, until I reached, opposite *l'abside de Notre Dame* (an appropriate spot for a first perusal of Nostradamus) the little restaurant of the *Cloche d'Or*, grubbily uninviting without but full of good savours within. Having deciphered with some difficulty the blue print menu, I ordered my luncheon and, with the first mouthful of the *paté maison* and the first *gorgée* of Chateauneuf du Pape, I opened the book.

My first feeling was one of intense disappointment. I had expected a certain obscurity but the reality was worse than I had feared. It was not that the text was difficult, in spite of the crabbed French with its strange inversions and abbreviations. It reads rather like a literal translation from Latin and some scholars believe this to have been the case. No! It was rather an obscurity of theme, a lack of connecting link. I had thought in my ignorance that the *Centuries* were centuries of years and not merely centuries of quatrains, arbitrarily jumbled together. Whatever the clue to Nostradamus might be it was obviously not a chronological one, for there seemed to be little or no connexion between one quatrain and the next. Was this the work which had been taken seriously by some of the most eminent minds, was this the book that had had a place in the library of Pascal?

I began dipping into it at hazard. Rumours of war, hints of famine, prophecies of pestilence, the death of monarchs, disasters by sea and land, portents and signs in heaven, assassinations and tumults, monstrous births, astrological conjunctions, swarms of bees – all these moved before my eyes in a series of dissolving views, dissolving before one could quite grasp their outline, or understand their place in time.

> *La grande famine que je sens approcher*
> *Souvent tourner, puis estre universelle,*

> *Si grande et longue qu'on viendra arracher*
> *Du bois racine, et l'enfant de mammelle.*

Earthquakes and great hail:

> *Le tremblement si fort au mois de May,*
> *Saturne, Caper, Iupiter, Mercure au bœuf:*
> *Venus aussi, Cancer, Mars, en Nonnay,*
> *Tombera gresle lors plus grosse qu'un œuf.*

Not all are as vague. In some there is almost a plethora of names:

> *La tour marine trois fois prise et reprise,*
> *Par Espagnols, Barbares, Ligurins:*
> *Marseille et Aix, Arles par ceux de Pise,*
> *Vast, feu, fer, pillé Avignon des Thurins.*

What can be made of such a catalogue of disasters? How can one hope to relate them to particular historical events?

Suddenly my eye was caught by the name Varennes. Now, as Dumas *père* justly remarks in the little-known book in which he describes his attempt to reconstruct one of the most famous episodes in French history, the little town of Varennes is remembered for one thing and one thing only, the flight of Louis XVI. It had never been heard of in history before, it is never likely to be 'in the news' again. What had Nostradamus to say about Varennes?

To my surprise I found that the quatrain in question was concerned with a nocturnal journey through a forest – by two people, one in white and one in grey, and that it ended with the astonishing line:

> *Esleu cap. cause tempeste, feu, sang, tranche.*

Could '*Esleu cap*' be the Elected Capet, the first Constitutional King of France? That granted, the word *tranche* leaps to the eye, or rather to the ear, like the sound of the falling knife between the tall uprights of the guillotine. My interest in Nostradamus began to revive.

It has been growing steadily ever since. As soon as I could I procured as many editions of the *Centuries* as possible, including some quite worthless publications of recent years when the sense of impending disaster induced a boom in cheap prophecy. I learned that Nostradamus was a Jew, that he died in 1566, that he was a noted and enlightened physician, and that, in spite of his protestations to the contrary, he certainly dabbled in Magic.

When the War came I had already begun to sketch out a life and a study of his prophecies. Another visit to St Remy and Salon had become difficult, but I still hoped to spend some time in Paris, working at the *Bibliothèque Nationale*. I had made arrangements for a seat in the plane which still flew in the early months of 1940, but the collapse of France put an end to that project also. So I was constrained to pursue my study of Nostradamus in the intervals of work of more national importance, reading the *Centuries* in railway waiting-rooms or the crowded corridors of trains and scribbling in the cellar of a London house while the sirens wailed and the 'crump' of bombs came audibly nearer –

> *Sera laissé feu vif, mort caché*
> *Dedans les globes horrible espouvantable.*

A great danger awaits any one who sets out to interpret the quatrains of Nostradamus. He becomes so completely engrossed in the fascinating crossword puzzle of the text, in the Sherlock Holmes pursuit of clues and cryptograms that in the end he is liable to become the victim of his own ingenuity, and to see connexions and meanings where none can reasonably be supposed to exist. All the commentators have succumbed in some measure to this tendency and I do not imagine that I have completely escaped it myself. But I have tried to play fair, and if there is some inconvenient fact which spoils the beautiful rotundity of a particular prophecy, I have stated it plainly to the best of my ability in the text or in a footnote.

Such a work as the present one would have been quite impossible without the researches of those who have gone before. In particular one must bear tribute to Bareste, to Le Pelletier, to the Abbé Torné-Chavigny and to Elisée du

Vignois. The last named, in spite of his occasional absurdities, is most useful for the prophecies covering the second half of the nineteenth century. Among the very few English commentators, Charles A. Ward should not be forgotten. His *Oracles of Nostradamus* came into my hands very late and was both a help and a disappointment to me, for I found he had anticipated some of the minor discoveries which I had thought to be my own. A list of the principal commentaries will be found at the end of the book.

The study of the Prophet certainly broadened the scope of my own reading and in that alone it more than repaid the difficult researches of the years of war. I read large numbers of books on every variety of occult phenomena and came to the conclusion that the occultists were not nearly such fools as my superficial rationalism had led me to suppose. I experimented with telepathy and crystal-gazing, I attended séances and visited a number of clairvoyants, some of whom told me remarkable things. The well-known astrologer Mr Louis de Wohl very kindly worked out my horoscope in my presence in order that I might understand the method of procedure. I read enough astrological and magical treatises to familiarize myself with their terminology. I turned a few tables. Lest the reader should think that I took a header into every kind of superstition, let me hasten to add that I am not yet convinced of the validity of the spiritualist hypothesis. But I came at least to the conclusion that the human mind and the human soul were very much more complicated than I had been willing to believe, and that in these twilight realms we are only at the very beginning of our knowledge. Complete scepticism is as unwarrantable as complete credulity, and while I feel obliged to reject much that others have found in Nostradamus, I find myself quite unable to explain him away. This blend of tempered belief and modified scepticism I have tried to preserve throughout the book.

I would like to thank M. Denis Saurat for information with regard to French booksellers and antiquarians of which I was unable to make as much use as I should have liked,

Mr Milton Waldman for enthusiastic encouragement in my long task, Mr Louis de Wohl for the service above mentioned, and Mr Jacques Reval for so kindly reading the complicated and difficult proofs.

CHAPTER ONE

Nostradamus the Physician

THE writer on Nostradamus faces a problem of peculiar – perhaps unique – difficulty. Is he to attempt a biography? The actual life of Nostradamus is the least interesting part of his story; his importance is only made manifest by events which occurred long after he was dead. Is he, with special emphasis on France, and some reference to England, to survey the field of European history for the last four hundred years? Such a task would be onerous and unnecessary. Is he to produce a study of Prophecy, or a discourse on Magic, or to attempt some kind of scientific and philosophic analysis of the Nature of Time? None of these things would singly be sufficient, yet all of them are in some sort necessary for the adequate understanding of this extraordinary man.

There is, however, one thing which may serve as a connecting link between all these different problems, one fact which perhaps will enable us to place them all in their proper relationship and see them in their right perspective: Nostradamus was a Jew.

Now, whatever may be thought of the Jews, they are certainly a very mysterious people. They seem to be eternal. Almost at the dawn of history they are already race conscious and separate from their neighbours; they are with us to-day. Why one particular Semitic tribe should have shown such powers of persistence must for ever baffle the rationalist historian. The Hittites have vanished almost without trace; the Amalekites are merely a name in the Hebrew scriptures; there is no Jebusite Problem in the modern world. But there is a Jewish Problem and perhaps there always will be.

This People has never been popular, yet all efforts to destroy them have failed. Enslaved in Egypt, they escape to found a nation. Carried into captivity in Babylonia they return bearing the spoils of their conquerors. Subjugated by the Romans they refuse to accept the blessings of the Pax Romana. When Titus destroyed their Temple he merely scattered their seed abroad. Nations exclude them, grudgingly admit them, persecute them, drive them out. But no nation's history can be written without some reference to the Jews. In the warp and woof of mankind's story they run like a single-coloured thread, a thread which is never broken.

This homelessness and this persistence in adversity gave rise to the symbolical figure of the Wandering Jew, the Wandering Jew who in each age was a living reality, staggering wearily from country to country, his head bent, his beard long on his bosom and on his bowed back the pack of the pedlar. The pack contained many things, trinkets, medicines, perfumes, anything that could be crowded into a small compass. It also contained the whole tradition of Magic.

In this enlightened age we are all convinced that Magic is nonsense – or are we? Which of us can lay our hands on our hearts and say that we are quite sure? As soon as we begin to investigate the matter we find at least a curious persistence (equalled only by that of the Jews) in its methods and traditions. It is now called by many different names and has adopted many disguises, yet the doctrines of a Madame Blavatsky differ only in unessentials from those of the Gnostic doctors; Paracelsus joins hands with both Pythagoras and modern Yoga, and tables are turned to-day by precisely the same methods as those used in ancient Rome. Whatever else Magic may be it is something very much more than a way of performing conjuring tricks without apparatus.

On its speculative side it is a very profound system of transcendental philosophy, a system which seems both eternal and universal, for it speaks the same language in first-century Alexandria, in Renaissance Europe and in the modern world. It is a hidden but vital part of the history of every religion; indeed the occultists would claim that it is, behind all religions, the reality of which they are but the distorted shadows, the formalized rituals of which the meaning has been forgotten, the richly carven cups from which the precious fluid has escaped.

On its practical side it is a technique for putting the will into contact with elemental forces, which, by the proper methods – so the doctrine runs – can be brought under control. Magic is not explained away by saying that much of it is hypnotism, or auto-suggestion, or the activity of the unconscious mind. These new names merely prove that modern psychology, in one of its aspects, is nothing more nor less than a rationale of Magic.

But, be Magic what it may, it is inextricably mixed up with the story of the Jews. When Abraham fled from Ur of the Chaldees (and the Chaldaeans were the Magi *par excellence* for the whole of the ancient world) he may have brought no learning with him; Moses was plainly an Initiate of the Egyptian temples, but he may have imparted nothing to his fellows; Solomon may or may not have been a magician, as all antiquity believed, but when the Jews returned from the Great Captivity they were certainly aware of Magic then. Scholars agree that in the time of Josephus there were writings in the hands of the Essenes which provide ample evidence of a continuous cabalistic tradition.

The very fact that the word 'cabalistic' is generally used as meaning magical is proof of the important part played by the Jews, for the Cabala is a Jewish creation. When it was created is a matter of dispute, but the extreme sceptical view that it was an invention of the thirteenth century, when it first produced an extensive literature, has been generally abandoned. Schalscheleth hakabbâlâh, the Chain of Tradition, stretches farther back than that.

It stretches back at least to first-century Alexandria, that melting-pot of the peoples of the ancient world, the home of merchants and scholars and philosophers and magicians, and Jews who were all these things at once. The finest minds among them, including some of the greatest of the Neo-

Platonists, sought to create a new Wisdom and to unite in one stupendous synthesis the mythologies of Greece and Egypt, the Jewish Cabala, Assyrian astrology, Babylonian magic, Arabian divination and Platonic philosophy. Those who tried to include Christianity also were called Gnostics, and the Church in the end repudiated them. They have been harshly judged and what we know of them is largely derived from the writing of their enemies. But their Science of Angels, which claimed to provide a key to the Universe and to raise the individual soul to the ecstasy of mystical contemplation, was not without its influence even on Christian thought. We find its echo in the Biblical phrase, 'Thrones, or Dominions, or Principalities, or Powers'. Orthodoxy itself is tinged with its conceptions, and when the Church was triumphant Gnosticism did not dry up but plunged underground, like the sacred river Alph, to become the occult tradition of the sorcerers, those sorcerers whom no persecution could quite exterminate.

In years of persecution it is always certain that Jews will be among the chief sufferers. From the fifth to the eighth centuries they had no rest and it was only the coming of the more tolerant Mohammedans that allowed them to thrive once more in lands that acknowledged the Prophet. It also enabled them to absorb Arabian culture and, by a curious irony of history, to be the bearers to Christian Europe of the forgotten learning of the Greeks.

New persecution in Babylonia drove them along the caravan routes to Spain and there for a time they enjoyed a golden age. If they were traders and negotiators, they were also physicians, and if they were physicians they were also astrologers. The First Crusade stirred up hatred against them, however, and the campaign against the Albigensians ruined their prosperity in Provence. It was then, in the late thirteenth century, that the Tradition began to be written down, in a peculiar Aramaic dialect, and in a manner wilfully symbolical and obscure. A key was necessary to the Cabala and that key was still the spoken word. Without that, what could be made of its diagrams, or its categories of

Angels, of its symbolic beasts or its meditations upon the letters in the unspoken name of God? In the written records that have come down to us there is much apparent nonsense and superstition, but there is much also of profound import, and there is little doubt that it embodies the whole tradition of Magic.

As the sky darkened above the Jews and persecution, especially in Spain, became incessant, the Cabala assumed even more importance. With the establishment of the Spanish Inquisition in 1480 the outward practices of Jewry grew difficult and dangerous; the occult flourished all the more. The Cabala was the Jew's mystical and magical escape. Soon there was hardly anywhere in Europe where Jews dared to show themselves openly, but one of the places where reasonable toleration was still shown was, once more, Provence, under the mild and enlightened rule of René of Anjou.

René of Anjou has passed into French legend and nursery story as 'Good King René', but to the English mind he is a puzzling figure. For of what country was so obvious a Frenchman king? He had in fact two kingdoms, of Jerusalem and Sicily, but one he never visited and to the other he was never able to make his claim good. He was also Count of Provence and Duke of Lorraine, but in the middle of the fifteenth century he ceded his Duchy to his son, and some twenty years later he was driven out of his own domain of Anjou by Louis XI. He fixed his court in Provence in 1473 and in 1480 died at Aix aged seventy-two, after forty-six years' reign.

His political and private misfortunes, however, never extinguished the gay and cultivated spirit of the man. He was himself poet, painter and musician, and although we must, no doubt, make large allowance for the flattery of his courtiers, it is not every monarch who even troubles to acquire a reputation for the arts. He had a passion for dramatic representations and is said to have written mystery plays himself. He loved pageants and tournaments, encouraged agriculture, glass-making, spinning and weaving. He surrounded himself with poets and learned men, who lived upon his bounty and made his court a centre of the arts and sciences.

Now at the court of King René was a certain Jewish physician and astrologer, Jean de St Remy, '*médecin ordinaire et conseiller du roi*'. The Jews of Provence had been allowed the free practice of their religion by an edict of 1454, and under the tolerant René were allowed for a while to forget their persecutors. There came to Provence therefore another Jewish physician in the suite of René's son the Duke of Calabria. His name is said by some to have been Pierre de Nostra-Donna, frenchified as Nostradame and latinized as Nostradamus. It is more likely, however, that this name was adopted by his son Jaume or Jacques, a notary of St Remy, from the name of the *quartier* in which he lived. Pierre himself practised at Arles, but accompanied King René on his progresses through Provence.

On René's death the affairs of the Jews took a turn for the worse. Provence became part of the domain of the French Crown, and in 1488 Charles VIII issued a peremptory order that all Jews should choose between conversion and the loss of all their possessions. Louis XII confirmed this order in 1501, and either at this or the former date the two physicians followed the example of most of the Provençal Jews and were baptized.

This story has, for centuries, seemed to rest upon the most unimpeachable authority. We find it first in a work by César de Nostradame, the son of the Prophet: *Histoire et Chronique de Provence*, published in 1614. César, no doubt, derived the details from another *Chronique de Provence*, by his uncle, Jean de Nostrame, which, strangely enough, remained in manuscript and was not published until 1913.[1] Unfortunately for the credit of both, recent researches by Dr Edgar Leroy, physician of Saint-Remy, and M. H. Chobaut, Chief Archivist of Vaucluse,[2] have shown that the noble and picturesque background which has been hitherto

1. *See* C. Chabaneau and J. Anglade: *Jehan de Nostredame*, Paris, 1913.
2. *See Mémoires de l'Institut historique de Provence*, vol. XVII, 1941.

accepted by every writer on Nostradamus has no basis in fact.

The truth is that the forebears of Nostradamus on both sides were simpler and less exalted people than it pleased him to make out. He would, after all, not be the first person in history to glorify his ancestry by the aid of a little pious fiction; but we must, regretfully, reject all his stories of celebrated physicians and honoured advisers of Kings. Rather was it a world of small commerce and minor officialdom in the neighbourhood of Avignon, where a Jewish community found it possible to exist in comparative security if its members, from time to time, went through the motions of adopting Christianity.[1]

Be that as it may, Pierre de Nostredame had a son, Jacques. Jean de Saint-Remy had a daughter called Renée. A marriage was arranged between Renée and Jacques de Nostradame, and at St Remy, at midnight on the 14th December, 1503,[2] a son was born to them. It would be an interesting exercise for the modern astrologer to cast the horoscope of this infant destined to be the most famous of all those who have given themselves to the Divine Science.[3] As his parents had changed their religion he was not circumcised according to the Law of Moses, but baptized according to the Christian rite. He was given the name of the Archangel Michael, which after all was a name as acceptable to the Synagogue as to the Church. To that Church he professed all his life the most fervent attachment, and we shall never now know how far the professing Christian concealed the crypto-Jew. But we cannot understand the strange career of Nostradamus unless we are continually striving to see him against the background of his Hebrew inheritance.

Little Michel was soon followed by another son who was

1. The actual family connexions of Nostradamus are given in full detail in Raoul Busquet: *Nostradamus, sa Famille, son Secret*. Paris, 1950.

2. By the Julian Calendar; 23rd December by the Gregorian Calendar.

3. Mr C. Nelson Stewart has drawn my attention to Nos. 795 and 932 in Alan Leo's *Notable Nativities* in which this task is undertaken.

called Jean, and the two boys grew up for a time together. Jean de St Remy, anxious perhaps that his science should not be lost, decided to devote himself to the education of one of his grandsons. He chose Michel. The younger boy followed his father's profession with such success that he became Procureur at the Parlement of Toulouse. He also wrote a great many Provençal songs of which nothing is now remembered except that they were extremely coarse.

Michel seems to have gone to live with the old man; at all events he was given over entirely into his charge and soon began to reap the benefit of his intimate relationship with such a fountain of learning. Whether or not he taught the boy mathematics, Greek, Latin, Hebrew, and the Humanities as Nostradamus alleged, he allowed him to assist in the preparation of medicines, the gathering of herbs, the manufacture of unguents. He instructed him in the use of the astrolabe.

We learn from Chavigny,[1] the pupil and biographer of Nostradamus, that even as a youth he had a passion for the study of the stars, chiefly then, it would seem, in what we should call their astronomical aspects. But we should remember that the sharp distinction between astronomy and astrology which the modern world takes for granted would scarcely have been understood by the sixteenth-century mind.

What more did the old man teach him? Since Medicine and Magic were still inextricably intertwined and Astronomy and Astrology regarded merely as two facets of the same science, we may be sure that if the young student learned of the virtue of herbs he learned also to pluck them under the right aspects, and that if the positions and movements of the stars were known to him he was not unaware of the influence which they were supposed to wield upon the affairs of men.

Nostradamus was still only a child when his grandfather and tutor died. Fortunately he had another grandfather

---

1. Chavigny: *La Vie et le Testament de Michel Nostradamus.*

who took up the task of instruction where Jean de St Remy had laid it down. Perhaps because the paternal grandfather lived with the family, Michel returned to his father's house in the Rue de Barri at St Remy.

St Remy-en-Crau has now a somewhat forlorn air. In the sixteenth century it was a flourishing little Provençal town nestling at the bottom of the valley of the Glanum and surrounded by rocky crags. It was girt by high walls, and overshadowed by the great tower of the *Maison de la Cour* in which King René had been wont to lodge when travelling from Aix to Tarascon. Outside the town, on the road to Arles, lay the ruins of the Roman mausoleum and the triumphal arch. The busy, open-air life of Provence filled its streets with noise and colour. But it was a tiny place and not at all a seat of learning. When Michel had come to the very early age at which boys then entered the University it was decided to send him to Avignon.

Avignon has changed comparatively little in the last four hundred years, and if we can abolish in thought the wide Rue de la République which runs like a backbone through the length of the city, the imagination should have little difficulty in restoring it to its sixteenth-century aspect. Then, as now, the great Palace of the Popes, with the Cathedral behind it, dominated the town.

The Pope no longer lived at Avignon, but a Papal Legate had been installed there since 1409 and still kept great state. He had his own guard of soldiers in their blue, red and orange liveries. He was indeed the real ruler of the place, for Avignon was not technically a part of France, and did not become so until after the French Revolution. It was therefore a city of refuge for bankrupts and criminals. It was also the seat of a University.

Michel's first task was to satisfy the examiners, as we should say, in Grammar, Rhetoric and Philosophy. The first two seem to have given him little difficulty, for mediaeval and Renaissance learning was largely a matter of citations and his memory was excellent. In the third he was far in advance of the other pupils, especially in all matters relating to the stars and other natural phenomena, such knowledge being then comprised under the heading of philosophy. According to Chavigny,[1] he knew and taught his fellows, that the earth was round like a ball and that the sun, when it seemed to set, illuminated the other hemisphere. If Michel also instructed them, as his first biographer states, 'of the movements of the planets and the annual revolution of the earth round the sun', he was in advance not only of his fellow-schoolboys but of the current scientific belief of the time. Nearly a century later Galileo was to be persecuted for holding a similar opinion.

The notary looked with some disquiet upon his son's activities. In spite of their conversion Jews were still Jews, as they were unpleasantly reminded in 1512 when King Louis XII, in desperate need of money for the Italian wars, imposed a special tax on recent converts. The name of Nostradamus appears in the list of those who paid the tax in St Remy and the notary had no wish to attract the attention of the Church also. He decided to make his son a physician.

Now at Avignon, while law studies flourished, there was no good School of Medicine. It was therefore decided to send Michel, once he had passed the necessary grades, to study at Montpellier.

Montpellier had then the best School of Medicine in France – possibly in Europe. Its professors were among the first to study anatomy by the dissection of corpses, for the Duke of Anjou had given them the right, in 1376, to demand every year the body of one executed criminal. It was not perhaps a very generous allowance, but many schools had not even that, and the whole practice was still frowned upon as savouring of necromancy.

The University was in a most flourishing state and the students were in possession of many privileges which they did not fail to use, and abuse. It is hard to say why future physicians have throughout the ages so often proved the most turbulent of all student bodies. At Montpellier they

---

1. *La Vie et le Testament de Michel Nostradamus.*

were exempt from nearly all taxation and could not be cited before the ordinary magistrates. In former times they had been governed by a 'King' of their own choosing, but he proved himself such a Lord of Misrule that his office was abolished by the statutes of 1340. Nothing daunted, the students elected an 'Abbé' and this functionary was still in control in the time of Nostradamus. A few years later, in 1527, he too was abolished, only to be replaced by a 'Procureur' until in 1550 the assembly of professors, tried beyond further patience, contrived to put an end to the office as well as the name.

The students were in the habit of parading their Abbé about the streets with a guard of armed men, and the inevitable 'Town and Gown' riots frequently ended in bloodshed. The good bourgeois of Montpellier must often have wondered whether the city's increase in business and prestige by the presence of the university was really worth the danger to their windows and merchandise and to the morals of their wives.

Nostradamus, we may be sure, took little part in these extravagances. He was a 'reading man' if ever there was one, and his only anxiety was to squeeze the orange of learning dry. At Montpellier he was able to attend the lectures of some of the most celebrated physicians in Europe, and if he found in their teaching a strange mixture of medicine, alchemy and magic he was not conscious that a future age would consider the one valid and the other two mere superstitions.

For three years he followed the course prescribed by the Faculty until, at last, the time had come to be examined for his 'baccalauréat'. Written examinations had not yet been invented by the Jesuits, the Order itself being still in the future, and so the examination was still conducted in the mediaeval manner by means of a dispute. From eight in the morning until midday Nostradamus parried the questions of the professors, avoided their traps, gave proof of a learning equal to their own. At the end he was allowed to exchange his student's gown for a red robe with a hood, a garb which was still the dress of the period for persons of dignity and standing, and which has lasted as an academic survival down to our own day.

For three months he was required to teach in the schools, under surveillance, and was then allowed to sit for the four examinations called 'per intentionem', in which four different professors interrogated him concerning four different maladies. It was not easy to become a doctor in the University of Montpellier. Eight days later he presented himself before the Chancellor and 'pricked' a great medical treatise in order that chance might decide the fifth disease for which it was his duty to prescribe remedies. Even this was not the end. Before the doyen of the University he was presented with an aphorism of Hippocrates selected also at hazard, and given until the morrow to prepare a thesis upon it.

Next day in the church of Notre-Dame-des-Tables, in the Chapel of St Michel (throughout the life of Nostradamus his own name pursues him in the most extraordinary fashion) from midday until four o'clock he remained closeted with the professors, and this final trial over, he went a week later to receive his 'Licence' from the hands of the Bishop of Montpellier *'in aula episcopali'*, that is to say, in a room in the palace which the Bishop of Maguelone possessed in the ancient part of Montpellier, of which he was *Seigneur*. Officially Michel's student days were over, but, unlike some other physicians, he remained a student all his life.

A disastrous event was soon to give him the opportunity for new experience. Throughout the Middle Ages and for long afterwards the Plague was endemic in Provence, but every now and then it broke out with increased virulence. It devastated the whole countryside, it raged in the towns, trade and industry were brought to a standstill, and the people died by thousands. Scarcely had Nostradamus become a qualified physician than a savage outbreak of the pestilence occurred at Montpellier.

Plagues still break out in modern times and still cause many deaths. It has been estimated that more people died of the so-called Spanish influenza in 1918 than had been killed in the preceding four years of war. But such outbreaks no longer cause the same degree of panic, for modern sanitation reduces their virulence and modern medical practice in sterilization and the use of disinfectants gives confidence that the peril can be resisted and finally overcome. In the sixteenth century sanitary conditions were everywhere deplorable, disinfectants were unknown and every outbreak of disease was regarded with a superstitious terror which extended to the medical profession itself. The doctors whose duty it was to succour the afflicted were as terrified of the disease as their patients and the garb which they assumed for the purpose was more calculated to inspire horror than confidence. They clothed themselves in shirts soaked in magical juices and stained with seven different coloured powders, and over these tunics of leather supposed impervious to the passage of the tainted air. With spectacles on nose, a sponge tied over the nostrils and with a sprig of garlic in the mouth they hurried through the infected streets pursued more often than not by the insults and even the stones of the citizens who with an inverted logic held the medical profession in some part responsible for the outbreak.

Nostradamus was one of the most assiduous and one of the most successful. Why he should have been so is a matter of speculation. His self-confidence may have had a heartening effect, for he was a man of unquenchable courage in the presence of disease; but it seems likely that he was also in possession of some kind of disinfectant, for we hear much from his early biographers of a mysterious powder which he used to purify the air.

It certainly seems to have been efficacious, for his services were soon in demand not only in Montpellier but in the surrounding countryside. Like the plague itself, Nostradamus followed the course of the rivers – the Garonne and its tributaries – and visited hamlet after hamlet exercising his skill and gaining experience. He worked thus for four years, and whatever else may be thought of Nostradamus, this much at least is admitted even by his enemies, that he was a physician not only of more than common skill but of quite extraordinary devotion to duty.

Other towns claimed him, notably Carcassonne, where he had the satisfaction of curing the Bishop of various disorders by means of a pomade of his own manufacture. The composition of this pomade, which is given in his *Traité des Fardemens*, reminds us that we are still in the period of magical medicine, for it was compounded of lapis lazuli, coral and leaf gold and according to the learned doctor himself was a veritable elixir of life. 'This composition,' he says, 'rejuvenates the person who uses it: if he is sad or melancholy it makes him light and joyful; if he is timid, it makes him audacious; if he is taciturn it renders him affable by changing his qualities; if he is surly, it makes him sweet and kindly, as if he were but thirty years old; if his beard is turning grey it retards old age by much, preserves the colour in spite of the years, rejoices the heart and the whole person ... preserves from headaches and constipation, and augments the sperm in such abundance that a man can do whatever he wishes without damaging his health; and conserves the four humours in such symmetry and proportion that if a man had it from birth, he could live for ever; but He who has taught us to be born has taught us also to die.'[1]

It is impossible to say which of these remarkable qualities commended it most to '*Monseigneur Ammanien de Fays, le Reverendissime Evesque de Carcassonne,*' but there is no doubt of the high favour which the purveyor of the pomade henceforth enjoyed. Nostradamus indeed seems always to have been on good terms with the ecclesiastical authorities, perhaps because he took so much pains to keep so. For the plague was not the only pestilence now ravaging Provence. The Lutheran heresy had spread there also and was already dividing the cities into warring factions each accusing the other of having by their practices called down upon their fellow-citizens the vengeance of heaven. More than ever it behoved even a baptized Jew to walk warily and Nostra-

---

1. *Traité des Fardemens.* Chap. XXVI.

damus never left it in any doubt that in the quarrel between the Church and the Huguenots he was on the side of the Church.

From Carcassonne he passed to Toulouse, where he stayed long enough to set up house in the Rue de la Triperie, not far from the Place du Capitole. He spent some time at Narbonne where there were many Jews and where the schools of the Talmudists and the alchemists flourished. Like Nostradamus himself they had, at least outwardly, embraced Christianity, and we may be certain that he entered into close relations with them, and took the opportunity of adding to his knowledge. We do not know that he ever practised alchemy as it is now understood but we should remember once more that the distinction which the modern mind makes between the alchemist and the scientific laboratory worker had no meaning for the contemporaries of Nostradamus.

He visited Bordeaux and other towns and some time during these wanderings found himself back at Avignon, where so much of his youth had been spent. Here, in the intervals of tending the sick, he found time to prepare a certain 'quince jelly, of a sovereign beauty, goodness, taste and excellence proper to be presented to a king.' This he offered both to the Cardinal of Clermont, Legate of Avignon, and to the Grand Master of Rhodes who happened to be staying in the city. Later, to make good his boast, he was to present a sample of it to François I.

He was increasing his knowledge all the time. While in Avignon he made great use of the library, he gained clinical experience in tending his patients and he frequented the shops of the apothecaries. This was indeed his practice wherever he went and he soon collected a vast body of receipts in which medicine, gastronomy and mere superstition are strangely mingled and which he has preserved for our instruction in his extant writings.

After four years the plague seemed to have run its course and Nostradamus returned to Montpellier to take his degree as doctor. He was inscribed anew upon the books of the

University on October 23rd, 1529. He had to submit to a whole new series of examinations and he found that his success in curing the sick had by no means endeared him to the Faculty. Even such celebrated doctors as Antoine Romier, who was among his judges, showed that they were not at all anxious to receive among themselves one who had shown himself willing to use unauthorized remedies, and what was perhaps worse, to effect cures by them. However, the learning of Nostradamus could not be gainsaid, and, in the end, he was admitted to the doctorate. Clothed in their robes, and preceded by musicians, the whole Faculty went in procession to his house, and, leading him to the Church of St Firmin, where such ceremonies were usually performed, placed on his head the square cap of his new condition, put a ring on his finger and a girdle of gold round his waist and presented him with a bound volume of the works of Hippocrates.

Such an honour might have meant much more to Nostradamus before his wanderings, but now he had already enjoyed four years of liberty, using his own remedies and relying upon his own increasing knowledge. He found the restrictions of practice in Montpellier irksome, and, as one of his duties was to teach, he found it more and more difficult to do so along traditional lines. For some of his colleagues, for Antoine Suporta, for Guillaume Rondelet, for Honoré Castelan, he had a profound respect; for most of the Faculty nothing but contempt, and one day in 1531 he saddled his mule once more, got together his small baggage of books and instruments and left the town which had been his University and might have been the seat of a profitable practice.

For a further two years he wandered through Languedoc and Provence, visiting new cities like La Rochelle, revisiting old haunts like Bordeaux and Toulouse. He made the acquaintance of many of the notables of the district in their castles and country houses. Among these was no less a person than the Princess of Navarre, to whom he dedicated his transation in verse of the *Book of Orus Apollo, Son of Osiris, King of*

Egypt. The title is enough to show that his mind was already straying beyond the strict confines of medical learning, that he was already toying with the occult.

It was while he was at Toulouse that he received a letter from Julius Caesar Scaliger who had heard of his growing reputation and desired to make his acquaintance. This was a considerable compliment, for Scaliger was at that time the most celebrated scholar in Europe with the possible exception of Erasmus, with whom he had not hesitated to cross swords in controversy. In 1525 he had come to Agen in the suite, and as the physician, of the Bishop of Agen, Antonio della Rovere, and as he had liked the place he had stayed there. His Latin verse, of which he produced a prodigious quantity, is execrable, but his vast scientific learning was revered by his contemporaries, and he has been recognized even by such redoubtable later figures as Leibniz and Sir William Hamilton as one of the best modern exponents of the physics and metaphysics of Aristotle.

A man of such reputation and such congenial interests made a strong appeal to Nostradamus. Taking lodging in Agen he paid frequent visits to Scaliger, who owned the property called *de l'Escale* in a smiling valley near the little town, and the two *savants* found much pleasure in one another's company. That Scaliger afterwards turned against Nostradamus and referred to him in his writings in terms of calculated insult is no proof that they were not once on terms of intimate friendship, for that was the practice of Scaliger with all his friends.

He was so obviously happy in his wife, the beautiful Adriète de Loubéjac, and the two sons she had given him, that it would have been strange if the thoughts of Nostradamus had not turned to setting up house also. He had been for so long the Wandering Jew in his own person, and was, alas! to resume the role for an even longer period; but the Jew is not only a wanderer; he has, by nature, a strong sense of family and a desire even stronger than that of other races to leave descendants behind him. Nostradamus was now thirty years old; he was an acknowledged *savant*, he must already have received enough presents from rich clients to relieve him of the fear of poverty, and there was no reason why he should not practise his profession as profitably at Agen as elsewhere. He resolved to settle in the little place and to look about for a wife.

There was no lack of fathers in Agen who saw in the serious young physician a more than possible son-in-law. Nostradamus had, it is asserted, more than one chance of contracting a rich marriage. But his fancy had fallen upon a young girl 'of high lineage, very beautiful, very amiable', and it was her he married. Strangely enough the complimentary epithets are all that the biographers tell us. Her name is not mentioned and all that we know of her is that she made her husband happy and bore him two children, a son and a daughter.

There seemed no reason why Nostradamus should not remain at Agen for the rest of his days, watching his children grow up around him, becoming slowly richer as his fame spread throughout the district. For the things of the mind he had his own books and the friendship of Scaliger, and he might never have devoted himself to those more mysterious studies which were to give his name prominence. But it was not to be. The plague, against which he had fought so valiantly, broke out afresh and he who had saved so many from its ravages was unable to save his own kith and kin. Some critics have seen in this a proof of the vanity of his pretensions, but the gibe is hardly just and certainly less than generous. However it be, tragedy overwhelmed him in his own household. The pestilence slew his wife and his two children without his skill being able to do anything to save them, and Nostradamus was left once more alone.

His world had crumbled about him and there can be little doubt that he was profoundly unhappy. His reputation as well as his heart had suffered by the loss of those dearest to him, and he had to struggle with all those legal complications which so often seem to add a new terror to death. The family of his late wife started a lawsuit against him for the recovery of her dowry. But this was not the worst. Before the catastrophe (in 1534 to be exact) he had watched a workman casting in bronze the figure of the Virgin and had remarked that in manufacturing such images he was only making devils. It is probable that Nostradamus, essentially a man of the Renaissance, merely wished to imply that he found the Gothic form of the statue little to his taste, but the remark had been remembered and was now put forward as an accusation of heresy. Did not the Huguenots themselves declare that the images in the churches were so many idols and the honours paid to them the worship of devils?

The charge, for the moment, was not pressed,[1] but the paradise of Agen had been transformed into a place of torment. Nostradamus resolved to fly from it, and to become once more a wanderer.

His wanderings lasted eight years, and this time he was no longer content merely to traverse Provence from end to end revisiting his old haunts. He pushed farther afield, how far is a matter of uncertainty. But we know that he visited Guyenne and Dauphiné and Lorraine, travelled to Italy and even as far as Sicily. Wherever he went he established contact with the apothecaries and the physicians and with the Jews also, for many such were Jews. In every town there was a body of men who, although outwardly Christian, preserved much of the tradition of Israel, and if they practised medicine also dabbled in Magic.

While in Milan he came across an account in Latin of a feast given by a certain '*seigneur Trivulce*' on May 6th, 1488, and amused himself by translating it into French. It is printed at the end of some of the editions of his *Traité des Fardemens* and is a document of considerable interest for the historian of gastronomy, an interest which is not dissipated by the possibility that the date is invented, the translation a pretext and that Nostradamus had himself been present at such a banquet as he describes. His own taste, if he *were* present, must have been excited less by the procession of

---

[1] In 1538, when he had already set out on his travels, he was summoned before the Inquisitor sent from Toulouse to Agen to investigate charges of heresy. Nostradamus took good care not to appear.

roasted meats, venison, veal, capons, sucking pigs and peacocks than by a certain *confiture* of quinces '*avec sucre, girofle et cannelle*'. If we may judge by the receipts he collected for jams and preserves of all sorts, he had, in a marked degree, the sweet tooth of his race.

It was certainly during this period that his own gift of prophecy began to manifest itself. This gift, among the Jews, was traditionally associated with the tribe of Issachar, and Bareste, the early nineteenth century biographer of Nostradamus, claimed that he belonged to this tribe. But modern Jewish scholars are of opinion that this is an absurdity, since no Jew now knows from what tribe he is descended. Nostradamus himself says no more than that the gift was transmitted to him by his ancestors. However, that he had such a gift is very difficult to deny and is the whole *raison d'être* of the present study.

At first his gift seems to have resembled that 'second sight' so frequently recorded among the Scottish Highlanders. It is said that during his Italian journey he saw coming towards him a young Cordelier named Felix Peretti, born of poor parents in a little village in the March of Ancona, where he had been a swineherd. Nostradamus fell on his knees before him and when the surprised young monk asked him the reason replied that he knelt before His Holiness. The remark caused much amusement among the spectators; none the less the young monk became in time Cardinal of Montalto, and in 1585 was elevated to the Papacy under the title of Sixtus V.

The author of the *Testament* remarks that his gift, which he would have wished to keep hidden, none the less broke out from time to time like a fire under ashes. As he occasionally made predictions and these predictions came true he was considered by some as a genuine prophet and by others as a clever man who amused himself by a pretence of divination, although even these admitted that he was a very skilful physician. Among the sceptics was a certain Seigneur de Florinville with whom Nostradamus was lodging at his castle of Fains in Lorraine. This sceptical lord resolved to test the powers of Nostradamus and walking with him one day in the farmyard pointed out to him two sucking pigs, one black and the other white. He asked Nostradamus to prophesy the fate of both of them, and the latter replied that he, the Seigneur, would eat the black one and that a wolf would eat the white one. The Seigneur de Florinville thereupon went to his cook in secret and ordered him to kill the white pig and serve it for supper. The cook did so, dressed it and put it on the spit ready to be roasted in due course. It so happened, however, that the lord's men had captured a young wolf cub and were endeavouring to tame it. This animal penetrated into the kitchen and while the cook's back was turned seized the pig and began to eat it. The cook, coming back, was horrified at what he saw and, fearing the anger of his master, hastily killed the black pig, dressed it, cooked it and served it at table. The Seigneur de Florinville then informed Nostradamus that they were about to eat the white pig and that the wolf would never get it. Nostradamus replied, that on the contrary, it was the black pig they were about to eat. Then the Seigneur ordered his cook to bring the black pig and disprove the prophet. The unfortunate cook was compelled to confess what had happened, and the prediction of Nostradamus was thus triumphantly vindicated. There is, of course, no proof of the veracity of this story, but it is interesting as an example of the kind of tale which was current about him in his own lifetime.

Etienne Jaubert, author of *Eclaircissement des véritables quatrains de maistre Michel Nostradamus*, published in 1656, tells a story of a treasure known to be hidden in a mountain, and of which Nostradamus prophesied that it would never be found until the site was excavated for another purpose. It was finally discovered while digging for the ruins of a Roman temple.

Fascinating as these stories are it is as well to confess that most of them rest upon the faith of the later biographers. Some of the stories, which may, however, belong to a legitimate verbal tradition, appear for the first time in the seventeenth century, some of them even later. What are we to make of his supposed visit to the Abbey of Orval, of the Order of Cistercians in the diocese of Treves? While there he is supposed to have written the so-called *Prophecy of Orval* or the *Prophecy of Olivarius*, or both. They are separate works, although some modern writers on Nostradamus confuse them strangely. We shall, however, see reason to believe, in a later chapter, that both these works are nineteenth-century forgeries and that if Nostradamus ever stayed at Orval he did not leave there any manuscripts to be discovered only after the French Revolution. What Nostradamus did write, and publish in his own lifetime, is sufficiently remarkable without seeking to bolster up his reputation by dubious attributions.

In 1544 we find Nostradamus in Marseilles where a new outbreak of the plague had recalled him to his duties as a physician. In company with the celebrated Louis Serres he fought the malady, and with his old success. As if the plague were not enough, in November, 1544, Provence suffered from one of the most devastating floods in its history. The Rhone had become a raging torrent; half the Camargue was under water; Tarascon was cut off and the walls of Avignon breached; St Remy and other small places in the neighbourhood could only be reached by boat. As might have been expected, this catastrophe, by polluting the rivers with the corpses of men and animals, only served to spread the pestilence abroad, and Nostradamus and the other doctors of Marseilles had their hands full.

He seems to have been the most successful of all, and he had thoughts of settling permanently in Marseilles. There was much in the city to attract him, notably the excellent shops of the apothecaries who had at hand, in a great seaport, many medicaments which it was not easy to find elsewhere. It had also an important colony of Jews, among them many learned in medicine and astrology.

However, in 1546, when he had been two years in Marseilles, there came a deputation from the town of Aix-en-Provence, begging him to come with them and fight the plague which was raging there. The city was *in extremis*, the greater part of the inhabitants having either died or fled. For more than two hundred days the gates had been shut; there was no longer any Parlement or Courts of Justice, the churches were empty, grass grew in the streets. With the aid of the 'pure and sincere' apothecary Joseph Turel Mercurin, Nostradamus set to work and soon the pestilence began to abate. The grateful city voted him an annual pension as well as rich presents, most of which he distributed to the poor.

Then it was the town of Salon which claimed his services, and then the great city of Lyons. In the latter place he had to contend not only with the plague but with a rival doctor. This was Antoine Sarrazin,[1] and Nostradamus, finding it impossible to work with him, demanded that the city authorities should choose between them. It was Nostradamus who was chosen and with the aid of yet another worthy apothecary, one René Hepilierverd (Nostradamus delighted to preserve the names of those who had supplied him with drugs to his satisfaction) he succeeded in averting the plague. This was not likely to endear him to Sarrazin, who now began to accuse Nostradamus of practising Magic. However, for the moment, the citizens were too grateful for the cure to trouble much by what means it had been effected. Nostradamus returned to Salon loaded with rich presents.

It was in this place that he had finally decided to settle. It was the year 1547. He was now forty-four and tired of wandering, and in the last ten years the wound he had suffered had slowly healed. He was even able to contemplate a new marriage, destined to be more fortunate than the first. His choice lighted on a lady of some means and good connexions; her name was Anne Ponsart Gemelle and she was the widow of a certain Jean Beaulme. The marriage contract was signed on November 11th, 1547, before Master Etienne Hozier, notary of Salon, and the couple took up

[1]. Perhaps the father of the celebrated Jean Antoine Sarrazin who passed his baccalaureat at Montpellier in 1565, that is some eighteen years after the epidemic at Lyons.

their abode in a house in the Ferreiraux quarter, dominated by the crenellated towers of the old castle on its steep rock which overlooks the town.

In this house, which can still be seen in an *impasse* off the Place de la Poissonnerie, Nostradamus was destined to live for the remainder of his days. The street was dark and narrow, but a fine spiral staircase led up to a top room, which he had decided to make his study and from which he could see the stars. For, although he still continued to practise as a physician, the little town of Salon was not likely to overwhelm him with patients, and he was now sufficiently rich to be able to devote his time to other studies if he so desired. We know that he did so desire, for it is plain from internal evidence that he must have begun to compose his prophecies very shortly after the date of his marriage.

The first fruits of his settled leisure, apart from some prophetic almanacks, was not, however, a book of mysteries except in the very minor sense of secret remedies and receipts. His *Traité des Fardemens* appeared in 1552, and, as its name implies, was concerned largely with those unguents and face-paints which Catherine de'Medici had made *à la mode*. It is odd to find Nostradamus so deeply immersed in the concoction of beauty creams and even odder to discover his interest in every kind of jam and preserves. Here the careful housewife would find much to interest her and if by chance she also wished to experiment in the manufacture of a love-philtre Nostradamus would be of considerable assistance to her in that also.

One day a young man knocked at the door of the Jewish physician. His name, he said, was Jean Aymes de Chavigny, of Beaune. His master in the study of Greek had been Jean Dorat, a great admirer of Nostradamus, and he had inspired his pupil with such enthusiasm that Chavigny had come to Salon solely to study at the feet of the Master. He remained there as pupil and disciple, and it is from him that we learn almost all we know of the biography of Nostradamus. Perhaps it was his encouragement that led the careful Jewish physician to give his prophecies to the world.

CHAPTER TWO

Nostradamus the Prophet

IT was in the year 1555 that the first edition of the *Centuries* appeared. We know, on the good authority of Chavigny, who knew him intimately, that Nostradamus had been at work on them for some years. 'There it was,' he says (i.e., at Salon), 'that, foreseeing the signal mutations and changes which should come throughout Europe, and even the bloody civil wars and pernicious troubles of this Gallic realm which fatally drew near, full of an enthusiasm and as it were rapt in a new madness (*fureur*) he set himself to write his *Centuries* and other *Présages*.... He kept them a long time without wishing to publish them, thinking that the novelty of the matter would not fail to arouse infinite detractions, calumnies and attacks (*morsures*) more than venomous as indeed it fell out. In the end, vanquished by the desire which he had to be useful to the public, he published them; and immediately their noise and renown ran through the mouths of our compatriots and of strangers with the greatest wonder.'

A printer of Lyons, one Macé Bonhomme, was entrusted with the publication. The authorities, having been assured that the book contained nothing contrary to the Catholic Faith, gave their permission for the printing on the last day of April, 1555, and the volume fell from the press on the fourth of May following. Bibliographically we are on solid ground.

Strangely enough the book contained only three complete *Centuries* and fifty-three quatrains of the fourth. But this fragment of the final work was enough to catch the public interest, and Nostradamus, whose celebrity had hitherto been purely local, found himself famous throughout Western Europe.

It is a little difficult to see why this should have been so, since none of the predictions had yet been fulfilled and they were all of what must have seemed an impenetrable obscurity. Even to-day when we open the book for the first time, it is difficult not to cast it aside in disgust. These four-line stanzas of crabbed French verse, obeying neither prosody nor syntax, arranged in no intelligible order and bristling not only with words in half a dozen foreign languages but with initials, anagrams and made-up names – how can there be a hope of finding any meaning in such a publication at all? And if there were, would it be worth the trouble?

The book is provided with a preface by Nostradamus in the form of a letter to his son César. The child, however, was at the time of publication but a few weeks old, and the preface may therefore be considered to be addressed to his spiritual son and disciple, Jean Aymes de Chavigny, and to all who should seek to interpret the prophecies in future ages. It sets certain matters down clearly enough:

'Although for a long time I have frequently predicted a long time in advance what has afterwards come to pass. . . . I was willing to be silent and to pass over what might be harmful, not only as relates to the present time, but also for the greater part of future time, if committed to writing, since kingdoms, sects and religions will pass through stages so contrary, and indeed diametrically opposite to their present state, that if I were to relate what will happen in the future, governors, sectaries and ecclesiastics would find it so little in accord with their auricular fancy that they would immediately condemn what future centuries will know and perceive to be true. Considering also the words of the true Saviour, "Cast not your pearls before swine".'

It will be seen that Nostradamus was not over-complimentary to the established authorities of his day. He continues:

'This has been the cause which has led me to withhold my tongue from the vulgar, and my pen from paper, – then I thought I would enlarge a little as touching the Vulgar Advent, and show by abstruse and twisted sentences the future causes, even the most urgent, as I perceived them, whatever changes might be, so only as not to scandalize their fragile hearing, and write down everything under a figure rather cloudy than plainly prophetic.'

Here Nostradamus gives his own reasons for his wilful obscurity. He purposely concealed the meaning of his prophecies in order that it might not be guessed too soon and get him into trouble. Especially interesting in this connexion is his reference to the Vulgar Advent, *le commun advenement*, as he calls it, or as it might be phrased, the accession of the people to power.

Fantastic as it may seem, this Vulgar Advent, this accession of the people to power, is none other than the French Revolution which he foresaw quite plainly more than two hundred years before it happened. Even the most sceptical writers on Nostradamus have been compelled to admit that he knew something about the French Revolution; we shall see reason to believe that he knew almost everything about it, even to the names of some of the principal actors. He even knew when it would happen, for in the Epistle to King Henri II which appears in the second edition of the *Centuries*, speaking of the great persecution of the Church which was to accompany it, he mentions the date, 1792.

If we can swallow this, what are we to make of his claim, in the same Epistle, that he could easily have dated *all* the quatrains, if he had wished? Whether this be so or not, he was certainly wise to be cautious, for not only would he have offended the great ones of the earth but he would have laid himself under the not unreasonable suspicion of being in league with the devil.

Even as it was, and for all his careful obscurity, he knew himself to be in constant danger of persecution as a sorcerer, and he attempts, rather desperately, to clear himself from this charge in the Epistle to César. Claiming to have been inspired solely by God, he begs his son not to indulge in occult practices, in a curious passage which is, in all likelihood, purposely ambiguous:

'And further, my son, I implore you not to attempt to employ your understanding in such reveries and vanities which wither the body and bring the soul to perdition, troubling the feeble sense: even the vanity of that most execrable magic, denounced already by the Sacred Scriptures and by the divine Canons of the Church – from which judgement is excepted Judicial Astrology, by means of which, and the Divine inspiration and revelation, by continual calculations we have reduced our prophecies to writing. And, notwithstanding that this occult Philosophy was not reproved by the Church I have not wished to divulge their wild persuasions, although many volumes which have been hidden for centuries have come before my eyes. But dreading what might happen in the future, having read them, I presented them to Vulcan, and as the fire began to devour them the flame, licking the air, shot forth an unaccustomed brightness, clearer than natural flame, like the flash from an explosive powder (*comme lumière de feu de clystre fulgurant*) casting a strange illumination over the house, as if it had been in sudden conflagration; so that none might come to be abused by searching for the perfect transmutation, lunar or solar, or for incorruptible metals hidden under earth or sea, I reduced them to ashes.'

It is impossible to read this passage, disingenuous as it is, without a certain quiver of the imagination. Is the whole thing mumbo-jumbo or a mere poetic flight of fancy, or was Nostradamus really in possession of books which it would have been dangerous to allow to fall into the hands of others? And if such books existed, what was their nature? If they were really Hermetic volumes it was an act of unforgivable vandalism to destroy them; if they were merely treatises on alchemy or astrology he would never have burned them. Had they been vulgar *grimoires* or books of ceremonial magic their destruction would hardly have called for such solemnity. Were they the Coptic treatises of the Gnostic Schools; were they some particularly significant fragments of the great Hebrew tradition of Magic?

That he, the Jew, was deeply read in the Cabala, we may take for granted. Did he also possess a copy of the mysterious *Keys of Solomon* which Goethe speaks of in the first part of

Faust, and the existence of which was an abiding tradition throughout the Middle Ages? Nicetas Chonensis,[1] a Byzantine historian of the twelfth century, declares that an Empress of Constantinople possessed a copy, a *Biblos Solomônteios*, which enabled her to call up demons and to converse with them. Much earlier, in the time of the Emperor Vespasian, Josephus mentions a book of incantations attributed to Solomon, and declares that a Jew called Eleazar was able to cure the sick and the possessed by the aid of a talismanic ring and a few words from this magic book.

Michael Psellus speaks in the eleventh century of a work of Solomon on demons, and we learn from the twelfth century Byzantine author above mentioned that the Jew, Aaron Isaac, imperial counsellor, possessed a copy. According to Nicolas Eymeric, towards 1350, the Pope Innocent VI caused to be burned a large volume containing formulae for the evocation of demons and known as the Book of Solomon.

Actual texts of so-called *Keys of Solomon* have come down to us, including one in the Library of the Arsenal, in Paris.[2] It is a strange *grimoire*, written in a language full of Latin, Greek, Hebrew, Arab and even Chaldean words. Who shall say if it be identical with the book which Empresses studied and Popes burned, which reaches back to Byzantine days and beyond? The traditions of Magic are strangely persistent, and some at least among the Jews seem always to have possessed them. Was this one of the books which the man of Salon used for his nocturnal conjurations? Was this one of the volumes he thought it wiser to burn?

For all his protestations, his habitual caution and his desperate efforts to keep on the right side of the Church, there can be little doubt that Nostradamus was deep in Magic. His only Latin quatrain, the one with which he concludes *Centurie VI*, has all the flavour of a magical imprecation:

---

1. Nicetas Chon. *De Manuele Comneno*. Lib. IV, p. 95.
2. MSS. 2350.

Legis Cantio Contra Ineptos Criticos

> *Qui legent hosce versus mature censunto,*
> *Profanum vulgus & inscium ne attrectato:*
> *Omnesque Astrologi, Blenni, Barbari procul sunto:*
> *Qui aliter facit, is rite sacer esto.* (VI, 100)

Let those who read these verses give them mature reflection! Let not approach the profane and ignorant crowd! Keep off, all ye astrologers, fools and barbarians! May he who acts otherwise be devoted to the Infernal Gods, according to the rites (i.e. the rites of Magic).

There are three other quatrains which must be considered here because they contain, as it were, the reluctant evidence of his practices. In one he seems to have perpetrated a deliberate mutilation of his original text as if to throw his enemies off the scent. In the very first quatrain of *Centurie I*, he writes:

> *Estant assis de nuict secret estude,*
> *Seul, reposé sur la sele d'aerain,*
> *Flambe exigue sortant de solitude,*
> *Fait prosperer qui n'est à croire vain.* (I, 1)

Alone at night in secret study, seated on the brazen tripod, a little flame illuminates my solitude and makes to succeed that which I have not believed in vain. And in another verse, immediately following:

> *La verge en main mise au milieu de Branches,*
> *De l'onde il mouille & le limbe & le pied:*
> *Un peur & voix fremissent par les manches:*
> *Splendeur divine. Le Divin près s'assied.* (I, 2)

The wand of the magician is placed upon the tripod (also, as it were, in the midst of that temple at the gates of Miletus called the Temple of Branchus, the young man to whom Apollo gave the gift of prophecy); he moistens in the water his feet and the hem of his robe; he hears a voice and his arms tremble with fear. The sacred light gleams; the envoy of the Gods sit down beside him.

The ultra-Catholic Elisée du Vignois, anxious to save the

good name of the Prophet, insists on a more prosaic rendering. The wand in question is, he thinks, nothing but the pen wet with ink. 'A shiver runs through his body; the divine splendour surrounds him, and God himself gives him inspiration.'[1] But this is not quite good enough, for both passages are derived directly from *De Mysteriis Egyptiorum*, a work of the fourth century, attributed to the Neo-Platonist Iamblichus. *Foemina in Branchis fatidica, vel sedet in axe, vel manu tenet virgam, vel pedes aut limbum tingit in aquam; et ex his modis impletur splendore divino, deumque nacta vaticinatur.* The prophetess of Branchus sits in the sanctuary, holds in her hand the wand, bathes the foot and the hem of her robe in water and by these means she is filled with the divine illumination and, finding herself in communication with the divinity, she prophesies. The close parallel between the Latin text and the quatrain of Nostradamus needs no stressing. And in another passage Iamblichus speaks of the priestess of Delphi who, seated upon the tripod (*super sedem aeneam*), receives a ray of the divine illumination (*radio divini ignis*) which is none other than Nostradamus' 'little flame'. He either knew Iamblichus by heart or had the book before him as he wrote.

The following mysterious and ambiguous passage occurs in the Epistle to his son César with which he prefaced the first edition of the *Centuries*:

'*L'entendement crée intellectuellement ne peut voir occultement, sinon par la voix faicte au limbe moyennant la exigue flamme, en laquelle partie des causes futures se viendront à incliner.*'[2]

The intellectual understanding (or, as we should say, the conscious intelligence) can perceive nothing of the occult

---

[1] This was also the view of the seventeenth-century commentator Garencières. He explains 'branches' as the writer's fingers, and interprets the second line as meaning that the page is wet with ink from the top to the bottom.

[2] Some apology is perhaps due to the reader for the citing of such passages in the original text; but it is his only guarantee that he is not being misled. It is so easy to cheat, consciously or unconsciously, in making translations to prove a point.

without the aid of a voice *'faicte au limbe moyennant la exigue flamme.'* This is a curious phrase. Le Pelletier interprets: 'Without the aid of the mysterious voice of a spirit appearing in the vapour floating above a vessel of water, and without the illumination of the magic flame in which future events are partly revealed as in a mirror.' The reasonableness of this expansion must be left to the reader; it is, however, supported by what is known of magical rites.

We have seen that Nostradamus was acquainted with the writings of Iamblichus. We have reason to believe that he was also familiar with the work entitled *De Demonibus*, by the twelfth-century author Michael Psellus, and was a little uncomfortable in his knowledge.

> *Le dix Calendes d'Avril de faict gotique*
> *Resuscité encor par gens malins:*
> *Le feu estainct, assemblée diabolique*
> *Cherchant les os du Damant & Pselin.* (1, 42)

It is thought that he originally wrote –

> *Cherchant les os du Demon de Psellus*

and blurred the passage for fear of frightening the authorities.

The tenth day of the Kalends of April, calculated in the Gothic fashion, magical practices are revived by the sorcerers (*gens malins*); the lights are extinguished, the diabolic assembly seeks the bones of the Demon of Psellus.

Now in the writings of Psellus we find a description of such evocations. He even uses the phrase *extinctis luminibus* of which *le feu estainct* seems an echo. And what he describes corresponds to the practices hinted at in the quatrains previously quoted.

Before we examine the relevant passages, however, we must pause for a moment over the first line:

> *Le dix Calendes d'Avril de faict gotique.*

Why is Nostradamus so careful to insist that the calculation shall be made 'in the Gothic fashion'? Did he foresee the day when the calendar would be changed, by the adoption in

1582 (sixteen years after his death) of the Gregorian system? The tenth day of the Kalends of April corresponds to the twenty-third day of March in the new calendar and it may be that he means a particular year in which Good Friday (a favourite day for magical evocations) fell on March 23rd. Such a year would be 1543 or 1554, and one or other of these may have been the date on which he commenced his own prophetic work, by the aid of the 'Demon of Psellus', present before him in bodily shape, or as the French would say, *en chair et en os*.

Psellus writes:

'The diviners take a basin full of water appropriate to the use of the demons.... This basin full of water seems first to vibrate as if it would emit sounds; nevertheless the water in the basin does not differ in appearance from natural water, but it has the property, by the virtue which is infused into it, of being able to compose verses (!) which renders it eminently apt to receive the prophetic spirit. For this sort of demon is capricious, earth-bound (*atque terrenum*) and subject to enchantments; and so soon as the water begins to give out sounds, manifests its satisfaction to those who are present by some words still indistinct and meaningless, but, later, when the water seems to boil and spill over, a faint voice murmurs words which contain the revelation of future events.'

There is something slightly comic in the notion of a basin of water composing verses, but we seem to be on the track here of a mode of divination approaching Nostradamus's own methods. Divination by gazing at a bowl of water was well known in antiquity and is still practised among primitive people. The fakirs of India are said to be able to make water appear to boil and bubble beneath their gaze. Is it all anything more than a technique for going into a trance? We touch on the one hand the Pythoness of Delphi and on the other the practices of modern Spiritualism, and overleap, as it were, all the complicated rituals of ceremonial magic. Were such rituals themselves ever anything else than a method of drugging the conscious mind?

And when the conscious mind is drugged asleep, when that guardian of what we miscall the Self no longer bars the way, then another personality (phantasm from within or demon from without) takes control of the body, agitates the larynx and speaks. And he would be a very resolute, and indeed impenetrable, sceptic who would deny that what is spoken is ever prophetic. But we must return to these difficult matters in a later chapter.

Chavigny tells us that after the publication of the first edition of the *Centuries* the fame of Nostradamus came to the ears of King Henri II, and that he summoned the prophet to court in order to consult him. It was, however, more probably the Queen than the King who desired to see him.

Catherine de'Medici's interest in things occult was an abiding passion, if not almost a mania. Such an interest was indeed traditional in her family, and astrology was taken seriously by those around her from her very earliest years. In 1519 her father, Lorenzo II, had her horoscope cast by Bazile the mathematician, and her parents had also consulted on her behalf and on their own the celebrated Luc Gauric.

As the prophecies of this extraordinary man confirm – and anticipate – those of Nostradamus concerning one very important event in French history some details of his career may not be out of place. He was born at Gifoni in the Kingdom of Naples in 1476, and, having come to man's estate, at first earned his living by teaching mathematics to the sons of the local lords. At the end of the fifteenth century there was nothing astonishing in the fact that a mathematician should be also an astrologer – it was indeed a very usual combination – but not all practitioners were as successful as Luc Gauric. Sometimes he was too successful for, being consulted by Giovanni Bentivoglio, tyrant of Bologna, he rashly prophesied his exile and death. Bentivoglio, with imperfect logic, condemned him to 'five turns of the strappado', a horrible torture from which the unfortunate astrologer did not recover for some years. The tyrant was none the less chased from Bologna, for the citizens, in November, 1506, opened the gates to the armies of Pope Julius II.

The Medici had already become interested in Gauric, and

in 1493 he had been required to cast the horoscope of Giovanni de'Medici, then a juvenile cardinal of some fourteen years. Gauric declared that he would be Pope, which duly came to pass in 1513, when he assumed the title of Leo X. It is small wonder that the prophet's credit stood high with the Medici family and that they should consult him in the following year concerning the fate of the infant Catherine who was a grand-niece of the new Pontiff.

Gauric was the most celebrated astrologer of his time and travelled much in the exercise of his profession. On a visit to Scotland he told Hamilton, Archbishop of St Andrews, that he would die on the scaffold, which shows that even the five turns of the strappado had not taught him discretion. Perhaps he relied upon the protection of Rome, where his credit always seems to have been high. Paul III even gave him the bishopric of Civita Castellana and conferred on him the rank of Knight of St Paul. This did not prevent him from prophesying the malady from which the Pope would die, as he did, on the day duly indicated, November 20th, 1549.

When Catherine became Dauphine of France she, not unnaturally, sent for Gauric and consulted him concerning the fate of her husband. The prophet declared that he would be King, that his succession to the throne would be marked by a sensational duel and that another duel would bring both reign and life to an end.

The first duel in question was that between Gui Chabot Jarnac and François Vivonne la Châtaigneraie at Saint Germain-en-Laye, on July 16th, 1547, when the young king was present and saw Châtaigneraie killed. Double prophecies of which one half has already been fulfilled are very disturbing things and it was natural that Catherine should be anxious for further particulars. At her request Gauric sent a letter to the King in which he warned him 'to avoid all single combat in an enclosed place, especially near his forty-first year, for in that period of his life he was menaced by a wound in the head which might rapidly result in blindness, or even in death'.

Various accounts have come down to us of Henri II's reception of this letter. Claude de l'Aubespine, Baron de Châteauneuf, and Secretary of State under Francis I, Henri II and Charles IX, died in 1567 and left behind him, in manuscript, a work entitled *Histoire particulière de la Cour de Henry II*.[1] In it he declares that on the evening when the Truce of Naucelle was announced (February 5th, 1556), 'there was a despatch from Rome containing the horoscope of the King, composed by Gauricus. I translated it from Latin into French in order that the King might understand it. This horoscope was neglected until the day of the King's wound, when I showed the copy which caused much astonishment.'

Brantôme, who was a contemporary, describes the King's reactions. He says[2]: 'Monsieur the Constable was present there, to whom the King said: "See, my *compère*, what death is predicted for me." "Ah Sire", replied the Constable, "would you believe these rascals? They are nothing but liars and babblers. Throw it in the fire." "My *compère*," replied the King, "why so? They sometimes tell truth. I care not if my death be in that manner more than in any other. I would even prefer it, to die by the hand of whomever he might be, so long as he was brave and valiant, and that I kept my honour." And without paying any heed to the Constable's words he gave the prophecy to M. de l'Aubespine to keep for him until he should ask for it. Alas! neither he nor the Constable thought of the single combat in which he should die, but rather of another kind of duel in an enclosed space and to the death as such serious duels should be fought.'

Although Henri II treated the matter lightly it undoubtedly weighed on the mind of the Queen. *La Princesse de Clèves* is, of course, a novel, and its authoress, Madame de la Fayette, lived in the seventeenth century, but the traditions of the Court of the Valois still lingered in her circle, and

1. *Archives curieuses de la France*, 1st Series, Vol. III, pp. 295 and 296, 1835.
2. Brantôme: *Œuvres, publiées et annotées par Ludovic Lalanne. Edition de la Société de l'Histoire de France*, Vol. III, p. 280.

although her story has not the value of contemporary evidence it is none the less of considerable interest.

'One day,' she writes, 'the King being with the Queen at the hour of reunion, the conversation turned to horoscopes and predictions. Opinion was divided concerning the credit which should be given them. The Queen professed great faith in them. She maintained that so many things had been prophesied and had come true that it was impossible to doubt that there was some certitude in that science. Others maintained that among an infinite number of predictions the few that did come true made it evidence that it was all a matter of chance. "I used to be very curious concerning the future," said the King, "but I have been told so many false and improbable things, that I have become convinced that one cannot know anything for certain. A few years ago a man came here who had a great reputation in astrology. Everyone wanted to see him, and I went like the others, but without telling him who I was. I took with me only Messieurs de Guise and d'Escars; I made them go in before me; the astrologer none the less addressed himself to me, as if he judged me to be the master of the others. He predicted that I should be killed in a duel. He later said that Monsieur de Guise would be slain from behind, and that d'Escars would have his head broken by the kick of a horse. Monsieur de Guise was half offended by this prediction, as if he had been accused of running away. D'Escars was not much better pleased to learn that he would end by such an unfortunate accident. In fact we all three came away extremely annoyed with the astrologer. I don't know what will happen to Messieurs de Guise and d'Escars," added the King, "but there is not much likelihood of my being killed in a duel. We have just made peace, the King of Spain and I, and even if we hadn't, I doubt that we should fight together, or that I should call him out, as the King, my father called out Charles V."'

It will be seen that Madame de la Fayette's story says nothing of the reception of a letter, but rather of a visit to an astrologer who may or may not have been Luc Gauric.

There was no lack of such men. According to Pierre de l'Estoile there were, under the Valois, thirty thousand sorcerers, alchemists, prophets and astrologers in Paris alone, not to mention those attached to the Court: Regnier, Oger Ferrier and the Italians, Cosmo Ruggieri and Gabriel Simeoni, both of whom played an intimate part in Catherine's occult practices. Gauric himself seems to have been only an occasional visitor but, as if to anticipate the natural scepticism of the modern reader concerning his alleged prophecies, he had them printed at Venice in 1552, that is some seven years before the death of Henri II.[1]

If Claude d'Aubespine gives us the right date (February 5th, 1556) for the reception of Gauric's letter reiterating his warning to the King, it would seem as if Catherine de' Medici lost no time in sending for the new prophet, Nostradamus, brought to her notice by the publication of his *Centuries* in the previous year. She wrote to Claude de Savoie, Comte de Tende, Governor of Provence, and asked him to persuade Nostradamus to come to Court. Claude, who was a personal friend of the Prophet of Salon, transmitted the message. Nostradamus accepted it as a command, and set out on his long journey on July 14th, 1556.

It took him a month, and would have taken him longer but for the '*poste royale*' from Pont-Saint-Esprit established by Louis XI. As it was, he arrived in Paris on August 15th, and put up – by happy augury – at the Auberge St Michel near Notre-Dame.

The abbé Torné-Chavigny, the nineteenth-century commentator of Nostradamus, claimed to have read, in the *Bibliothèque Nationale*, a letter written by the prophet in 1561 to a certain M. de Morel, returning to him the two rose-nobles and the two *écus* which he had been compelled to borrow on his arrival in Paris. Whether this be authentic or not, we can well imagine that he arrived in Paris impoverished by his long journey and feeling – he the Provençal and the Jew – completely out of place in the northern city.

---

1. Luc Gauric, *Opera*, Vol. II. *Tractatus Nativitatum*, 3 vols. in fol. Venice, 1552.

However, his arrival had been announced and soon no less a person than Monsieur the Constable came to fetch him to Court then, since the month was August, established at St Germain-en-Laye.

Most of the commentators assume that he had been summoned chiefly to explain a single quatrain in the *Centuries*, the quatrain which was to cause so much comment three years later:

> *Le lyon jeune le vieux surmontera*
> *En champ bellique par singulier duelle:*
> *Dans cage d'or les yeux luy crevera*
> *Deux classes une, puis mourir, mort cruelle.* (1, 35)

It is possible that the King had noticed the resemblance between this and the other prophecies – in which case his later behaviour is even more incomprehensible. But Henri was no great scholar and it is unlikely that he had read the *Centuries* with very much attention. Moreover, Nostradamus had wrapped up his prophecy in symbolism and if the King did question him about it he probably replied with his usual discretion. He lacked altogether the forthrightness of Luc Gauric, realizing perhaps that as a Jew and a subject he risked something worse than the strappado. His interview with the King seems to have been a short one, and when it was over he was ushered into the presence of Catherine de' Medici.

He saw before him a woman still young – she was thirty-seven – a woman who had never been beautiful, with thick lips, crinkly hair and receding chin, but with eyes that were intensely alive and with a skin dazzling in its whiteness. She saw in him a man of the south, bearded and dressed in the long gown and square cap of the doctor, speaking with a warm Provençal accent, and with gesticulations which reminded her of Italy. They would have had much to talk about even apart from the object of his visit. Had she read his book on cosmetics; did she share his sweet tooth and his passion for jam? But sooner or later the conversation must have veered round to the subject which interested both of them so profoundly: fortune, destiny, the influence of the stars. Perhaps he confessed to her, if to no one else, his deep study of magic.

In any case, Catherine was favourably impressed, and on his return to Paris he was lodged, not at the inn, but at the town residence of the Archbishop of Sens. The King sent him a purse of velvet containing a hundred *écus* and the Queen added thirty. It is true that Nostradamus thought this a very miserable recompense, as he had spent a hundred *écus* on his journey. But further proofs of the royal favour were not long delayed.

Meanwhile the whole Court had got wind of his arrival, and his apartments were besieged by all kinds of clients; old lords who wanted a prescription for the gout or the stone, young ladies who hoped to learn a secret remedy against the decay of their complexions, anxious mothers who demanded the horoscopes of their children. They brought with them gifts, clothes and plate and jewels and money. The royal presents were soon a very negligible part of his gains.

We hear stories of his strange powers of second sight quite apart from the calculations of astrology. One night when Nostradamus had already shut himself in his study a page in the employment of the Beauveau family came knocking at his door. He had lost a valuable hound which had been left in his charge, but before he had had time to announce his errand, Nostradamus called out: 'You are making a great deal of noise for a lost dog. Go away and look on the road to Orleans. You will find it there on the leash.' This story passed from mouth to mouth and increased the fame of the Prophet. He was the sensation of Paris.

Suddenly he received the royal command to go to Blois, where the children of Henri and Catherine were living, and to cast their horoscopes. He must have done so with very mixed feelings, for, in the cloudy language of the *Centuries*, were not their desperate fates already written? That boy of thirteen who shall one day be Francis II, who shall be married while still a child to that other unhappy child Mary Stuart, and who shall die miserably after one year of reign;

that girl of eleven, destined also to die young, the child-wife of gloomy old Philip of Spain; that girl of nine who will die in her twenties as Duchess of Lorrain; that melancholy little boy of six, the future Charles IX, in whose staring eyes shall one day be reflected the fires of St Bartholomew, that boy of five who shall be twice a King, but in both kingdoms unhappy, and whose body will be pierced by the assassin's dagger, and that other boy of two, François, Duc d'Alençon, the perpetual *Malcontent*, titular sovereign of the Netherlands, suitor of Queen Elizabeth, laughing-stock of Europe – what a nursery to prophesy for! The only child with any soundness and sweetness in the whole brood was the tempestuous Marguerite, then a girl of four, who was to be married to the enemy, Henry of Navarre, to be repudiated by him for her adulteries, to outlive them all and to go down to history as the raffish, ragtaggle but not unlovable *Reine Margot*.

If we believe in Nostradamus at all we must believe that he knew all about them. How much he knew we shall see when we come to study the *Centuries* more closely. For the moment his problem was not to see but to conceal, to pronounce a true oracle without offending the Queen. She was known to have ambitions for her sons both outside and inside France. He contented himself with telling her that they should all be kings.

He had scarcely returned from Blois when one night he was visited by a 'very honest woman' who had the air of a lady of quality and who warned him that '*ces Messieurs de la Justice de Paris*' had the intention of calling upon him and of inquiring what kind of science it was that he practised with so much success. Relying upon the protection of the Queen, he might have stayed and braved it out, but Nostradamus merely replied that he hoped they would not give themselves so much trouble as it was his firm intention to leave Paris the very next day. When morning came he was already on his way back to Salon. The volatile Parisians turned to new sensations, and for a time he was forgotten in the capital – by all except the Queen.

The return of Nostradamus to his home was triumphal. The presents he brought back with him, the fact that he had been received by the King, gave him new lustre in the eyes of his fellow citizens. His friends received him with open arms. He had become, as if by Royal Warrant, the Prophet of Salon. As if to remind the world that he was a physician as well as a soothsayer he busied himself in preparing for the press his translation of the *Paraphrase of Galien*.[1] He was interested in public affairs, especially in the construction of a canal to supply the town with water, an enterprise undertaken by his friend Adam Cramponne, to whom Nostradamus had lent two hundred crowns for the prosecution of the work. His door was crowded by those who came to seek advice, either medical or prophetic.

An amusing story of his powers of second sight is told of him at this period of his life.[2] One evening he was seated in a chair outside his front door taking the air and perhaps dozing a little. The daughter of one of his neighbours passed him on her way to the wood just outside the town, to gather sticks or on some other errand. Very politely she greeted him: '*Bonjour, Monsieur de Nostredame.*'

'*Bonjour, fillette,*' he answered.

An hour later the girl returned and as she passed him once more said sweetly: '*Bonjour, Monsieur de Nostredame.*'

'*Bonjour, petite femme!*' said Nostradamus slyly.

Unfortunately the health of the Prophet was beginning to break down, although he was scarcely yet in the middle fifties, and many annoyances embittered his life. The success of his almanacks had produced a crop of imitations in which there was nothing of Nostradamus but the name, and that they tended to bring into discredit. He had already had to prosecute a Lyons printer in 1553 for a similar offence. Then his very success had sharpened the jealousy of his fellow-physicians and others.

The most absurd stories were circulated about him. A

1. Published at Lyons by Antoine de Rosne, February, 1557.
2. The story is of doubtful authenticity, but too charming to be omitted.

certain Laurens Videl brought out at Avignon in 1558 a special pamphlet in which he attacked him violently, as may be gathered from the forthright title: *Déclaration des abus, ignorances et séditions de Michel Nostradamus*. In this the writer declares that having been consulted by a man who suffered from ulcers of the bladder, Nostradamus advised him to sleep with 'a small black woman'. This treatment, says the indignant author, made the ulcers worse!

More formidable opponents came into the field as the satirical poets took up the cudgels. The famous Jodelle produced a Latin distich which flew from mouth to mouth, as indeed it deserved to for its neatness and wit:

> *Nostra damus cum falsa damus, nam fallere nostrum est,*
> *Cum falsa damus, nil nisi nostra damus.*[1]

It was in vain for the friends of the Prophet to riposte with another distich:

> *Vera damus cum verba damus quae Nostradamus dat,*
> *Sed cum nostra damus, nil nisi falsa damus.*

Even if the reply had been as clever as the original the damage was already done.

Nostradamus strove to forget their insults in the preparation for the press of the second, and enlarged, edition of the *Centuries*, and he proposed to include, as preface, an epistle to no less a person than the King himself: Carefully he studied the language which should commend the book to the approval of the monarch:

A l'invictissime
Tres Puissant et tres Chrestien
Henry Roy de France Second:
Michel Nostradamus
Tres-humble, et tres obeyssant serviteur et subject,
Victoire et Felicité

Some Royalist commentators have seen a mystery here

[1]. We give that which is ours when we give lies, for to deceive is our business, and when we give false things we only give what is proper to us.

where no mystery is, and have tried to prove that '*Henry Roy de France Second*' does not mean Henri II at all but that Messianic 'Second King' who shall come in the fulness of time to deliver them from the Third Republic. This dream of a Royalist restoration has been the main motive of several of those who have devoted their lives to the study of Nostradamus. But while we may not dismiss the idea entirely there seems little support for it here.

Nostradamus genuinely wished to address the King who sat on the throne of France when he wrote, although it may well be wondered whether he ever expected him to wade through the whole preface. For if, as some writers have held, the Epistle to César is *en clair*, the Epistle to Henri II is certainly in code – a code of which the key has been lost. It is almost fantastically obscure, containing as it does a whole series of elaborate calculations apparently based on Biblical chronology. One ingenious author [1] holds that this is only a colour. The epistle, he says, 'gives, under the pretext of Biblical chronology, two series of numbers quite arbitrary at first glance, but constituting the key which, by a series of additions, permits us to link up the verses and the date and extract a meaning. This is the key which Nostradamus gave to Catherine de'Medici and to Henry II, but it stops in 1792, foreseeing the replacing of the Julian calendar by that of the Republic. When he gave his key, *Centurie VII* comprised forty-two quatrains. He added two, of which the forty-fourth is very clear and announces that Louis XVI will be guillotined. It is from this date that it is necessary to take up the numerical system of the key. It stops again, however, in 1924.'

The only objection to all this is that there is not an atom of proof for it. If only there were!

It is extremely unlikely that Nostradamus gave any key to Henri II; it is even probable that the King never saw the Epistle at all, for the volume which contains it was never published in his lifetime – or in that of Nostradamus.

1. P. V. Piobb, *Le Secret de Nostradamus*, 1927.

The bibliographers have made rather a mystery of the fact that the Editio Princeps of the *Centuries*, which appeared in 1566, is found on examination to consist of two fascicules, each with its title. It seems probable that one of these, which the learned Le Pelletier thinks was printed in 1558, was in fact the edition which Nostradamus was preparing and which was to have come out shortly afterwards with the dedication to Henri II. But before it could do so, the King came to his strange and violent end. Nostradamus, who had prophesied the event but was apparently unaware of the date when it would happen – or why should he have written his preface? – took fright and suppressed the whole edition. It might not now be a recommendation that he, along with other prophets, had foreseen the tragedy so clearly. The moment for bringing out a new edition of the *Centuries* might, perhaps, more safely be deferred. Yet no event contributed more than this to spread the fame of Nostradamus. The historical facts are these.

In the summer of 1559 the Royal House of France was to celebrate a double marriage, that of Henri's daughter Elizabeth to Philip II of Spain and that of his daughter Marguerite to the Duke of Savoy. The first was celebrated by proxy (Philip being too grand to appear in Paris) on June 22nd. The marriage contract for the younger sister was signed on the 28th, and on the same day began a three-day tournament and general festivity.

The lists had been set up in the Rue St Antoine, near the Palais des Tournelles, and the King, who was still in the prime of life, was himself one of the jousters. On the first two days he distinguished himself above all the others by his prowess and skill. On the third, towards evening, he rode against Montgomery, the Captain of his Scottish guard, and, failing to unseat him, insisted that the bout should be ridden again. Montgomery demurred, but the King would take no denial. The two men circled the lists twice, met, and missed one another. In the third encounter they both splintered their lances in the approved fashion, but Montgomery, in passing, failed to drop the haft in time and the jagged point pierced the King's visor and entered his eye. He reeled, clutched the pommel desperately and was caught in the arms of his grooms as he fell.

It was the end of the festivities, but not yet the end of Henri II. With indomitable courage he lingered for ten days, enduring the worst that the clumsy surgeons of the age could do to him. But on July 10th that contest too ended, and he was dead.

Then men remembered the quatrain of Nostradamus published three years previously:

> The young lion shall overcome the old,
> In warlike field in single fight:
> In a cage of gold he will pierce his eyes,
> Two wounds one, then die a cruel death.

The tilting helm strangely resembles a cage, and the King's visor was gilded. 'Two wounds one': a splinter of the lance is said to have entered the King's throat. But whatever the authenticity of the details the stanza was only too likely to strike the imagination of those who had just witnessed the singular fate of their King, and some of them clamoured for vengeance against the man who had prophesied both so well and so ill. The rumour flew that he was not only a sorcerer but a Protestant, which was even worse. In the suburbs of Paris the populace made a figure of straw in his likeness and burned it,[1] calling upon the Church to do the same to Nostradamus himself. Catherine's anger, with a more feminine logic, was directed against the innocent author of the tragedy.

Henri II had ordered that no harm should come to Montgomery, but kings are not killed with impunity even by accident, and there was every reason to believe that Catherine would be avenged if she could, in spite of her dead husband's clemency. Montgomery fled to England and stayed there for nearly fifteen years. He became a Protestant and, when the Huguenots of Normandy revolted, he crossed the Channel again and put himself at their head. Having

---

1. César Nostradamus. *Histoire et Chronique de Provence.*

captured the towns of Saint Lô and Carentan he found himself surrounded by the Maréchal de Matignon in his own fortress of Domfront and was compelled to yield the place. Under the terms of the capitulation his life was to be spared, but on the night of Thursday, May 27th, 1574, on the express orders of the Queen, he was arrested in bed by six noblemen of the royal army.

Even these happenings Nostradamus seems to have foreseen with extraordinary particularity:

> *Celuy qu'en luitte & fer au faict bellique*
> *Aura porté plus grand que luy le prix,*
> *De nuict au lict six luy feront la pique,*
> *Nud, sans harnois, subit, sera surpris.* (III, 30)

He who in fight on martial field shall have carried off (*porté* for *remporté*) the prize from one greater than he, shall be surprised by six men by night, suddenly, naked, and without armour.

The quatrain could scarcely fit more closely if it had been written by an historian instead of a prophet. Montgomery was taken from Domfront to Caen and from thence to the Conciergerie in Paris where he was delivered over to the vengeance of Catherine.

Against Nostradamus she rightly enough felt no anger whatever. Had he not shown himself a good prophet, and might not good prophets be extremely useful to a Medici and a Queen?

CHAPTER THREE

The House of the Seven

CATHERINE'S worst fears had come true, her forebodings had been fulfilled, her belief in astrology justified. Small wonder if she surrendered herself to a belief in Magic more completely than ever before. In the first flood of her grief she had changed her arms to a mourning device: on a black ground, between two bezants (presumably the golden balls of the Medici), a broken lance with the motto, *Lacrymae hinc, hinc dolor*. Now she changed them again: on a blue ground a star surrounded by a serpent biting his tail – a purely magical emblem. The motto was *Fato prudentia major*. She had recovered her courage and meant to fight for her power, by the aid of her own wits and such help as sorcery could give her.

We have already mentioned Luc Gauric's prophecies. He lived in Italy but was consulted by letter. Gabriel Simeoni, another astrologer, is said to have played a part in Catherine's occult practices. Cosmo Ruggieri seems to have been her chief familiar.

This extraordinary man, whose father had been a physician at the Court of the Medici, came to France in Catherine's suite and supplied her for many years with horoscopes, talismans, love-charms and other enchantments. He warned her to 'beware of St Germain', and, as the Louvre is in the parish of St Germain l'Auxerrois, she refused to live there after Henri's death (as also in the Palace of the Tournelles with the memories of the fatal tournament) and built the new Hôtel de Soissons. In this she constructed an observatory for Ruggieri and this, strangely enough, still exists, attached to a corner of the Paris Bourse.

She also constructed for him a laboratory in part of her château at Chaumont-sur-Loire, demolished in the eighteenth century, and it is here she is said to have conducted her famous séance, known as the Consultation of the Magic Mirror. Nicolas Pasquier[1] has left an elaborate description of this ceremony in which the angel Anaël was invoked and the Queen saw, in the glass, the images of her sons as if they had been in an adjoining room. Francis moved round the room once, Charles fourteen and Henry fifteen times. Then she saw Henry of Navarre who made twenty-one turns and vanished.

Whatever we may think of this story, and it has all the marks of fiction, there is no reason why Nostradamus should have been concerned in it except that his more romantic biographers would like to think so. On the contrary there is every ground for supposing that he did not at any period of his life form part of that gang of intriguers, poisoners and traitors who practised astrology and other arts at the Court of the Valois. Nostradamus had a strange gift, but he was not a criminal. He had nothing in common with a scoundrel like Trois-Echelles or Cosmo Ruggieri.

Catherine might, however, have consulted him with advantage concerning the fate of her offspring, for there can be little doubt that he knew all about it, and of the difficulties with which Catherine would have to contend after the death of her husband.

> *En l'an qu'un œil en France regnera,*
> *La court sera en un bien fascheux trouble.* (III, 55)

In the year when France shall have a one-eyed King, the Court shall find itself in a very troubled state. The one-eyed King was of course Henri II during the ten days between the tournament and his death.

> *La Dame seule au regne demeurée*
> *D'unic esteint premier au lict d'honneur,*
> *Sept ans sera de douleur explorée,*
> *Puis longue vie au regne par grand heur.* (VI, 63)

[1]. Quoted by Eugène de France. *Catherine de Médicis, ses astrologues et ses magiciens-envouteurs*. Paris, 1911.

The Lady shall be left alone in the kingdom of her only spouse, dead before her on the field of honour. After mourning him for seven years she shall live long for the welfare of the kingdom.

It is not often Nostradamus speaks quite so clearly. As a matter of historical fact Catherine left off her mourning on August 1st, 1566 (that is, seven years after the death of Henri II) on her return from the royal progress with Charles IX. She lived until 1589. Whether her long control of the state really contributed to its welfare may well be disputed, but Nostradamus was fanatically royalist and anti-Huguenot, and had a strong personal loyalty to Catherine. He even calls her in one place '*la vefve saincte*', the sainted widow, and this in spite of having foreseen the Massacre of St Bartholomew.

On the death of their father seven of the children of Catherine de Medici were still surviving. This number seven is insisted on by Nostradamus in several quatrains, which will be considered in their chronological sequence.

> *De maison sept par mort mortelle suite,*
> *Gresle, tempeste, pestilent mal, fureurs:*
> *Roy d'Orient d'Occident tous en fuite,*
> *Subjuguera ses jadis conquereurs.* (Présage, 40)

The death of the House of the Seven (i.e. the House of Valois) shall come about by a series of deaths. (Other readings might be given, but the sense is clear enough.) Tempest, hail, fury and pestilence (i.e. civil strife and the *pestilent mal* of heresy). The last two lines are very important. A King of the Orient will put the Occidentals all to flight and will subjugate his former conquerors. The King of the Orient is Soliman the Magnificent, Emperor of the Turks (1520–66), who threatened the whole of Christendom and recovered all the Holy Places that the Crusaders had taken from his predecessors the Saracens. It is interesting to note that if Nostradamus foresaw the triumphs of Soliman he also foresaw the disasters which should overtake the Turks after his death.

THE HOUSE OF THE SEVEN

> *Pres du rivage d'Araxes la mesgnie*
> *Du grand Soliman en terre tomberont.* (III, 31)

Near the shores of Cape Araxum, the House (old French, *mesnie*, house, family, vassals) of the great Soliman shall fall to earth (the verb is in the plural, as *mesnie* is a collective noun). The Battle of Lepanto (October 5th, 1571), in which the fleet of Don John of Austria annihilated that of Selim II, son of Soliman, was fought near Cape Araxum, to-day called Cape Papa.

Another quatrain may conveniently be linked with this; blending, like the *Présage* quoted above, the history of France and contemporary events in the Orient:

> *Le grand pillot par Roy sera mandé,*
> *Laisser la classe pour plus haut lieu atteindre:*
> *Sept ans apres sera contrebandé,*
> *Barbare armée viendra Venise craindre.* (VI, 75)

He who obtained from the King a commission as Grand Pilot (that is, Gaspard de Coligny, created Admiral of France by Henri II in 1552) shall leave the fleet (Latin, *classis*) for a higher command. Seven years after he shall be in arms against him. Venice will come to fear the coming of the barbarians.

Coligny resigned his charge in 1559, on the death of Henri II, in order to place himself at the head of the Huguenots. In 1569 he was commander-in-chief of the Protestant forces at the Battle of Moncontour. In 1570 the Sultan Selim II took the Island of Cyprus from the Venetians.

The rank of Admiral of France implied, of course, no specific naval function. Is there a touch of irony in Nostradamus's transcription, '*le grand pillot*'?

Catherine had a very difficult task before her. As Queen-Mother she had, in the strict sense, no rights at all. The conduct of the realms and the guidance of the sickly boy who was now its King should have fallen, in accordance with custom, to the Princes of the Blood, that is to the Bourbons, with the King of Navarre at their head. But they were absent from Paris, and the men in possession were the members of the upstart and unscrupulous House of Guise. When the royal party emerged from the Palace of the Tournelles after Henri's death they were shepherded by the Cardinal of Lorraine and the Duc de Guise who carried the youngest of the royal children in his arms. The new King Francis II and his wife Mary Stuart were both little more than children; Catherine seemed to be there merely by courtesy. What could she do in the hands of the most astute and unscrupulous politicians of her day? She had none the less determined in her own mind to defend the royal prerogatives at least until the majority of her son, and to this end, to play off the Guises and the Bourbons against one another.

The period is so confused that even the historian, with all the documents before him, has some difficulty in finding his way through the labyrinth. For the man writing *before* the event, whatever his powers, the difficulty would seem insuperable. Yet every now and then the prophetic eye of Nostradamus seems to have caught some incident, perhaps unimportant in itself, and to have set it down with all the detail of an eye-witness and a contemporary.

In September, 1560, five citizens of Lyons and twenty others, including some German Protestants, entered into a conspiracy to hand over the city to the Huguenots. It was suspected that the real instigators of the plot were noblemen, the Prince de Condé and the Vidame de Chartres. It was, however, discovered by the watch, called vulgarly *aboyeurs* or 'barkers'. Here is what Nostradamus says about it:

> *Dedans Lyons vingt et cinq d'une haleine,*
> *Cinq citoyens, Germains, Bressans, Latins,*
> *Par dessous noble conduiront longue train,*
> *Et descouverts par abois de matins.* (x, 59)

In the town of Lyons, twenty-five persons with a single intention (all of one breath), five citizens, with Germans, men of Bresse and Italians; underneath the nobility organizing a long train (like a train of powder); and discovered by the baying of watch-dogs (mastiffs).

Sometimes he sees and sets down an actual name or title:

> *Le grand Balif d'Orleans mis à mort*
> *Sera par un de sang vindicatif,*
> *De mort merite ne mourra ne par sort*
> *Des pieds et mains mal le faisait captif.* (III, 66)

The Grand Bailli of Orleans will be condemned to death (Latin, *mittere aliquem ad mortem*, to condemn someone to death; the rest of the quatrain makes it plain that the sentence was not carried out) by a man avid of blood; he will not die by this deserved death, nor by his natural death; his bonds, on hands and feet, will not succeed in keeping him captive.

Jérôme Groslot, Grand Bailli (that is, chief magistrate) of Orleans, attempted in November 1560, to deliver the city to the Prince de Condé and for this he was condemned to death at the demand of the public prosecutor, but he succeeded in breaking his bonds and making his escape.

Condé himself, the inspirer of all these plots, is not mentioned by name in the *Centuries*, but is glanced at sufficiently clearly. Nostradamus had a particular detestation of the great Protestant leader as a heretic and a rebel.

> *Bossu sera esleu par le conseil.*
> *Plus hideux monstre en terre n'appareu,*
> *Le coup voulant prelat crevera l'œil,*
> *Le traistre au Roy pour fidelle receu.* (III, 41)

The hunchback (Condé was, in fact, a hunchback) will be elected by the Council; a more hideous monster was never seen on the earth. The deliberate shot (*coup* means either a blow or a shot) straight at him (Latin, *praelatus*, carried forward) will pierce the eye of this traitor whom the King received as faithful.

The Huguenot Assembly proclaimed Condé chief on March 19th, 1560. He was several times reconciled with the Court but continued his insurrections. He was taken prisoner at the battle of Jarnac on March 13th, 1569, and Montesquiou deliberately killed him by a pistol shot in the head. But much was to happen both to France and the Monarchy during the intervening nine years.

In November 1560 the Court was at Orleans. On Sunday, 17th, Francis, having touched for 'the king's evil' (a custom which persisted, even in England, to the end of the seventeenth century), went with his suite to the Chapel of the Jacobins to hear vespers. During the service he was taken with a shivering fit and fell into a syncope. The doctors diagnosed the formation of a fistula in his left ear, and although some thought he had been poisoned by his barber or a Huguenot valet, the medical opinion was probably right. The Spanish ambassador described him as 'remarkably consumptive' and this may have been the reason why he grew steadily worse and worse. On December 15th, Francis died. Nostradamus had written:

> *Premier fils vefve malheureux mariage*
> *Sans nuls enfans deux Isles en discord,*
> *Avant dix-huict incompetent âge.*
> *De l'autre près plus bas sera l'accord.* (x, 39)

The eldest son of the widow will die a minor before the age of eighteen, without children, setting two Isles in discord. His next eldest brother will be affianced even younger. This is a very remarkable quatrain. As Francis was born on January 19th, 1543, he was, at his death, some six weeks short of reaching the age of eighteen. He had no children, and his young widow, Mary Queen of Scots, returned to her kingdom, setting at discord the 'two Islands', that is, the two realms comprised in the British Isles. The last line is equally exact, for Francis's younger brother Charles had been affianced to Elizabeth of Austria at the age of eleven although he did not marry her until 1570 when he was twenty.

There is some remarkable contemporary evidence that the quatrain was known and understood at the French Court. 'Each courtier', wrote Michieli, the Venetian Ambassador, 'remembers the thirty-ninth quatrain of *Centurie X* of Nostradamus and comments upon it under his breath'; and, in the following May, he remarks, 'There is another prediction very widespread in France, emanating from the famous astrologer called Nostradamus and which menaces the three brothers, saying that the Queen will see them all Kings.' The Spanish Ambassador wrote to Philip II in a similar strain, and the Tuscan ambassador also. There is ample evidence of the Prophet's fame in his own lifetime.

Francis II was succeeded by Charles IX, a boy of ten, and the old struggles recommenced with even greater bitterness. They were not least violent in the town in which Nostradamus had hoped to live out his days in peace.

In the spring of the year in which Francis II died the Sieur de Mauvans, one of the Protestant leaders of Provence, had been assassinated at Draguignan. The common people of Salon, who were fanatically Catholic, gave vent to wild rejoicings, but many of the wealthier citizens, among them the kinsmen of the murdered man, were already touched with Lutheranism, and a bitter fight broke out between them and the 'cabans' or peasants. There were riots and pillagings, followed by violent repressions, and party strife became every day more violent.

Nostradamus, both as Jew and magician, was in a dangerous situation. The Huguenots were angered by his punctilious discharge of his religious duties, but these did not serve to endear him to the Catholics, who accused him of hypocrisy and, not without reason, of practices little in conformity with orthodox Christianity. He could not seek the protection of the Protestant nobles, and his wealth made him an obvious prey in the eyes of the tumultuous peasantry. During May 1560 many of the better class houses in Salon were sacked and Nostradamus must have trembled not only for his goods, but for the secrets of his study. He must often during this troubled period have smelt the faggot, and perhaps have wished that the Royal protection on which he could count were nearer at hand. He did not go to the King, however. Strangely enough the King came to him.

Early in 1564, in the interval between two civil wars, Catherine conceived the idea of a Royal Progress throughout the provinces of France, a kind of propaganda tour in the company of the fourteen-year-old Charles IX, to culminate in a meeting with her daughter, the Queen of Spain, at the Spanish frontier. The first signs of Spring were no sooner visible than she set out, followed by a train reduced, for purposes of economy, to the miserable total of no more than eight hundred people. The Court, including the famous 'Flying Squadron' of thirty-five of the most beautiful and most noble young women in France, the Royal Council, four companies of *gens d'armes*, a company of light horse, a regiment of guards, lackeys, cooks, grooms, huntsmen, on foot, on horseback, in coaches and litters, started from Fontainebleau on a tour lasting two years.

Slowly they made their way through country ravaged by war and pestilence, until in the Autumn of 1564 they had reached Provence, and the 'consuls' of the little town learned to their satisfaction – and also probably to their astonishment – that the royal party intended to call at Salon. Everything was prepared, arrangements made for receiving all the men and horses accompanying the King, carpets and tapestries were hung from the windows of the houses, triumphal arches were erected, speeches prepared, and, on the afternoon of October 17th, Charles IX made his state entry into Salon by the gateway of St Lazare. The boy king was mounted on a grey arab steed with trappings of black velvet trimmed with gold and was clad in a mantle of violet velvet embroidered with silver. His cap of the same colour was thickly set with diamonds and, suspended from his ears, by chains of gold, two immense diamonds fell upon the double ruff around his neck.

On a dais of white and violet damask were grouped the notables of the town, including Nostradamus. The chief magistrate read a complimentary oration to the King, but the latter, with the frankness of youth, replied: 'I came to see Nostradamus.'

Accounts of the meeting differ. Some say that the King ordered one of the courtiers to give the Prophet a horse so that he could ride in the royal procession. In any case he was treated with singular honour and that evening was summoned to the royal apartments together with his entire family, even to the child still in the cradle.

The moving spirit behind all this was, of course, Catherine, and early next morning she sent for Nostradamus and ordered him to draw up the horoscope, not of the King but of his younger brother the Duc d'Anjou. The Prophet declared that he would one day succeed to the throne.

But there was another boy in the royal train who interested Nostradamus even more. This was the ten-year-old Henry of Navarre. The Prophet asked his tutor to have him undressed, but the boy, fearing that he was going to be beaten, refused. Next morning, Nostradamus was introduced into his room before he was up – even princes in those days slept naked – and having examined him declared that he would have the whole inheritance. It is probable that Nostradamus wished to see the boy naked in order to examine the moles on his body, as these were thought to serve as a check on the planetary position at birth. If the exact time of birth were unknown, or if the rising sign were in doubt, then the bodily marks might be a valuable guide.[1] That the boy's horoscope *was* drawn up seems certain on the authority of the *registre journal* of the future Henri IV himself, and the whole incident is vouched for by the historian Gaufridi.

Charles IX left Salon during the afternoon of October 18th, to spend the night at Lambesc. At Arles, however, he found the Rhone in flood and, unable to proceed farther, stayed there for a time. Catherine seized the opportunity to send once more for Nostradamus. The Spaniard Francisco de Alova, who was in the Royal suite, wrote of the trust which the Queen placed in the Prophet, and declared that when she quoted his words she had an air as confident as if she were citing St John or St Luke. Whatever it was he told her she bestowed upon Nostradamus a hundred gold *écus*, to which the King added two hundred, and in addition

[1]. I owe this suggestion to Mr C. Nelson Stewart. See also Raphael's *Horary Astrology*, London, 1920, Chapter XV, 'Of Marks, Scars and Moles'.

created him *'medécin et conseiller ordinaire de roi'* with the wages, prerogatives and honours attached thereto. Nostradamus had every reason to be pleased with the consideration shown him by the House of Valois.

He had, however, no delusions concerning its fate. He had already foreseen the succession of Henry IV, and he foresaw too that he would never come to the throne as a Huguenot. At Marseilles the young King was about to enter the Cathedral to hear mass. Henry of Navarre stopped at the threshold and the King (they were both children) seized his cap and threw it into the church in order to compel him to cross the threshold to retrieve it. When this was reported to Nostradamus he declared that it signified his ultimate return to the Church.

Nostradamus had seen Catherine and her sons for the last time. He was now an old man, and seemed older than his years. Long study and the gout had made him so infirm that he was unable to edit the new edition of the *Centuries* which he had been preparing. It is a proof of the excellent relations which existed between him and the ecclesiastical authorities that he should have entrusted the task to the Franciscan friar Jean Vallier. It is strange that he did not employ the faithful Chavigny, who was at his bedside daily. He confided to him, however, the arrangements for his burial. Not wishing, even when dead, to be trodden under foot by the people of Salon, he desired to be buried upright in the thickness of the wall of the Church of the Cordeliers between the great door and the Altar of St Martha, and Chavigny promised that it should be so.

His gout had now changed to dropsy and he knew that he had not long to live. He had himself propounded a remedy in his *Traité des confitures* – an infusion of the rind of the bugloss or *lingua bovina* – but it was powerless to help him now. In June, 1566, he wrote in the ephemerides (what we should call the autograph album) of Jean Stadius the motto, *Hic propre mort est*, My death is near. On the 17th he sent for Master Joseph Roche, royal notary at Salon, and dictated to him his last will and testament.

On July 1st he sent for Brother Vidal of the Friars Minor at Salon, who heard his confession and administered to him the last rites of the Church. He knew that he would not survive the night. Chavigny says, 'And the day before he exchanged this life for the other, I having assisted him for a considerable time, and very late taking leave of him until the next morning, he said these words to me, "You will not see me alive at sunrise".'

He had foreseen his own death down to the smallest details:

> *De retour d'Ambassade, don de Roy mis au lieu,*
> *Plus n'en fera, sera allé à Dieu,*
> *Parens plus proches, amis, freres du sang,*
> *Trouvé tout mort près du lict et du banc.* (Prés. CXLI)

On return from his embassy (he had gone to Arles as the representative of the town of Salon), the King's gift safely put away, he will do no more, for he will have gone to God. By his near relations, friends and brothers he will be found dead near the bed and the bench. The bench in question was one which he had had made in order to assist him in hoisting his dropsical body into bed. He had evidently striven to rise in the night, for he was found in the morning on the bench.

On the same day (July 2nd, 1566), the feast of the *Visitation de Notre-Dame*, he was carried to the grave supported by Palamède Mark, Sieur de Châteauneuf, and by Jacques Suffren, citizen of Salon, surrounded by candles and with books and a writing desk beside him, as was suitable to so learned a doctor. As he had directed, he was immured in the masonry of the Church of the Cordeliers, and Anne Ponsart, his wife, had the following inscription cut in the stone:

'Here repose the bones of the most illustrious Michel Nostradamus, the only one, in the judgement of all mortals, worthy to write with a pen almost divine, under the influence of the stars, of the future events of the entire world.

He lived sixty-two years, six months and seventeen days.

He died at Salon in the year 1566. Let Posterity trouble not his repose.

Anne Ponsart Gemelle, his wife, wishes her spouse true felicity.'

So Nostradamus disappeared from human sight, but soon a rumour began to circulate among the superstitious citizens of Salon that he was not really dead at all, but had had himself immured as in a kind of magic cabinet in order to finish his prophecies. They put their ear to the wall and fancied that they heard a movement inside. But none was so hardy, for many years, as to open the tomb.

This was scarcely to be wondered at, for Nostradamus, in the *Centuries* themselves, had pronounced a curse against any who should disturb his bones:

> *Qui ouvrira le monument trouvé*
> *Et ne viendra le serrer promptement,*
> *Mal luy viendra ...*   (IX, 7)

He who opens the discovered monument and does not close it quickly, evil will come to him.

In another passage he says:

> *Est caché le thresor*
> *Qui par long siècles avoit esté grappé:*
> *Trouvé mourra, l'œil crevé de ressort.* (I, 27)

The treasure is hidden which during long centuries has been sought for. He who finds it will die, his eye pierced by the spring.

These ambiguous words have led some to believe that he had had buried with him in the tomb the manuscript key of his predictions, or the prose prophecies of which he speaks in another place, and which have never been found, or the missing forty-eight quatrains of *Centurie VII*.

But perhaps the monument in question was elsewhere. *Trouvé* seems to imply that it had yet to be found and the quatrain quoted above (I, 27) begins quite clearly:

> *Dessouz le chaine Guien du ciel frappé,*
> *Non long de là est caché le thresor ...*

Beneath the Guyenne mountain smitten by heaven, not far

from there the treasure is hidden. It is another mystery to add to the many that surround this extraordinary man.[1]

There is another strange quatrain which may throw some further light – or further darkness – on the matter:

> *Quand l'escriture D.M. trouvée,*
> *Et cave antique à lampe descouverte,*
> *Loy, Roy, & Prince Ulpian esprouvée,*
> *Pavillon Royne & Duc sous la couverte.* (VIII, 66)

If 'D.M.' stands for '*du manuscrit*' we may read: When the manuscript is found and the antique cave explored with a lamp, the Law, the King and Prince Renard shall be tried, and the standard of the Queen and the Duke hidden away.

Is this equivalent to saying that the tomb will be opened at the French Revolution? That is certainly what happened, for during the troubles of that period the Church of the Cordeliers at Salon was destroyed. The remains of Nostradamus were later removed to the chapel of Notre-Dame in the Church of St Laurent, and in 1813 the epitaph was re-engraved on a marble plaque.[2] But no manuscript of any kind is known to have been discovered.

The Prophet of Salon was dead, but the scroll of history which to him had been transparent, continued slowly to unroll itself as he had foretold, and the House of Valois to move to its predestined end.

It would be out of place in a work like the present one to attempt to trace in any detail the history of the French Wars of Religion. They are a welter of battles and skirmishes,

---

1. One of the present author's correspondents, Major Herbert R. Sykes, makes the interesting suggestion that *chaine* should be *chêne*, and that Guien is an adjective derived from *gui*, mistletoe. The line would then read: 'Beneath the mistletoe-clad oak, struck by lightning'.

2. *D. M. Clarissimi Ossa MICHAELIS NOSTRADAMI, unius omnium mortalium judicio digni, cujus pene divino calamo totius Orbis, ex Astrorum inflexu, futuri eventus conscriberentur. Vixit annos LXII menses VI dies XVII. Obiit Sallone an. MDLXVI. Quietem Posteri ne invidete. Anna Pontia Gemella Conjugi opt. v. felicit. Reliquiae Michaelis Nostradami in hoc sacellum translatae fuerunt post annum MDCCLXXXIX. Epitaphium restitutum mense iulio MDCCCXIII.*

marchings and counter-marchings, unsuccessful sieges, indecisive campaigns, unlikely alliances, treasons, assassinations, broken truces, uneasy peace. The Court, which means Catherine de' Medici, swung from one policy to another, now seeking to exterminate the Huguenots, now to come to some arrangement with them in the teeth of the Catholic League.[1] Both sides called in foreign mercenaries, both intrigued with foreign powers. The House of Guise was always a potential ally of the Crown, always its greatest danger; the House of Bourbon was the hope of the Protestants, yet, on more than one occasion, the salvation of the Catholic King. It is like a rich tapestry shot through with threads of black and scarlet, but the passions which wove it have now grown so dim that it is difficult to distinguish one figure from another or make out its pictured histories. Yet in the middle of this faded hanging there is a dark stain which Time has not obliterated – the Massacre of St Bartholomew. To many an English reader it is the sole fact still visible, the only rememberable incident in the confused reign of Charles IX.

Another civil war had been ended by the Peace of Saint-Germain in 1570. The Edict of Tolerance was re-established so that, from the Catholic standpoint, the whole campaign had been in vain. What military glory there was had accrued to the Duke of Anjou, and the King was already violently jealous of his brother. He began to dream of an attack on Spain in Flanders, as a diversion in which both parties in his own realm might be united. An intrigue was begun to draw in England by a marriage between Queen Elizabeth and Anjou.

For all these projects, however, it was necessary to come to terms with the Huguenots. Coligny, Admiral of France, was now their leader, and with his friends had fortified himself in the Protestant stronghold of La Rochelle. The King invited him to Blois, and greatly daring – for there had

1. The 'Holy League' was established in 1576, under the leadership of Henri de Guise. It was opposed to any compromise with the Protestants, even at the cost, in the end, of dethroning the king.

already been repeated attempts on his life – the Admiral came. He was graciously received and there was even a reconciliation with the Queen-Mother and Anjou.

With the frankness and fearlessness of his nature, Coligny took very few precautions, so few that even his enemies took it upon themselves to warn him. Meeting him one day alone in a dark passage, the Duc de Montpensier, a fanatical Catholic, remonstrated with him and insisted on accompanying him to the public room. 'I am in the King's house', protested Coligny. 'Where the King is not always master,' replied Montpensier. 'Where are your men?'

Still, outwardly, all was well. Coligny received a grant of 100,000 livres from the King's private purse to indemnify him for his losses while he had been fighting against the King. He resumed his seat in the Council and even presided over it in the King's absence. Something like intimacy sprang up between him and Charles, who called the old man *mon père*, and confided to him his distrust of Catherine and Anjou. His advice was sought with regard to the projected campaign in Flanders.

It was in the midst of these negotiations that there occurred the Battle of Lepanto, of which, as we have seen, Nostradamus had foreknowledge.

In French internal politics the effect of the battle was to strengthen the hands of the Huguenots, since Catherine had everything to fear from a triumphant Spain. Yet always, at the back of her mind, lay the notion that she might one day, by a happy stroke, rid herself of the troublesome heretics in her own kingdom. Her daughter Elizabeth, Queen of Spain, was dead; she had tried to induce the widower to marry her second daughter Marguerite, and, having failed in this project, she asked Coligny to negotiate a marriage with the young Henry of Navarre in spite of his Protestantism, and to persuade his mother the Queen of Navarre to come to Court for the final arrangements.

With some misgiving she came and after six weeks of negotiations the marriage was arranged, and the espousals were celebrated in the Louvre on August 17th, 1572. The marriage took place the following day and the next four were given up to feasting, jousting and masquerades. The Duc d'Anjou, the future Henri III, was, as befitted his character, in charge of these entertainments and, in the light of later events, may be seen to have taken a perverse pleasure in sinister double meanings. In one *divertissement*, the King and his two brothers, dressed as knights errant, defended Paradise and drove their opponents towards a stage property representing the mouth of Hell, into which they were dragged by devils. The King might not know what he was doing, but Anjou did.

Coligny's advice to the King had been to escape from the tutelage of his mother and to get rid of his dangerous brother by supporting his candidature to the crown of Poland. This did not suit either of them, and in concert with the Guises they determined on Coligny's death. A bravo named Maurevert was stationed in a house adjoining the cloister of Saint-Germain l'Auxerrois, on the route between the Louvre and the Admiral's lodging. After seeing the King it was Coligny's custom to return on foot to his house, and in the morning of August 22nd he was walking slowly along reading a petition when Maurevert fired an arquebus from behind the curtain of his window. The ball carried away the index finger of Coligny's right hand and lodged in his arm. But he was not killed and his first act was to send word to the King of what had happened.

When the news reached the King he was playing tennis. In an access of rage he broke his racquet, crying, 'Shall I never have peace?' It is unlikely that he was acting a part. He had a genuine regard for Coligny, and was almost certainly sincere in his desire to punish the perpetrator of the outrage. Accompanied by his mother and brothers he visited the wounded man and had a short interview with him alone. Pressed on the way back by Catherine and Anjou to relate what had passed he flew into a rage and said that the Admiral had warned him against them. It was enough; it was more than enough.

The attitude of the King lulled the Huguenots into

security. The Guises presented themselves before Charles, and said a surly farewell. But they did not leave Paris. Catherine and Anjou held a conference with four of their adherents and when they were ready went to see the King. They told him that the Huguenots were plotting a new rebellion, that Coligny, whom he had trusted, was planning to make himself King. Charles was frightened and wavered. Then Catherine played her trump card. She revealed [1] that she and Anjou were the authors of the attempt on the Admiral's life, and that the Guises were merely accomplices. 'We struck at the Admiral to save the King. The King must finish the work or he and we are lost.'

The neurotic Charles had a brain storm and broke out into a tempest of anger, but, when it had subsided, the evil counsellors were still around him. He struggled, gloomy and hopeless, for an hour and a half, and at last consented. And then his mad rage returned and he cried out that if they killed Coligny they must kill all the Huguenots in France, that none might live to reproach him with the deed.

The conspirators completed their preparations. The massacre was to commence at daybreak on August 24th and the signal was to be given by the bell of the Palais de Justice. The first death was to be that of Coligny at the hand of Guise himself.

Several Protestant lords assisted at the *coucher* of the King. One of them, La Rochefoucauld, was the boon companion of Charles, who tried to persuade him to spend the night in the palace. La Rochefoucauld made a joke and departed. Before dawn the King, Catherine, and Anjou took up their places on the side of the Louvre which looked towards Saint Germain l'Auxerrois 'to see the beginning of the execution'. It is said that Charles had yet another revulsion of feeling and would have stopped the signal from the Palais de Justice. Catherine forestalled him by having it rung from the nearby church.

Coligny was murdered in his bed and his corpse flung out

1. According to Marguerite of Navarre the actual revelation was made not by Catherine herself but by her creature, Retz.

of the window, to be dragged through the streets of Paris. Then Paris itself went mad, and nobles, royal guards, and populace vied with one another in the work of butchery. Most mad of all was the King who began shooting out of a window of the Louvre with an arquebus, crying, 'Kill! kill!'

> *Le Noir farouche quand aura essayé*
> *Sa main sanguine par feu, fer, arcs tendus,*
> *Trestous le peuple sera tant effrayé*
> *Voir les plus grans par col & pieds pendus.* (IV, 47)

When the ferocious King (throughout Nostradamus *Noir* is used as the anagram of *Roi*) shall have exercised his blood-stained hand with fire and sword and the bended bow (the arquebus was only just beginning to replace the cross-bow) all the people will be frightened to see the greatest in the land hanged by the neck and the feet.

There was a streak of sadism in the neurotic Charles which led him, while hunting, to disembowel the game with his own hand, and to blow out the brains of all the donkeys and pigs he met with. *Farouche* is therefore a very suitable word, for which 'ferocious' is not a very happy translation. With regard to the final line of the quatrain it is interesting to note that the body of Coligny, having been dragged through the gutters of Paris, was hanged by the foot from the gibbet of Montfaucon.

A number of '*Sixains*' are said to have been found among the papers of the Prophet at his death, but, as they were not published until the next century, they have not the authenticity of the quatrains printed during his lifetime. One of them refers to St Bartholomew by name:

> *La grand Cité qui n'a pain à demy*
> *Encor un coup la sainct Barthelemy*
> *Engravera au profond de son ame:*
> *Nismes, Rochelle, Geneve et Montpellier,*
> *Castres, Lyon, Mars entrant au Belier,*
> *S'entrebattront: le tout pour une Dame.* (Sixain 52)

While the planet Mars enters the sign of the Ram, the great city which famine threatens will engrave deeply in its memory the festival of St Bartholomew. Nîmes, La Rochelle, Geneva, Montpellier, Castres, Lyons will be the scene of civil war, all by the orders of a great lady.

Dame stands invariably in Nostradamus for a Royal lady except (and this is here particularly apt) where it stands for the Catholic Church. Secret orders were sent to the provincial governors to kill the Huguenots, and the inspirer of this move was the Queen-Mother, Catherine de' Medici. Both meanings therefore fit.

The King never recovered from the shock of St Bartholomew. It was in vain that, prompted by his mother, he spoke of a Huguenot plot and urged more massacres and more violent persecutions. He knew only too well where the responsibility lay. The Republic of Venice was the best informed government in Europe and the reports of its representatives abroad are a valuable source of information even concerning the intimate details of the lives of Kings. The Venetian ambassador in Paris wrote home to the Signori concerning Charles IX: 'He never looks one in the face when one addresses him, he stoops ... and contracts his shoulders, and he has a habit of lowering his head and narrowing his eyes. ... Besides being morose and taciturn, they say that he is also vindictive and never forgives any one who offends him, and it is feared that from being merely severe he will become cruel.' He hunted furiously, sometimes remaining twelve or fourteen hours in the saddle, and his health, never robust, began to give way under these exertions, and under the strain of remorse. Consumption set in and in the autumn of 1573 it became plain that he had not long to live. He died on May 30th, 1574. He was not quite twenty-five.

Two of Catherine's children had now been Kings of France. The third, Anjou, had been elected to the crown of Poland, and the Queen-Mother, once more Regent, sent urgent messages to recall him to his own country. The Poles were very unwilling to let him go, but he escaped, and travelling by way of Venice, Turin and the Mont Cenis, arrived in France, where he assumed the title of Henri III.

He is the *Roy-Roy* of the Nostradamus prophecies, and, since his younger brother Alençon was to die before him, the last of the Valois Kings.

Henri III returned to a distracted kingdom. The Massacre of St Bartholomew had thrown the Huguenots more and more into open revolt, but this was not all. Alençon (who had now, for the further confusion of the reader, succeeded to the title of Anjou as his brother had succeeded to the title of King) was very much discontented with his position in the State, and ripe for treason. Other rebellious elements crystallized around him, and so began the so-called War of the Malcontents which lasted from 1574 until 1576.

> *Des sept rameaux à trois seront reduicts,*
> *Les plus aisnés seront surprises par mort,*
> *Fratricider les deux seront seduicts . . .* (VI, 11)

The Seven Branches will be reduced to Three, the eldest having been surprised by Death; the Two male survivors will be seduced to fratricidal strife. The death of the four elder children of Henri II left (besides Marguerite of Navarre), only Henri III and François, his brother.

Nostradamus returns to the same theme in even plainer language:

> *Deux royals frères si fort guerroyeront*
> *Qu'entre eux sera la guerre si mortelle:*
> *Qu'un chacun places fortes occuperont,*
> *De regne et vie sera leur grand querelle.* (III, 98)

Two royal brothers will wage war so fiercely against one another and between them shall be such mortal strife that both will occupy fortified places. Their dispute will concern not only the realm but their very lives.

The King had reproached Anjou with conspiring against his life, and had told him that he merited death. He had even made the strangest propositions to Henri of Navarre, suggesting that the disappearance of Anjou would be to the benefit of both the King and his Protestant rival. After a number of battles and truces Henri III was compelled to accord a number of fortified towns both to the Huguenots and to the Malcontents. The Duke of Anjou returned to Court and the King was constrained to dissimulate his resentment.

But if Henri had pacified two enemies for the moment he found a third ready to rise up against him. The extreme Catholic party distrusted him profoundly, suspecting that, rather than depend upon its partisans, he was willing to make an alliance with Henri of Navarre. For a while he held them in check.

> *Par lors qu'un Roi sera contre les siens,*
> *Natifs de Blois subjuguera Ligures...* (x, 44)

When a King, native of Blois, shall be opposed to his own, he shall subjugate those of the League. Henri III was descended from the Counts of Blois and in another quatrain is called *le Grand de Blois*. That the quatrain above quoted refers to him is shown clearly by the last line, which refers to 'the Seven', who, as we have seen, were the children of Henri II:

> *Des sept puis l'ombre à Roy estrennes et lemures.*

Then the shadow only of government will remain to the King, last branch of the tree of the Seven – branches cut off and shades of the dead! The line is more than usually congested and abbreviated but the sense is clear.

The suspicions of the Leaguers were well founded for, in 1577, Henri issued the Edict of Poitiers, by which the Protestants were authorized to practise their cult and the marriage of their pastors was recognized. This latter provision seems to have shocked the Prophet profoundly. He writes:

> *Pour le plaisir d'edict voluptueux,*
> *On meslera le poison dans la foy:*
> *Venus sera en cours si vertueux,*
> *Qu'obfusquera du Soleil tout aloy.* (v, 72)

For the pleasure of the voluptuous Edict, poison will be mingled with the Faith. At the Court Venus will be so virtuous or so vigorous (debauchery itself being almost, as it were, a virtue) that the glory of the sun of Righteousness will be obscured.

Henri's Court did indeed give a pattern of debauchery to the whole of Europe, although it would be unfair as well as unwise to take at their face value all the accusations which were brought against him by the pamphleteers of the League. His homosexuality probably gave most offence to his subjects, especially as his Mignons flaunted their wealth in fantastic attire and made no secret of their condition. But it was probably their open practice of sorcery which armed the hand of Jacques Clément against the King.

Henri was alleged to have a familiar spirit named Terragon and to have given him as a husband to the Comtesse de Foix. But his flesh was so hot that she could not endure his embraces. Such fancies are proof at least of the hysterical hatred which the King had now provoked against him. He is described in another pamphlet not without wit as 'Henry, by the grace of his Mother, useless King of France and of imaginary Poland, Door-keeper of the Louvre. . . . Friend of the Devil, Barber of his Wife, Haberdasher to the Palace . . .' with a string of other epithets even less complimentary. It was obvious that the throne of France was tottering to its fall, whatever shifts and temporary alliances might prolong its life for a little. Nostradamus wrote:

> *Les sept en trois seront mis en concorde*
> *Pour subjuguer les Alpes Apennines,*
> *Mais la tempeste et Ligure coüade*
> *Les profligent en subites ruines.*   (III, 39)

The Seven reduced to three will come to an agreement to subjugate (him of) the Apennines; but the tempest and the cowardly Leaguer will soon cast them down in ruin.

The seven children of Henri II were now reduced to three: Henri III, the Duke of Anjou and Marguerite of Navarre. They sank their quarrels in an attempt to conquer the Netherlands, then occupied by Spanish troops under the command of the Duke of Parma, whose estates were traversed by the Apennines. At first the project seemed to succeed, and in 1582 the Duke of Anjou was acknowledged as Duke of Brabant and Count of Flanders. But in the following year he was driven back to France by the tempest of opposition he had provoked, and died there soon afterwards. The 'cowardly' Leaguer is Jacques Clément who was to slay Henri III by treachery seven years later.

The hostility of the Leaguers to Henri III became more and more pronounced, and as Paris was entirely in their hands the King was no longer safe in his own capital. Meanwhile France was invaded by an army of 36,000 German and Swiss troops, and the only effort to oppose them was made by the Duc de Guise, the darling of the League, which was even beginning to favour his succession to the throne.

> *Nouvelle et pluye subite, impetueuse,*
> *Empeschera subit deux exercites,*
> *Pierre ciel feux faire la mer pierreuse,*
> *La mort de sept terre et marin subites.* (II, 18)

This quatrain, hopelessly dark to the general reader, is none the less one of the most interesting in the whole of the *Centuries* once the historical background is understood. Literally, it might be translated: News! – and sudden, impetuous rain will prevent two armies (from *exercitus*, an army) from coming to grips. Stones and musket shots (like fire from) heaven. (The man of) earth and sea will make the stony sea. It is obscure enough in all conscience until we have the clue. But when the news of the invasion came to Guise he hastened to Montargis where there might have been a decisive battle but for a most violent rainstorm which compelled both sides to break off the fight. Soon after, on May 12th, 1588, occurred that rebellion of the Parisians against their King which is known to French historians as the *Journée des Barricades*. During this the King's partisans were assailed with stones and musket shots by the citizens, led by Brissac who had been told by Henri that he was good for nothing 'either on earth or sea'. He replied that he had now found his element, lifting the very paving stones of Paris in a wave of popular resentment. These details, unimportant in themselves, are very astonishing when we compare them with the language of Nostradamus in the above quatrain. It is as if he had known the very words of both and had tried to set them down in a form too abbreviated to carry the meaning. The triple repetition of *subit* links the quatrain with that already quoted which prophesied *subites ruines*.

The King tried to take vigorous counter-measures, but was overwhelmed by the force of the agitation and compelled to leave the city. Later Paris had cause to repent of driving him out, for he returned with an army and besieged it. Nostradamus knew all about this also:

> *La republique de la grande cité*
> *A grand rigueur ne voudra consentir,*
> *Roy sortir hors par trompette cité*
> *L'eschelle au mur, la cité repentir.* (III, 50)

The popular government of the great city will not be willing to accept the King's repressions. The King, leaving the city, will swear to summon the city to repentance by the sound of the trumpet and with the assaulting ladder placed against the wall.

Paris was now almost completely in the hands of the 'Seize', its revolutionary government of sixteen persons, sworn to obedience to the principles of the Catholic League, and favourable to the Duc de Guise. The very day before the *Journée des Barricades* the King had resolved to rid himself of this dangerous rival. How dangerous he was might be seen from the joy with which he was welcomed in Paris, to which he had come in spite of the royal prohibition. He went to see Henri in his apartments. Henri had concealed a soldier ready to kill him when he should give the signal. He never gave it. Instead he fled from Paris and summoned the Estates to meet at Blois. Catherine managed to effect an apparent reconciliation, but her own son had neither forgiven nor forgotten.

Guise knew that his life was threatened, but he thought

he understood the psychology of Henri III. 'He is a King who wants frightening,' he remarked to one of those who warned him. On December 21st, the King and he went together to visit Catherine who was ill in bed. She was cheered by the sight of their apparent reconciliation. The King invited Guise to attend a meeting of the Council early next morning and Guise agreed. That night he found an anonymous note, tucked into his napkin at supper, warning him once more that his life was in danger. He read it aloud, scribbled on the paper, 'He would not dare,' and at eight o'clock in the morning was in his place in the Council. From there he was summoned to the King's apartments and as he entered the passage leading to them hesitated for a moment at the sight of the King's bodyguards. A moment later he was stabbed. Unarmed but desperate, he struggled fiercely, crying, 'Treachery'. Henri III appeared in the doorway in time to see him fall. The next day the Cardinal of Guise suffered the same fate as his brother.

Catherine heard of these things with horror. She was already ill in bed, and in her discouragement she made her will and sent for a priest. She asked him his name and he replied that it was Julien de St Germain. '*Mon Dieu!*' cried Catherine, 'I am dead'. For she remembered the prophecy of Cosmo Ruggieri when he had warned her to beware of St Germain. On the night of January 5th, 1589, she died.

Not only Catherine disapproved of her son's action. The Estates assembled at Blois addressed to him the strongest remonstrances at the risk of their lives:

> *Par la response de dame Roy troublé,*
> *Ambassadeurs mespriseront leur vie:*
> *Le grand ses freres contrefera double,*
> *Par deux mourront, ire, haine & envie.* (1, 85)

The last two lines are interesting. The Duc de Mayenne, after the assassination of his two brothers (the Two will die by anger, hate, and envy) will so act as to take their place (contrefera double). He was, in fact, proclaimed chief of the

League and took the title of Lieutenant-General of the Kingdom.

Thus the murder which Henri III had plotted to commit in Paris took effect at Blois, and Nostradamus comments:

> *Paris conjure un grand meurtre commettre*
> *Blois le fera sortir en plain effect:*
> *Ceux d'Orleans voudront leur chef remettre;*
> *Angers, Troye, Langres leur feront un meffait.* (III, 51)

The second half of the quatrain is as exact as the first. The men of Orleans wishing to set up again their chief, rose against Balzac d'Entragues, the Royal Governor, and placed at their head Charles of Lorraine, Chevalier d'Aumale, one of the chiefs of the League; Angers, Troyes and Langres, on the other hand, took the side of Henri III.

> *Le grand de Blois son amy tuera;*
> *Le regne mis en mal & doute double.* (III, 33)

Certainly the second line describes the condition of France after the 'Great One of Blois' had killed his 'friend'. The breach between Henri and the League was now irreparable. The King found himself increasingly alone.

Distrusted by the Court, hated by the League, driven out of his capital, he turned in desperation to the last possible if unlikely ally, Henri of Navarre, the leader of the Protestant party and his own chief rival to the throne. The world saw with stupefaction an alliance in arms between the two Henris, one of whom had been one of the main instigators of the Massacre of St Bartholomew, and the other so very nearly one of its chief victims. In the eyes of the Leaguers this was the King's crowning infamy. They resolved to rid themselves of him for ever and they pressed the Papacy for a sentence of excommunication.

Pope Sixtus V had already in 1585 excommunicated Henri of Navarre and pronounced him incapable of succeeding, under any circumstances, to the throne of France. For five months he hesitated to excommunicate Henri III, and even when he did so, in May 1589, he did not release his subjects from their oath of allegiance. The Papacy had seen only too well the effects of excommunication. England and half Europe seemed already lost. Was the Church to be stripped naked? Was France itself to be lost?

> *Quand chef Perouse n'osera sa tunique*
> *Sans au couvert tout nud s'expolier,*
> *Seront prins sept . . .* (v, 67)

When the Chief of Perugia (in the Papal States) dare not see his tunic taken away for fear of being completely naked, Seven shall be taken.

Once more the 'Seven'. Marguerite of Navarre being excluded from the succession by the Salic Law, Henri III was the last of the Seven capable of ruling, and he too is now approaching his violent end. The last line of the quatrain reads:

> *Le pere et fils morts par poincte au colier.*

Father and son dead by mortal blade. *Au colier* is not physically exact. The wound of Henri II was near enough to the throat, but Henri III was stabbed in the lower bowel. It is possible that a play is intended on the Greek word κοιλια, a cavity, the stomach, the belly.

Allied with Henri of Navarre, Henri III approached Paris with 40,000 men and would probably have taken it. The League resolved on a last extremity, the killing of the King. A Dominican, Jacques Clément, made his way to St Cloud where Henri was encamped and under the pretext of conveying a secret letter to the King was admitted to his presence. He found Henri III on the *chaise percée* – it is extraordinary to the modern mind that a King should have received anyone in such circumstances – and profited by the occasion. Leaning towards the King, as if to impart some secret, he drew a knife from his ample sleeve and stabbed him, as we have said, in the lower bowel. Clément was immediately slain by the courtiers, but the King himself died the following day, August 2nd, 1589.

Three days before he was killed at St Cloud Henri III

had had a strange dream. He dreamed that he saw all the regalia, sandals, tunics, dalmatics, the blue satin mantle, the great and the little crown, the sceptre and the Hand of Justice, the sword and the gilded spurs, all bloody and trodden under foot by monks and populace, and this incensed him against the secretary of the Abbey of St Denis, in whose charge these symbolic objects were. Yet although this dream might have warned him of his fate, the precautions he took were insufficient to prevent it.[1]

Nostradamus has a very curious line concerning the murder of Henri III:

Le Roy-Roy n'estre, du Doux la pernicie ... (Prés. 38)

The King-King will be no more on account of the homicide (*pernicie* from the Latin *pernicies*, killing, destruction) committed by Le Doux.

Now, as we have seen, Henri III had been King of Poland as well as of France, so that '*Roy-Roy*' is particularly apt. But even stranger is the use of the name Le Doux, for *doux* is the synonym of *clément* and Jacques Clément was the assassin of the King.

Paris being still in the hands of his enemies, Henri III was buried provisionally in the abbey of St Corneille at Compiègne and it was not until 1610 that his coffin, with those of Henri IV and Catherine de Medici, was transported to the traditional vault of the Kings of France at St Denis. Nostradamus, in a striking quatrain, pictures the ancestors of the last of the Valois welcoming him behind the iron grille of their tomb.

> *Serpens transmis en la cage de fer*
> *Ou les enfans septains du Roy sont pris,*
> *Les vieux & peres sortiront bas de l'enfer*
> *Ainsi mourir voir de fruict mort & cris.* (1, 10)

When the coffin (Greek σαρπος, a coffin) shall pass into the iron cage in which the Seven children of the King are held,

---

1. Louis Guyon, *Diverses Leçons*, liv. II, ch. XXIV. Quoted by the Bibliophile Jacob in his *Curiosités des Sciences Occultes*.

the ancestors will emerge from the depths of Hell and cry aloud to see die the last of their line like a dead fruit, leaving no issue.

So ends the House of Seven by the succession of deaths which Nostradamus had foreseen:

> *De maison sept par mort mortelle suite;*
> *Gresle, tempeste, pestilent mal, fureurs* ... (Prés. 40)

By a mortal sequence the House of the Seven will die, troubled by the pestilent evil of heresy and the storms of civil strife. One by one the children of Henri II whom Nostradamus had seen in their own nursery, came to their gloomy and predestined ends. Time was weary of them and France also; weary of wars and intrigues and assassinations, and ready to welcome with open arms a King who would give it some semblance of national unity and some hope of peace. But Henri of Navarre had still some hard fighting to do and some grave decisions to make before being accepted as the Saviour of France.

CHAPTER FOUR

The House of Bourbon

HISTORY, we have been told by Dr Inge, does not repeat itself, it merely resembles itself, yet sometimes it resembles itself very strangely. In 1589, exactly two hundred years before the French Revolution, Paris was in the hands of a real revolutionary government, the so-called *Faction des Seize*, the Sixteen. In 1789 the name Jacobin suggested a revolutionary, but in 1589 the real Jacobins were equally in revolt against constituted authority. Indeed the Parisian clergy as a whole had denounced both Henri III and Henri of Navarre with so much vigour that they could hardly avoid a tinge of republicanism. By their encouragement and justification of the murder of Henri III by Jacques Clément they were all tarred with the brush of regicide. One king had been got rid of; they were unlikely to welcome another in the person of a relapsed heretic. So Henri of Navarre found it necessary to undertake a regular siege of Paris, which lasted for six months.

Nostradamus, as if foreseeing that Paris would one day be called *la ville lumière*, and also with a reference to Campanella's imaginary 'City of the Sun',[1] where there was absolute community of goods and all adult citizens were members of the assembly, speaks of the *cité solaire*.

> *Combien de fois prinse cité solaire,*
> *Seras changeant les loix barbares et vaines,*
> *Ton mal s'approche, plus seras tributaire,*
> *Le grand Hadrie recouvrira tes veins.* (1, 8)

Nostradamus compliments Henri by calling him 'Hadrie', and thus implying that he possessed the virtues of the

[1]. Campanella (1568-1639) was of course born after the death of Nostradamus, but what is that to a prophet?

Emperor Hadrian, in a whole series of quatrains. This one might be interpreted. How many times, O City of the Sun, will you change your vain and barbarous laws! Your evil hour approaches, you shall be yet more enslaved. The great Hadrian will cover your veins again with flesh. The middle lines glance not only at the innovation of the *Seize*, but at the much more drastic changes of the later Revolution. The last line is a reference to Henri's allowing food to pass to the starving citizens.

Henri encamped before Paris from the end of April to the beginning of September 1590, when he was compelled to raise the siege by the advance of the Duke of Parma, general of Philip II, from Flanders. This annoyed not only Henri, but the Pope himself, who was now hostile to the Spaniards and therefore favourable to the Navarre claims. In the very next quatrain to the one just quoted Nostradamus comments:

> *De l'Orient viendra le cœur Punique,*
> *Fascher Hadrie et les hoirs Romulides* . . . (I, 9)

From the east will come the man of bad faith, to trouble Hadrian and the heirs of the Romans (i.e. the Papacy).

In yet another of the Hadrian quatrains, Nostradamus makes further reference to the shortness of the siege:

> *Amour alegre non loing pose le siege*
> *Au Sainct barbare seront les garrisons.* (x, 38)

The Prophet, as if he had foreseen Henri's nickname of *Vert-Galant*, here calls him 'Light o' Love'. Light o' Love will not make a long siege; the garrison of the city shall be devoted to that which is holy and that which is barbarous, that is, they will be clerical revolutionaries. *Amour alegre* gains a particular aptness from the fact that during this siege of Paris, Henri was conducting that furious love-affair with Gabrielle d'Estrées which gained him the title of the *Vert-Galant*. He was at the same time engaged in another *amour* with the wife of Balagny, Governor of Cambrai, and as a sop to the husband, promised him the hereditary possession of that town, a charge of which Balagny showed himself utterly unworthy.

Fantastic as it may seem, Nostradamus seems to have been aware of all these particulars:

> *L'ombre du regne de Navarre non vray*
> *Fera la vie si fort illegitime:*
> *La veu promis incertain de Cambray* ... (x, 45)

For once the Prophet uses no nickname but calls Henri roundly 'Navarre'. Navarre, being in possession not of the true government but only of its shadow (since his claim to the throne was not yet universally recognized) will lead a very irregular life. The construction of the third line may make exact translation difficult, but with its 'vow' and its mention of Cambrai and its suggestion of doubt it is, at least, in view of the circumstances we have related, extremely curious.

Meanwhile the League, which had used the factions of Paris and the hatred of the minor clergy against Henri III for its own purposes, had no intention of allowing the revolutionary ideas of the capital to triumph. The Duc de Mayenne, one of the claimants of the throne on behalf of the House of Guise, carried out a *coup d'état*. He invited the leaders of the Seize to a banquet in order to disarm their vigilance and on the following night put the principal members to death. He then hoped to defend Paris for the League.

> *Dans le conflict le grand qui peu valloit*
> *A son dernier fera cas marveilleux,*
> *Pendant qu'Hadrie verra ce qu'il falloit,*
> *Dans le banquet pongnale l'orgeilleux.* (II, 55)

In the conflict the Great One who was worth little (Mayenne being no match for the astute Henri of Navarre) will, towards the end of his power, perform an act of great éclat, in a banquet will make away with the Proud (i.e. the Commons who had arrogated to themselves the government). Some editions have '*pongnarde*', stabs, which may have been

THE HOUSE OF BOURBON

the manuscript reading. Meanwhile Hadrian will see what must be done.

Henri realized that he could never be King of a united France so long as he remained a Protestant, and he saw 'what must be done'. 'Paris,' he cried, 'is worth a mass.' He negotiated with the Papacy and asked for 'instruction' in the Catholic faith. There is a quatrain dealing with these events, but it should be noted that as it is from the *Présages* it has not quite the same authority as those previously quoted.

> *Par le legat du terrestre & marin*
> *La Grande Cape à tout s'accommoder:*
> *Estre à l'escoute tacite Norlarin,*
> *Qu'à son advis ne voudra accorder.* (Prés. 76)

The Great Capet will agree to everything proposed to him by the Legate of Him who is Lord of Earth and Sea. In order to be released from the excommunication launched against him by Sixtus V, Henri abjured Protestantism at St Denis, on July 25th, 1593, in the presence of the Archbishop of Bourges, *ad hoc* Legate of the Holy See. The taciturn Lorrainer Mayenne perceived (listened to) these proceedings and tried to persuade the Parisians not to yield to Henri, but his advice was not taken.

Paris held out for a very brief period longer, but Mayenne's moral authority was gone. The Gay Gascon – for this was another of the Prophet's nicknames for Henri, succeeded in installing himself behind the wall of the old palace (of the Louvre) and the new palace (of the Tuileries).

> *Le vif Gascon...*
> *Derrier mur vieux et neuf palais gripper.* (IX, 39)

We have seen that Nostradamus had a whole series of nicknames for a King whom he had known personally and who seems often to have excited his prophetic powers. He calls him Hadrian half a dozen times, he calls him Light o' Love, he calls him the Gay Gascon. He also gives him the strange name of Mendosus, in many ways the most curious of all.

Before his accession Henri bore the title of Duc de Vendôme, or Vendosme, as it was then spelt, derived from his father Antoine de Bourbon, Duc de Vendôme and King of Navarre. Now Mendosus is the anagram of Vendosme, u and v being reversible in the old orthography. It will be remembered that Voltaire availed himself of a similar liberty in constructing his pen-name from Arouet le jeune. Mendosus has the additional advantage (Nostradamus loved a *double entendre*) of meaning *défectueux* – a suitable epithet, since Henri was not only a heretic but a relapsed heretic. Born a Protestant, he became a Catholic in 1572 in order to escape the Massacre of St Bartholomew and reverted to Protestantism in 1576, when he placed himself at the head of the Huguenots. What does Nostradamus say about *Mendosus-Vendosmus*, the heretic Vendôme?

> *Mendosus tost viendra à son haut regne,*
> *Mettant arrière un peu les Norlaris:*
> *Le rouge blesme, le masle à l'interregne,*
> *Le jeune crainte & frayeur Barbaris.* (IX, 50)

This is a most interesting quatrain, for if Mendosus is the anagram of Vendôme, Norlaris is the anagram of Lorraine, that is, the Guises. We have already seen Mayenne referred to as Norlarin. Vendôme, therefore, will soon come to the throne and will push into the background the House of Guise. *Le rouge blesme*, the man who is at once red and pallid, is the old Cardinal of Bourbon, pallid by reason of his age and red by reason of his robe. He was proclaimed King by the League in 1589, under the title of Charles X, and died in the following year. The *masle* is the Duke of Mayenne, Lieutenant-General of the realm during the interregnum. The young man *crainte*, or *craintif* (a very frequent inversion in Nostradamus) is the young Duke of Guise, son of the more redoubtable *Balafré*, and Barbaris is Philip II of Spain, who also claimed the throne of France for his daughter Isabella, niece of Henri III through her mother Elisabeth, daughter of Henri II.

Does this seem too ingenious? In another quatrain Nostradamus speaks more clearly:

Le rang Lorrain fera place à Vendosme,
Le haut mis bas, & le bas mis en haut,
Le fils de Mamon sera esleu dans Rome,
Et les deux Grands seront mis en defaut. (x, 18)

The House of Lorraine will give place to the Duc de Vendôme; Mayenne, chief of that House shall be brought low and Henri of Navarre, called in derision '*le petit Béarnais*' (or, as we should say, the 'little provincial') shall be raised on high; the heretic prince (the son of the false god Mammon – Nostradamus was, or pretended to be, fanatically Catholic) will be elected, or accepted, in Rome as King of France, and the two Pretenders will be set aside. The Cardinal of Bourbon having died in 1590 and Isabella of Spain being excluded by the Salic Law, the two Great Ones, passed over at Rome after the conversion of Henri, were the Duc de Mayenne, and the young Duke of Guise as above mentioned.

The main task of Henri IV was now accomplished, but much still remained to be done. He had not only to pacify the rest of the country but he had to contend against foreign hostility also. Philip II of Spain whose interest it was to keep France weak and divided, sent, in 1596, a fleet under the command of Charles Doria to seize Marseilles. The small neighbouring islands of the Chateau d'If and of Ratonneau were occupied, in order to cut off any hope of French interference by sea, and Charles de Casau attempted to betray the city to the Spaniards. He was, however, assassinated by Pierre Libertat, whereupon Marseilles chased the Spaniards away and opened its gates to Henri IV. Here is the very remarkable quatrain in which Nostradamus recorded these events a whole generation before they took place:

De Barcelonne par mer si grande armée
Toute Marseille de frayeur tremblera,
Isles saisies de mer aide fermée,
Ton traditeur en terre nagera. (III, 88)

It might almost be a literal translation – into Nostradamian telegraphese – of the foregoing passage. The final line may present some difficulty. Literally, it means 'Thy betrayer will swim on land.' Casau swam on land because he swam in his own blood!

It is known that Nostradamus, at his death, left quantities of papers. He mentions them in his will and directs that no inventory should be made of them but that they should be put into baskets and kept in a room in his house until his sons are old enough to profit by them. It would be strange if among these papers were none of a prophetic nature, and Vincent Sève of Beaucaire (the little town on the other side of the river from Tarascon) who brought out an edition of the works of Nostradamus in 1605, professes to have included in it a certain amount of material from this source and not hitherto published. Sève's volume contains twenty-seven quatrains not found in the original editions printed at Lyons by Pierre Rigaud between 1558 and 1566 or in that brought out by Benoist Rigaud in 1568. In addition there are two new works: the *Présages* (*Presages tirez de ceux faicts par M. Nostradamus, és années 1555 et suyvantes iusques en 1567*) and the *Sixains* which are entitled *Autres prophéties de M. Nostradamus, pour les ans courans en ce siècle*. The *siècle* in question is, of course, the *seventeenth* century.

The *Présages* follows the same form as the quatrains in the *Centuries*. They are, in general, of much less interest. We shall have occasion to quote only one or two in the course of the present work.

The *Sixains* are not only in a different form of verse but are completely different in style. Instead of the usual telegraphese of Nostradamus they are more leisured, more eloquent, more *poetical*. The prophet may, of course, have been wilfully curt and arid in the *Centuries* and have regarded the *Sixains* as a kind of relaxation. Or he may not have written them at all.

> *Considerant la triste Philomelle*
> *Qu'en pleurs & cris sa peine renouvelle,*
> *Racoursissant par tel moyen ses iours,*
> *Six cens & cinq, elle en verra l'issue,*
> *De son tourment, ia la toille tissue,*
> *Par son moyen senestre aura secours.* (Sixain 18)

This is poetry, or at least in the idiom of poetry, and if Nostradamus wrote it, there was a side to his nature which would not have been suspected from a reading of his other works.

Another possibility is that the *Sixains* represent the lost *prose* prophecies of Nostradamus versified by another hand, possibly that of Chavigny. But this is pure conjecture, just where certitude would be particularly valuable. For if *Sixain 6* was written by Nostradamus, in whatever form, then it contains a very remarkable piece of detailed prophecy; if it was written by somebody else its value is negligible because, as we have seen, it was not published until 1605 and the events to which it refers took place in 1602. It reads as follows:

> *Quand de Robin la traistreuse entreprise,*
> *Mettra Seigneurs & en peine un grand Prince,*
> *Sceu par la Fin, chef en luy tranchera . . .*
>
> (Sixain 6)

When the treacherous enterprise of Biron (of which Robin is the perfect anagram) shall put in pain, or danger, a great Prince and his lords, the plot shall be revealed by Lafin (or 'in the end') and they will cut off his head.

Biron, a bold and impetuous soldier and for that reason employed and trusted by Henry IV, was also an excessively vain and foolish man. He allowed himself to be tempted to betray his master by the promise of sovereign rights in Burgundy, 500,000 crowns and the daughter of the Duke of Savoy in marriage. These negotiations with Spain passed through the hands of one Lafin who revealed the terms to the King. Biron was condemned and executed in the courtyard of the Bastille on July 31st, 1602.

Any quatrain to which Nostradamus assigns a date is worthy of attention, especially when he does so as clearly as in the following:

> *Croistra le nombres si grand des astronomes*
> *Chassez, bannis et livres censurez,*
> *L'an mil six cens et sept par sacrées glomes,*
> *Que nul aux sacres ne seront asseurez.* (VIII, 71)

The number of astrologers or astronomers (the distinction is foreign to sixteenth-century thought) will become so great that they will be pursued and banished and their books condemned, in the year 1607, by ecclesiastical assemblies (*glomes* from *glomas*, a troop) and none of them will be assured of impunity in relation to the priests. The curious fact is that astrology was condemned in strong terms by the Council of Malines and that this took place in 1607!

An event of three years later is also touched upon by the all-seeing prophet:

> *Par les contrées du grand fleuve Bethique*
> *Loin d'Ibere, au Royaume de Grenade,*
> *Croix repoussée par gens Mahometique,*
> *Un de Cordube trahera la contrade.* (III, 20)

In the countries of the great river (Guadalquivir means the great river) which the Ancients called Boetis, far from the Ebro (the word Iberia itself is derived from Ebro, according to some authorities), the Cross having been rejected by the Mohammedans, one of Cordova will break the contract.

After their defeat in 1492 the Moors were allowed to occupy a small corner of their old Kingdom of Granada, but later they were required to accept Christianity or retire to Africa. Those who remained were accused of not being sincere in their profession, and in 1610 they were turned out of Spain by Philip III, in the teeth of the contract which had been made with them by Gonsalvo Fernandez of Cordova, entrusted by Ferdinand and Isabella with the negotiations. It may be objected that it was not the Man of Cordova himself who broke the contract, but the general validity of the quatrain is clear enough.

In the same year as the expulsion of the Moors Henri IV was about to embark upon a new campaign against the Spanish Netherlands. Driving through Paris, his coach was held up with a number of other vehicles in the Rue de la Ferronnerie. A young man named Ravaillac pushed his way through the crowd and with a sudden blow stabbed the King to the heart.

> *Un grand Roy prins entre les mains d'un jeune,*
> *Non loin de Pasques confusion coup cultre* ... (ix, 36)

A great King taken in the hands of a young man, not far from Easter – confusion, a blow with a knife (from the Latin *culter*). Henri was fifty-seven, Ravaillac thirty-two. The assassination took place on May 14th, thirty-three days after Easter, 1610.

As Shakespeare pictures the death of Julius Caesar accompanied by omens and signs in heaven:

> And graves have yawned and yielded up their dead;
> Fierce fiery warriors fought upon the clouds.
> In ranks and squadrons and right forms of war,
> Which drizzled blood upon the Capitol. ...

so Nostradamus writes of Henry IV:

> *Les armes batre au ciel longue saison*
> *L'arbre au milieu de la cité tombe,*
> *Vermine rogne, glaive en face, tison,*
> *Lors le monarque d'Hadrie succombe.* (iii, 11)

The noise of battle is long heard in the skies; the tree in the middle of the city falls; vermin, plague, a sword before his eyes, thunder-bolt; then the monarch Hadrian has succumbed.

The phrase *monarque d'Hadrie* is curious. French commentators compare it with the familiar construction '*sa respectable femme de tante*'. We have already seen Nostradamus compare Henri with the Emperor Hadrian in other quatrains. Elisée du Vignois suggests for the third line: 'a diseased remnant of the League strikes with a blade like a thunderbolt'. The 'tree' is presumably symbolic although some commentators have sought to relate it to the fall of an ancient tree at that time.

Hadrian, Mendosus, Navarre, the Gay Gascon, the Great Capet, Light o' Love – Nostradamus has yet another name for Henri IV. He calls him '*Le Grand Chyren*'. 'Chyren' is the anagram of Henryc, a not unusual spelling of the period, and that Henri was 'le grand' is a commonplace of French history-books, although the phrase 'Henry the Great' is somewhat unfamiliar to English readers.

> *Au chef du monde le grand Chyren sera,*
> *Plus outre après aymé, craint, redouté;*
> *Son bruit & los les cieux surpassera,*
> *Et du seul titre victeur fort contenté.* (VI, 70)

The great Henryc will occupy the highest place on earth (i.e. the throne of France); he will be loved and feared in his lifetime and even more after his death (*plus outre après*); his renown and glory (*los*) will mount to heaven, and his subjects will be very happy to give him the title of victor. Voltaire in his *Henriade* has the apposite line:

> *Il fut de ses sujets le vainqueur et le père.*

He was both the father and the conqueror of his subjects.

It is fair to add that some modern French commentators, especially of the ultra-Royalist camp, have seen in the above quatrain a reference not to Henri IV but to that problematical and indeed mythical Henri V who shall, one day, they believe, restore the Monarchy of France, combat Antichrist and inaugurate the Golden Age. These fancies will be dealt with in a later chapter; for the moment it is sufficient to note that there is nothing in the verse which would have savoured of excessive adulation to a contemporary and subject of Henri Quatre.

Louis XIII, a dim king, overshadowed in his lifetime by Cardinal Richelieu and ever since by the glory of Louis Quatorze, has the honour of only one quatrain in the whole of the *Centuries*. Even then only half the verse is devoted to him, and the reference is chiefly for the sake of giving a date.

> *Le lys Dauffois portera dans Nanci*
> *Jusques en Flandres electeur de l'Empire;*
> *Neufve obturée au grand Montmorency,*
> *Hors lieux prouvés delivré à clere peyne.* (IX, 18)

Louis XIII, the first bearer of the royal lilies to have borne also the title of Dauphin since the time of Nostradamus, entered Nancy on September 25th, 1633. The Imperial city of Trèves or Trier had been captured in 1632 by the Maréchal d'Estrées, who re-established the authority of the Elector. But in March 1633 the Elector was carried off by the Spaniards and taken as a prisoner to Brussels (*jusques en Flandres*) and it was this which caused Louis to declare war on Spain.

At the same time (1632) there was a revolt in the south of France led by the last and most illustrious of the Montmorency, *known to history* as well as to Nostradamus as 'le grand Montmorency'. His family vainly solicited his pardon; all that they could obtain was that he should be executed in private and not by the common executioner. Instead, therefore, of meeting his end in the open square of Toulouse as the sentence of death had ordered, he was beheaded in the court of the prison in the Hotel de Ville recently built.

Obturée is from the Latin *obturare* to enclose, and therefore means the enclosed place; *hors lieux prouvés* implies 'not in the approved or usual place'. All this, *some seventy years before the event*, is sufficiently remarkable, but more is to follow. *Delivré à clere peyne* means 'delivered to his clear or obvious punishment', but there is a double meaning, a Nostradamian pun, for, according to Etienne Jaubert and the Chevalier de Jant, who were both contemporaries of the event, the soldier who struck off Montmorency's head was named Clerepeyne!

Even if we refuse to believe either of them – and as commentators on Nostradamus they are perhaps suspect – the quatrain remains sufficiently astonishing, and one is tempted to ask if it is really to be found in the early editions of the *Centuries*. It is! It is not an interpolation. There can be no doubt about it whatever, and it must therefore rank as one of the prophet's most spectacular triumphs. Indeed it is difficult to see how those who disbelieve entirely in his powers of prediction can possibly explain it away.

It is small wonder that the reputation of Nostradamus grew steadily throughout the seventeenth century. Louis XIII himself visited his tomb in 1622, as Louis XIV was to visit it in 1660. Attempts began to be made to annotate the *Centuries*. That of Etienne Jaubert was entitled *Eclaircissement des véritables quatrains de maistre Michel Nostradamus*, and appeared, without the name of the author or the place of publication, in 1656; that of the Chevalier de Jant, *Prédictions tirées des Centuries*, in 1673. Both these works testify to the interest aroused by the Prophet of Salon during the period we are considering. Even Kings and statesmen might well think there was something to be learned from the *Centuries*. We do not know if Richelieu was acquainted with the works of Nostradamus; Nostradamus certainly knew something about Richelieu, fantastic as such a statement may seem. The formidable cardinal is indeed the subject of one of his most striking quatrains.

Richelieu at the end of his days entrusted his young protégé Cinq-Mars with the delicate task of spying upon the King. Cinq-Mars succeeded so well in gaining the confidence of Louis XIII that he grew ambitious on his own account. He began to intrigue with Gaston d'Orléans, the King's brother, and to plot the downfall of his old master the Cardinal. The latter saw himself deprived of his office and of the command of the army when, at Arles, he received from his agent a copy of the secret treaty between Gaston and the King of Spain arranged by Cinq-Mars. Richelieu had Cinq-Mars arrested, brought back to Paris and executed. Here is the quatrain which deals with these events:

> *Vieux Cardinal par le jeusne deceu,*
> *Hors de sa charge se verra desarmé,*
> *Arles ne montres double soit apperceu,*
> *Et Liqueduct & le Prince embausmé.* (VIII, 68)

Old Cardinal deceived by the young man, he will see himself disarmed and put out of his office if you do not show, Arles, so that it can be perceived, a copy (*double*) of the treaty. There is no need to translate the quatrain; it is itself the translation of the paragraph which precedes it. But what of the last line? What is the meaning of the strange word 'Liqueduct'?

It means, and can only mean, 'carried by water'. Now Richelieu was so desperately ill after his triumph over Cinq-Mars that he was compelled to take to his bed. The bed, placed on a barge, was carried up the Rhone from Tarascon to Lyons, and then down the Seine from Fontainebleau to Paris. *Liqueduct!* Two months afterwards (on December 4th, 1642) he died, and Louis XIII followed him to the grave six months later. Both were embalmed.

> *Et Liqueduct & le Prince embausmé.*

And a quarter of a century before Richelieu was born, an old Jew in the upper chamber of his house at Salon saw, as in a crystal, a clear picture of that slow journey up the Rhone, saw that 'he who was carried by water' wore the red robes of a cardinal, and saw too that he would soon be a corpse.

The power which Richelieu had wielded passed to Mazarin, likewise a cardinal, not so powerful but even more detested, and the early years of the reign of Louis XIV were marked by that bitter civil war which French historians call the *Fronde*. Elisée du Vignois, with his usual ingenuity, finds a quatrain (II, 14) which seems to bear upon it, but it does not perhaps carry sufficient conviction to be quoted here. The high esteem, however, in which Nostradamus was held at this period is proved by the fact that the Frondeurs, the lords who resisted the Cardinal, thought it worth while to issue a special edition of the *Centuries* in which they had fraudulently inserted two forged quatrains. So many copies of this were issued that the book is quite common, and the quatrains themselves have considerable historical interest.

> *Quant Innocent tiendre le lieu de Pierre,*
> *Le Nizaram cicilien se verra*
> *En grands honneurs mais après il cherra*
> *Dans le bourbier d'une civille guerre.*
>
> *Latin en Mars, Sénateurs en crédit,*
> *Par une nuict Gaule sera troublée,*
> *Du grand Croesus l'Horoscope prédit,*
> *Par Saturnus, sa puissance exillée.*

When Innocent holds the place of Peter (the Pope of the period was Innocent X) the Sicilian Mazarin (of which Nizaram is the anagram) will see himself in great honour but afterwards he will fall into the welter of a civil war. The second quatrain tries to be as obscure as Nostradamus and partially succeeds but from the murk emerges the fact (or rather the hope) that Mazarin will be exiled.

The forgery is not unskilful, although Nostradamus never varied his rhymes as is done in the first quatrain. But the contrivers made one or two trifling mistakes. The book, which was actually printed in 1649, bore the date 1568 and the place name 'Lyon'. But instead of basing themselves on the real edition of 1568, they used that of 1605, as can be proved by certain small typographical errors and also by the fact that they foolishly included the *Prédictions* which do not appear at all in the older edition. None the less, since these things would only be plain to scholars, the immediate propaganda value of the book must have been considerable. Yet the *Fronde* failed and its failure paved the way for the absolutism of Louis Quatorze.

Nostradamus, as he peered into Futurity, became so familiar with some of the phantoms of his vision that he was able to recognize them whenever he saw them, and even, as we have seen, to give them nicknames. So for that unborn child who would one day be Louis XIV he coined the name Æmathien. Now Æmathien or Emathion, as every schoolboy would have known even fifty years ago, was the child of Aurora the Goddess of the Dawn, that is, the Sun. But how in the name of magic and the stars the prophet knew that Louis would take the sun as his device and be called by his flatterers *le Roi Soleil* must remain a mystery. What has he to say concerning the 'Child of the Dawn'? He refers to him in several quatrains none of which yields its secret at first glance. But all fit exactly certain events in the reign of Louis Quatorze.

> *Au temps du deuil que le felin monarque*
> *Guerroyera la jeune Æmathien:*
> *Gaule bransler, perecliter la barque,*
> *Tenter Phossen, au Ponant entretien.* (x, 58)

THE HOUSE OF BOURBON

In the time of mourning (for Louis XIII) the astute monarch (Philip IV of Spain) will make war on the young Æmathien. France will be shaken (by the civil war of the Fronde) and the Ship (*la barque* in Nostradamus always means the Papacy) will be in danger (from the rise of Jansenism). Phossen, which he sometimes spells Phocen, is Marseilles, founded in 600 B.C. by a colony of Phoceans. Louis XIV entered the rebellious city by a breach in the walls on March 2nd, 1660. In the previous year he went to the extreme west of France (*Ponant* is an old word meaning the Occident) and, on an island in the Bidassoa, concluded with Philip IV the Peace of the Pyrenees and arranged his marriage with the Spanish Infanta Maria Theresa. The island is still called *l'Isle de la Conférence*. *Entretien* had in the sixteenth century exactly the same meaning. This is not one of the most spectacular or dramatic of the quatrains, but it is a positive gladstone-bag of facts. It is as if Nostradamus, like some fantastic press-correspondent from another world, were trying to squeeze into a single telegram the principal events of the early reign of Louis XIV.

There is another quatrain which is even more like a 'cable-despatch':

> *Le grand conflit qu'on appreste à Nancy;*
> *L'Æmathien dira: tout je soubmets;*
> *L'Isle Britanne par vin sel en soucy;*
> *Hem-mi deux Phi. long temps ne tiendra Metz.* (x, 7)

A great conflict is preparing at Nancy – it was taken in 1660 by the French, who turned out the Duke of Lorraine, Charles III, razed the fortifications of the city and incorporated it in France. Metz will lose (*ne tiendra pas long temps*) its rank as an Imperial city between the reign of two Philips (*emmy deux Phi*). The Treaty of Westphalia, concluded with the Emperor in 1648, during the reign of Philip IV, King of Spain and before the War of the Spanish Succession undertaken by Louis XIV on behalf of his own grandson Philip V, will cede Metz to France. *Le Roi Soleil* will say, 'I overcome everything', or 'Let all things obey me', in other words – *L'Etat, c'est Moi!*

One line remains, which indicates that the Island of Britain will be troubled by reason of wine and salt. It would be better perhaps to discuss this later with other quatrains referring to England. It is sufficient to note in this place that wine and salt were for Nostradamus the essentially *taxable* things and that trouble about wine and salt is therefore resistance to taxation. Such resistance was of course the main cause of the revolt against Charles I which culminated in his execution in 1649. But let us return to Æmathien.

> *Les ennemis du fort bien esloignés,*
> *Par chariots conduict le bastion,*
> *Par sur les murs de Bourges esgrongnés*
> *Quand Hercules bastira l'Hæmathion.* (IX, 93)

When the enemies of the strong man shall have been pushed well back (by the conquests mentioned above which considerably enlarged the borders of France), and bastions shall be constructed of earth brought in carts (in accordance with the system of fortification invented by Vauban), and the walls of Bourges shall fall into decay (the Grosse Tour of Bourges fell into ruin in the reign of Louis XIV) then Æmathien shall build like another Hercules. The Labour of Hercules referred to is the Languedoc Canal connecting the Mediterranean with the Atlantic. It was begun by Riquet in 1666 and finished in 1681 at a cost of 34,000,000 francs. It was the greatest engineering feat of the age, and the reference to Hercules has this additional interest, that by the construction of this canal the French made themselves independent of the western entrance to the Mediterranean. They turned, as it were, the Pillars of Hercules.

There is another quatrain concerning Louis XIV, a quatrain added to the *Centuries* in the edition of 1605, and in some ways the most curious of all, for it does what the quatrains so seldom do, it gives an exact date, albeit in somewhat obscure and symbolic fashion.

> *Quand le fourchu sera soustenu de deux paux,*
> *Avec six demy corps, & six sizeaux ouvers,*
> *Le très puissant Seigneur, heritier des crapaux*
> *Alors subjuguera sous soy l'univers.*
>
> (x, *additional quatrain*)

When the fork (V) shall be supported by two posts (*paux* is the plural of *pal*, a term of heraldry; English heraldry has the same word pale, and we still speak of palings, little posts), with six demy-cors (a *demi-cor* means half a hunting horn, which is the shape of a C), and six open scissors (X), then the very powerful lord who is the inheritor of the toads shall subdue beneath him the world. Now a fork supported by two posts is a capital M, and the six half horns are CCCCCC and the six open scissors are XXXXXX, and if these are put together we have MCCCCCCXXXXXX or 1660.

Toads were the ancient insignia of the Merovingians; the 'inheritor of the toads' is therefore the King of France. In 1660 Louis XIV assumed the personal direction of the realm, for Mazarin, under whose tutelage he had been, was dying, and early in the following year was dead. In 1659 Louis, as we have seen, signed the Peace of the Pyrenees, in 1660 he took Nancy and subdued Marscilles. If he was not exactly Lord of the Universe he was certainly the most powerful monarch of his time, and he became so in the year so picturesquely indicated by Nostradamus. This quatrain, on any view of the matter, must be regarded as one of the Prophet's triumphs.

The extraordinary particularity of his foreknowledge is shown in his description of an event which had nothing to do with Louis XIV personally, but took place during his reign. How Nostradamus managed to foresee such details baffles the imagination. It is as if he had had access to the newspapers of the future, long before newspapers were invented, and as he skimmed rapidly over their pages his eye had been caught occasionally by some happening not of great importance in itself but interesting precisely because he was able to foresee it. One such prophecy concerns a shipwreck.

> *Classe Gauloise n'approche de Corsegne,*
> *Moins de Sardaigne, tu t'en repentiras:*
> *Trestous mourrez frustrés de l'aide grogne,*
> *Sang nagera, captif ne me croiras.* (III, 87)

French fleet (from the Latin *classis*) approach not Corsica, still less Sardinia, or you will repent it; you will all die without being able to reach the cap du Pourceau (*Grogne* is the synonym of Pourceau); you will be drowned, because you have not believed me, you, the Captive.

Now for the historical fact. In 1655 a French naval squadron commanded by the Chevalier de La Ferrière foundered in the Gulf of Lions while sailing past Corsica and Sardinia. The ships were lost because they were unable to reach the cap du Pourceau and take refuge in its little port. And the strangest thing of all is that this prophecy, if it had been understood beforehand, might, as Nostradamus says, have served as a warning to Jean de Rian, the master-pilot, called *le Captif*, because he had been a slave among the Algerian pirates. Such a quatrain seems even more convincing than those concerned with the Kings of France and the major events of history.

The reign of Louis XIV, which had been so glorious, ended in gloom and disaster. The Revocation of the Edict of Nantes, by which Henri IV had granted freedom of worship to the Protestants, caused a new upheaval. The English were ready to help the people of La Rochelle, the great Calvinist stronghold, but such assistance was rendered impossible by the construction, in 1689, at the mouth of the Gironde of a fortification known as the *Pâté de Blaye*. This was a fort built on an islet near the town of Blaye and commanding the river. When Nostradamus notes, some 130 years before the event:

> *L'entrée de Blaye par Rochelle & l'Anglois,*
> *Passera outre le grand Æmathien,*

one can only rub one's eyes and wonder. But more is to follow. Early in the eighteenth century the Protestant Cevennes revolted – the so-called War of the Camisards of 1702-4.

> *Non loin d'Agen attendra le Gaulois*
> *Secours Narbonne deceu par entretien.*   (IX, 38)

The revolted Camisards expected help from their co-religionists in Agen and Narbonne, but they were disappointed in this (*deceu*) because of the submission of Jean Cavalier, the Protestant leader, after a conference (once more *entretien*) at Nîmes with the Maréchal de Villars, sent into Languedoc by Louis to pacify the country.

The conference was necessary because Louis was unable to crush entirely his rebellious subjects owing to the War of the Spanish Succession which absorbed his energies elsewhere. Nostradamus seems to have known all about this also.

In 1700 Charles II of Spain died leaving his realm, by will, to the grandson of Louis XIV who ascended the Spanish throne under the title of Philip V. 'The Pyrenees', cried Louis, 'have ceased to exist'. But the rest of Europe was unwilling to see such an extension of French power, and a coalition was formed, between England, Austria, Holland, Prussia, Portugal, and Savoy, to support the pretensions of the Archduke Charles. Nostradamus remarks:

> *Par mort la France prendra voyage à faire,*
> *Classe par mer, marcher monts Pyrenées,*
> *Espaigne en trouble, marcher gent militaire:*
> *Des plus grands Dames en France emmenées.* (IV, 2)

By reason of a death, France will undertake a foreign expedition; the fleet will put to sea and an army will cross the Pyrenees; Spain will be troubled and trampled over by the troops. The last line is puzzling until we remember that the French claim to the Spanish throne was founded on the fact that two Infantas had married French kings. Louis XIII and Louis XIV had indeed both married Spanish princesses, the first the eldest daughter of Philip III and the second the eldest daughter of Philip IV. These then were the two 'very great Ladies brought into France'. '*Dame*', in Nostradamus, nearly always means a Royal lady, but even if this were not so the sense would be plain enough.

The War of the Spanish Succession (bugbear of the English schoolboy, who tries in vain to see any connexion between the throne of Spain and the Battle of Blenheim) lasted from 1701 until 1713. It was unfortunate for France and clouded the last years of Louis XIV, troubled as he was by strife at home. This is Nostradamus's last reference to *le Roi Soleil*, child of the Dawn, now setting in murk and gloom:

> *L'Æmathion passer monts Pyrenées,*
> *En Mars Narbon ne fera resistance,*
> *Par mer terre fera si grand menée*
> *Cap. n'ayant terre seure pour demeurance.* (IX, 64)

Louis XIV will cross the Pyrenees (i.e. his troops will recross them, in retreat), will make no more resistance in Narbonne (the name of the town in Latin is *Narbo Martius*); he will make desperate efforts by sea and land in order to try to preserve his realm for the Capet,[1] who has now no corner of Spain where it was safe (*seure*, i.e. *sure*) for him to dwell.

That Louis XIV had a great respect for Nostradamus and his predictions is shown not only by his visit to the tomb of the prophet in 1660 but by the fact that when a certain François Michel of Salon was presented to him and when he learned that he claimed relationship with Nostradamus by collateral descent, the King exempted him from all taxes.[2]

Louis indeed could hardly help being aware of the *Centuries*. Between 1643 and 1698 there were at least eight editions and commentary on the prophecies became almost a fashionable pursuit. We have already mentioned Etienne Jaubert and the Chevalier de Jant. The former was simply a physician of Amiens, but the latter was an antiquary and *conservateur du cabinet des médailles* in the service of Monsieur, brother of Louis XIV. His *Prédictions tirées des Centuries de Nostradamus*, printed in 1673, was dedicated to the King.

There was, of course, an obvious advantage for a King as careful of what we should call publicity or propaganda as Louis, in encouraging commentary on Nostradamus. His greatness could not but be enhanced by the belief that it had been foreseen, and that the stars in their courses and the Fates themselves guaranteed the glory of *le Roi Soleil*. And

1. Nostradamus always abbreviates the word Capet to Cap. or Cappe.
2. Larrey, *L'Histoire de Louis XIV*, t. 6.

if among the prophecies of Nostradamus were any that might be interpreted in a contrary sense, it was quite certain that the courtier-commentators would either ignore them or be able to explain them away. Certainly such commentary went on in the very precincts of the royal palace, and not only scholars and librarians but nobles and fine gentlemen took a hand in the game.

Among the latter was a certain Sieur B. Guynaud who describes himself as '*Ecuyer et gouverneur des Pages de la Chambre du Roy*'. His *Concordance des Propheties de Nostradamus*, which first appeared in 1709 and was dedicated to the King, reveals a nice mixture of the courtier and the scholar. He refuses to discuss the future, remarking very judiciously: 'It is true, SIRE, that his Prophecies have this in common with thunder that they only burst out and make a noise when they are accomplished.' He understands many of the anagrams and his interpretation of some of the quatrains is in line with that accepted since. Strangely enough, owing perhaps to a corrupt text, he entirely misses the point of '*Quand le fourchu sera soustenu de deux paux*', which might have provided him with his most spectacular triumph.

The real attempt to place the interpretation of Nostradamus on a scientific basis was reserved for his successor, long known as 'l'Anonyme de Louvicamp', but now identified as Jean de Roux[1], curé of that place who brought out his *Clef de Nostradamus*[2] in 1710. The worthy curé in his Preface relates how, in 1688, at the beginning of yet another European war, he found himself in a company where the prophecies of Nostradamus were being discussed, and as he expressed a lively desire to study them an '*honneste Gentilhomme*' who was present offered to show him an old edition. The curé's first impression, like that of everybody else, was one of disappointment, and he concluded, as others have

1. Or, as he is sometimes called, Leroux.
2. La Clef de Nostradamus, Isagoge ou Introduction au véritable sens des Prophéties de ce fameux Auteur. Avec la Critique Touchant les sentiments & interpretations de ceux qui ont ci-devant écrit sur cette matière.... Par Un Solitaire. A Paris, Chez Pierre Giffart.... MDCCX.

done, that further study of the Prophet would be so much waste of time. However, soon afterwards, the death of his father threw him into such a state of despondency that he was unable to pursue his usual avocations and in an attempt to forget his troubles he took up the *Prophéties* once more. They became the preoccupation of the rest of his life.

He began to accumulate the various editions and the works of the commentators and soon found himself in a position to criticize the latter for their dullness of interpretation. Even Guynaud failed to satisfy him and he began to toy with the idea of bringing out a commentary himself. The work which he finally produced is an astonishing mixture of pedantry and insight, of logic-chopping, etymological minutiae and real scientific method. Knowing, as was natural enough, nothing of the French Revolution, he imagines the *commun advènement* to be a general peace following the anticipated victories of Louis XIV. He supposes the 'Epistle to Henri II' to have been really addressed to the same monarch. *Le Roi Soleil* indeed dazzles the eyes of the Solitary of Louvicamp almost as much as those of the courtier-commentators.

Jean de Roux, however, has two claims on our gratitude: he saw plainly that Nostradamus thought in Latin even when he was writing in French, and he understood something of the conventional names which the Prophet gives to his characters. With regard to the first, he even claims to have discovered the text-book which Nostradamus studied: the *Progymnasmata in artem oratoriam* published in 1528 by Franciscus Sylvius. With regard to the second he suffers from the disadvantage of writing too early. How should he recognize, in 1710, the nicknames which were to fit the personalities of Louis XVIII, or Napoleon III, or Victor Emmanuel? Nevertheless his work is on the right lines and he himself is a curious foreshadowing of that other commentator, like himself a country priest, who was to devote his whole life to the interpretation of the Prophet: the Abbé Torné of La Clotte. Strangely enough their two cures are only a few miles apart.

Louis XIV died in 1715 and was succeeded by Louis XV, then only five years old. During his minority France was governed by the Duke of Orleans as Regent. *La Régence* is glanced at in a single quatrain which is none the less of particular interest:

> *Cœur, vigueur, gloire, le regne changera,*
> *De tous points contre ayant son adversaire:*
> *Lors France enfance par mort subjuguera;*
> *Un grand Regent sera lors plus contraire.* (III, 15)

It is plainly a question of a Regent in France. Now the only male Regent in French history from the time of Nostradamus until to-day was Philippe, Duke of Orleans, during the minority of Louis XV. If 'heart, vigour, glory' may be regarded as a suitable description of the long and illustrious reign of Louis XIV, then certainly the rule 'changed' and the Regent, with his feeble policy and the cynical debauchery of his private life, was 'contrary' to his predecessor in every possible way. The important line is the third:

Lors France enfance par mort subjuguera,

which Le Pelletier interprets: 'Then (*alors*) a child will rule over (or subjugate) France by reason of the death of his ancestors'. Louis XV was the great-grandson of Louis XIV, his father the Duke of Brittany and his grandfather the Duke of Burgundy being already dead. Bareste sees a more sinister meaning, and thinks the line confirms the suspicions of those who believe that the Duke of Orleans had had a hand in removing those two scions of the direct line who stood most obviously between him and the throne.

There is another point, first noticed by Elisée du Vignois in his painstaking commentary. From the chronological viewpoint the quatrains of Nostradamus are sadly jumbled and no one has ever succeeded in rearranging them in their correct order, even if that order ever existed. The arrangement, however, does not seem entirely fortuitous and it is at least curious that, in their respective *Centuries*, the quatrains concerning the accession of Louis XIV, Louis XV and

Louis XVI, and the *de jure* accession of Louis XVII, should be numbered, respectively 14, 15, 16 and 17. It may, of course, be a coincidence, but one is forced to admit that coincidences occur so frequently in the works of the Prophet of Salon that the whole theory of coincidences tends to break down.

If there is only one quatrain for *la Régence*, the long reign of Louis XV is hardly treated more fully. There is indeed a gap in the prophecies at this point and some writers have wondered if it may not be explained by the missing quatrains of *Centurie VII* which have not come down to us. Or it may be that Nostradamus was content to indicate in a general way the character of Louis XV and the consequences which flowed from it. He gives a hint, also (albeit in an extremely obscure quatrain) of the origin of the King's debauchery.

Cardinal Dubois, at the instance of the Duke of Orleans, was placed in charge of the royal infant. He did not poison him physically, which is supposed to have been the fate of Louis's father and grandfather, but mentally and spiritually by his evil counsels and pernicious example. Although we will not attempt a detailed interpretation it does look as though Nostradamus were trying to say something of the kind in the following quatrain.[1]

> *De bois la garde, vent clos rond pont sera,*
> *Haut le receu frappera le Dauphin,*
> *Le vieux teccon bois uni passera,*
> *Passant plus outre du Duc le droit confin.* (IX, 27)

A few gleams shine through the fog. The first phrase *might* mean 'Guard it (the Monarchy) from the guard, Dubois' – a typical Nostradamus pun. '*Haut le receu*', received his charge from a high personage; '*frappera la Dauphin*' glances at the supposed fate of Louis's father. '*Vieux teccon bois*' means the old wooden ball, and has obviously a connexion with

---

1. The value of this quatrain as evidence of the prophetic powers of Nostradamus is, of course, *nil*. No sceptic will be convinced by it and it is inserted here merely as a curiosity.

the opening words. It may imply that the old rotten wood (Dubois himself) is still rolling about. The last line at least mentions a Duke and seems to mean that his instructions (whatever they were) were exceeded by the man into whose hands he had given the young king.

Fortunately the next quatrain to be considered is much clearer:

> *Ce grand monarque qu'au mort succedera*
> *Donnera vie illicite et lubrique,*
> *Par nonchalance à tous concedera,*
> *Qu'à la parfin faudra la loy Salique.* (v, 38)

As a description of Louis XV this could hardly be bettered even by those without the disadvantage of living a hundred and fifty years before he was born. He who succeeds at the death of this great King (inversion) will give an example of an illicit and erotic life, out of carelessness he will give way to every one, so that at the end the Salic Law will fail (Old French, *failler, je faux, je faudrai*). The Salic Law forbade the succession of women to the throne of France, but the weakness of Louis resulted in making a woman like Madame de Pompadour an uncrowned queen. It is a pity that Nostradamus did not always say what he meant in such unmistakable terms.

The Prophet having dismissed *Louis le Bien-Aimé* with such brief and contemptuous notice, it only remains for us to pass on in a later chapter to those world-shattering events of the French Revolution to which so many quatrains refer. But before we do so, it may be worth while to quote two lines of a verse concerning something which happened neither to Louis nor to France.

> *L'an mil sept cens vingt et sept en octobre,*
> *Le Roy de Perse par ceux d'Egypte prins. . . .*
> *Conflict, mort perte: à la croix grand opprobre.* (III, 77)

This would convey very little without the date, which is so unusually precise, and it is an historical fact that in October 1727 a treaty was concluded between Persia and the Turks, then in control of Egypt, by which the Shah was compelled to yield to the growing power of his neighbours and to recognize the Sultan as the legitimate successor of the Caliphs. *À la croix grand opprobre* is apt enough for, by this treaty, the Armenians and South Georgians, Christian communities, passed from the rule of the easy-going Persians to that of the fanatical Turks.[1] Why Nostradamus should have foreseen this with such particularity is a major mystery. The fact that he did so cannot be denied.

1. I am indebted for this suggestion to Mr W. G. Campbell.

CHAPTER FIVE

Nostradamus and the History of England

EVEN before his death the fame of Nostradamus had crossed the Channel, and two of his Almanacks were translated into English as soon as they appeared.[1] The *Centuries*, however, had to wait for more than a hundred years, for it was not until 1691 that a quarto volume, entitled *Predictions before 1558*, was brought out in London. Indeed the main English interest in Nostradamus in the sixteenth century seems to have been concerned with his non-prophetic writings, for one of his medical treatises was translated under the title of *An excellent Treatise on Contagious Infirmities* and appeared in London in 1559. The first English commentary by Theophilus Garencières was not published until 1672, the second, by D.D.[2] not until 1715. So far as the present author has been able to learn, there has been from that day until recently only one other English commentary, the valuable if somewhat eccentric work of Charles A. Ward,[3] composed at the end of the nineteenth century.

The main interest of Nostradamus in prophecy was centred, naturally enough, on France. But he occasionally turned his gaze to the neighbouring islands he had never seen, and although the quatrains concerning Great Britain are less numerous and, on the whole, less convincing than those concerning his own country, they are of particular interest to the English reader and it is proposed to give them in full.

1. *Almanacke for 1559*, London, 1559, 8vo; *Almanacke et Prognostications*, London, 1559, 8vo.
2. *The Prophecies of Nostradamus concerning the fate of all the Kings and Queens of Great Britain since the Reformation, and the succession of his present Majesty King George*.... Collected and explained by D.D., 1715.
3. *Oracles of Nostradamus*, by Chas. A. Ward, London, 1891.

The first reference concerns an event contemporary with the publication of the *Centuries* – the marriage of Mary, Queen of Scots. It is sufficiently explicit:

> *Premier fils vefve malheureux mariage*
> *Sans nuls enfans, deux Isles en discord,*
> *Avant dix-huict incompetant âge.*
> *De l'autre près plus bas sera l'accord.* (x, 39)

The quatrain has already been dealt with in the chapter concerned with the name of Valois. Francis II was the first son of the widowed Catherine de Medici. He was born on January 19th, 1543, and died on December 15th, 1560. He lived therefore seventeen years, ten months, and fifteen days, or as Nostradamus says 'before eighteen while still a minor' (*avant dix-huict incompetant âge*). He was married at the age of fifteen to Mary of Scotland and the marriage was brief, childless, and unhappy. The situation in which he left her resulted in discord between the two island kingdoms of England and Scotland.

The Prophet has nothing further to say about English or Scottish history until the next century. One might have expected him to have known about the Armada but no reference has ever been identified. But he knew something about the Stuarts and the troubles of the Great Rebellion.

> *Le jeune nay au regne Britannique,*
> *Qu'aura le pere mourant recommandé,*
> *Iceluy mort, Lonole donra topique,*
> *Et à son fils le regne demandé.* (x, 40)

The young prince born (*nay*, *né*) to rule over Britain (it is almost as if Nostradamus were choosing his words; he usually speaks simply of *l'Angleterre*), and who was recommended by his dying father (Darnley did in fact before his assassination recommend his infant son to the fidelity of the Scottish lords), he (the future James VI of Scotland and James I of England) being dead, Lonole will make speeches (*topique* means rhetorical commonplace) and will demand (or take over) the government from his son.

That seems sufficiently plain, but who was Lonole? The word is an anagram for Olleon, from 'ολλύων the present participle of the verb 'ολλυμαι, to destroy. Olleon is therefore the Destroyer. But had Nostradamus something else in mind? Oll – Oliver? Ward points out that Olleon is the anagram of 'Ole Nol' which is as near as a Frenchman might be expected to get to the 'Old Noll' of popular speech.

At this point it is likely that the impatient reader will fling the book away in disgust. What indeed is all this juggling with names, these Greek words turned inside out, these anagrams that mean two things at once? Do they not rather destroy than reinforce any possible belief in the prophetic powers of this Provençal Jew who apparently knew so much yet would not take the trouble to express himself clearly?

Yet we know that Nostradamus did make use of anagrams, including quite obvious ones like Rapis for Paris, and that such anagrams were very much in the taste of his time. And if he sometimes made puns in Latin and Greek that too was no novelty in the Renaissance period. But the question goes deeper than that. Everyone who has experimented with telepathy and has had any success at all knows that the subconscious mind often works in the most roundabout and apparently far-fetched way. Sometimes half a word is transmitted and then itself gives rise to a new chain of associations which may or may not have some reference to the original idea. If the power of prophecy is in some strange way related to the receptive mood which makes telepathy possible,[1] and there is reason to believe that it is, then something of the kind may have happened in this case. Perhaps Nostradamus 'got' only the first syllable of Oliver Cromwell's name and his conscious intelligence transformed it into Olleon, suggested by his knowledge of the Greek verb 'to destroy'. This argument is advanced, not as an attempt to *prove* anything, but merely for the light it may throw on the psychological processes involved. If Nostradamus had

1. For an admirably straightforward and convincing account of telepathic experiments, see Upton Sinclair's *Mental Radio*, London, 1930.

left a blank instead of writing Lonole the quatrain would still have had considerable interest. After all, the possibilities are sufficiently narrow. A king of *Britain* who dies and whose son is deprived of his throne – there are none who fit except James I and Charles I.

Nostradamus was much concerned with the death of Charles. To him regicide seemed the greatest of all possible crimes, and he refers to the fate of the martyred Stuart in one quatrain which is so plain-spoken that there can be no doubt about it at all. When reading the *Centuries* the line

> *Senat de Londres mettront à mort leur Roy*

leaps to the eye. That any 'senate' should have the power to put its king to death was not an idea that came very easily to the mid sixteenth century mind. That the English Parliament (a very unimportant body in 1555) should do so seemed outside the bounds of all probability. Yet here it is set down in black and white:

> *Gand et Bruceles marcheront contre Anvers,*
> *Senat de Londres mettront à mort leur Roy:*
> *Le sel & vin luy seront à l'envers,*
> *Pour eux avoir le regne en desarroy.* (IX, 49)

Ghent and Brussels will march against Antwerp; the Senate of London will put to death their king; wine and salt will be contrary, or reversed, and to have them the realm will be disorganized or thrown into disorder.

It is implied, but not stated, that the events of the first two lines will take place simultaneously. Charles was executed in 1649.[1] Holland had revolted from Spain as long before as 1579, but Philip IV made great efforts to reconquer the country up to 1648 when, by the Treaty of Westphalia, he abandoned his pretensions. Now in the time of Nostradamus the Low Countries were united under the rule of Spain, but

---

1. That is 'new style'. New Year's Day, down to 1752, was reckoned to begin on March 25, approximately eight weeks after the putting to death of the King. The actual warrant for his execution is therefore dated 1648. I owe this correction to the Rev. G. F. Pollard.

Antwerp lies on the extreme edge of what was to be the Spanish Netherlands once Holland had broken free. Any expedition therefore against Holland and based on Ghent and Brussels would naturally pass through Antwerp, and *contre* signifies not 'against' in the modern sense but 'in the direction of'. An exact picture of a frontier which does not yet exist is perhaps too much to ask of any prophet. The important thing for us is to note that such expeditions ceased in 1648, one year before the execution of Charles I. It has been pointed out by some commentators that the quatrain itself is numbered 49, but it would perhaps be preferable to regard this as a mere coincidence.

What of the 'wine and salt'? Nearly all the commentators interpret wine as meaning power and salt as meaning wisdom in accordance with the ideas of Catholic ritual. There is, however, another meaning already glanced at when discussing one of the quatrains referring to Louis XIV.

L'Isle Britanne par vin et sel soucy. (x, 7)

The Isle of Britain troubled by reason of wine and salt. It was there suggested that wine and salt were for Nostradamus the essentially taxable things (salt was never taxed in England, but the *gabelle* in France lasted until the French Revolution), and trouble concerning wine and salt is therefore resistance to taxation. The quatrain now under consideration says that wine and salt will be 'contrary' and that in an effort to have them (i.e. the taxes derived from them) the whole realm will be thrown into an uproar. Resistance to Charles's attempts to levy taxes without reference to Parliament was, of course, one of the main causes of the Great Rebellion. The alternative meaning is that Charles lacked both the power and the wisdom to carry out his designs.

Nostradamus has not yet finished with either Charles or Cromwell.

Du regne Anglois le digne dechassé,
Le conseiller par ire mis à feu,
Ses adherans iront si bas tracer,
Que le bastard sera demy receu. (III, 80)

Digne (which doesn't quite mean either 'worthy' or 'dignified') is a very happy word for Charles I.

> He nothing common did, or mean
> Upon that memorable scene...

The King, therefore, will be dispossessed of his realm. The counsellor, owing to the ire of the populace against him, will be delivered to their fury – and Strafford leaps at once to the mind. The Scots, his adherents, as he had thought them, will behave with such baseness that (they will sell Charles to the Parliament and) the usurper (*le bastard*) will be almost received as King – almost because he will have to content himself with the title of Lord Protector.

Nostradamus takes what might be called the pre-Carlyle view of Cromwell. He was unable to regard him as 'guiltless of his country's blood'; instead he saw him 'wade through slaughter to a throne.'

> *Plus Macelin que Roy en Angleterre,*
> *Lieu obscur nay par force aura l'empire,*
> *Lasche sans foy sans loy saignera terre,*
> *Son temps s'approche si près que je souspire.* (VIII, 76)

More like a butcher (Italian, *macellaio*) than an English king, born in an obscure place, by force he will seize power; coward without faith or law, he will make the earth to bleed; his time approaches so near that I sigh. This is hardly the modern estimate of Cromwell, but many a Royalist less fanatical than Nostradamus would have subscribed to every word of it, even to the '*lasche*', for the Protector was supposed by his enemies to wear a corselet under his coat in fear of assassination. The last line may seem strange in view of the fact that Cromwell was not born until 1599, forty years after the publication of the *Centuries*; but Nostradamus was either mistaken concerning the nearness of these events (which seems unlikely from his other references) or else a century was no long period to eyes that looked so far into the future.

There is one more quatrain which seems to apply to Cromwell:

> *Le grand criard, sans honte, audacieux,*
> *Sera esleu gouverneur de l'armée,*
> *La hardiesse de son contentieux,*
> *Le pont rompu, cité de peur pasmée.* (III, 81)

The great declaimer or demagogue, audacious and without shame, will be elected governor of the army. The insolence of his contentiousness will be such that the bridge will be broken and the city faint with fear. Elisée du Vignois thought that the bridge in question was the Parliament, the intermediary between the People and the Executive, and the reference was therefore to 'Pryde's Purge'. Professor Tancred Borenius, in a letter to the present writer, made the interesting suggestion that *pont rompu* means Pontefract, which held out for the King and endured two terrible sieges during the Civil War.

After Cromwell's time the interest of Nostradamus in the history of England seems to have waned. He regarded the English with some contempt as a people given to revolutions and drastic changes, unlike France, faithful (until 1789) to Throne and Altar. He says:

> *Sept fois changer verrez gent Britanique*
> *Teints en sang en deux cens nonante an;*
> *Franche non point . . .* (III, 57)

You will see the nation of Britain, tinged with blood, change seven times in 290 years; the French people not so. What are these seven times, and how are we to count the 290 years? Well, the French people certainly 'changed' in 1789, and if we count backwards from that date we reach the very beginning of the sixteenth century. Between 1500 and 1790 there were, in fact, seven fundamental 'changes' in English history:

i. In 1532, when Henry VIII broke with Rome and proclaimed himself Supreme Head of the Church. To Nostradamus this would have been equivalent to a revolution.
ii. In 1553, when Mary re-established the Catholic Church.
iii. In 1558, when Elizabeth proscribed Catholicism.
iv. In 1649, when Charles I was beheaded and a Commonwealth established.

v. In 1660, on the Restoration of Charles II.
vi. In 1689, when James II was dethroned by William III.
vii. In 1714, when the direct line of the Stuarts died out and the Hanoverians were called to the throne.

If these were the changes that Nostradamus had in mind he counted quite correctly.

The third of these changes was just happening when Nostradamus brought out the second edition of the *Centuries* with its 'Epistle to Henri II'. The sixth is glanced at somewhat obliquely in the following quatrain:

> *De l'Aquilon les efforts seront grands:*
> *Sur l'Ocean sera la porte ouverte,*
> *Le regne en l'Isle sera reintegrand,*
> *Tremblera Londres par voilles descouverte.* (II, 68)

This might have referred to the Armada, Van Tromp, or even to the recent war but for the third line. The meaning of the whole seems to be: In the north there will be great efforts, the door will be opened on the ocean, the rule or reign will be re-established in the Island and London will tremble at the sight of (hostile) sail. Now if the 'Island' means Ireland, then the quatrain applies to the efforts of James II to re-establish himself after the coming of William III. James, by the aid of a French fleet, which naturally alarmed the government in London, set up his rule again in Ireland. The word 'north' is explained by the situation of Nostradamus himself, deep in Provence, and of course Louis's fleet was operating to the north of its own bases. The Prophet gives no hint of the outcome of this unhappy expedition. He would presumably have preferred it to succeed.

Although he did not like the English heretics, he was under no illusion concerning their future greatness. Twenty years before the Armada it might have seemed a very daring prediction that they would one day be all-powerful. Yet this is the very word he uses:

> *Le grand empire sera par Angleterre*
> *Le pempotam des ans plus de trois cens:*

Grandes copies passer par mer & terre,
Les Lusitains n'en seront pas contens. (x, 100)

The great empire will be (held) by England. It will be all-powerful (*pempotam* is a made-up word derived from *pan*, all and *potens*, powerful) for more than three hundred years. Great armies will pass by sea and land, the Portuguese will not be pleased.

Why, one may well ask, should the Portuguese not be pleased? Earlier commentators have thought that the reference was to the Peninsular War when the great army (*copie* is from the Latin *copia*, a troop of soldiers) of Napoleon came by land and the armies of Sir John Moore and Wellington came by sea and met on Portuguese territory.[1]

Nostradamus promises England that she shall be all-powerful (presumably on the sea) for more than three hundred years and therefore, it is implied, as some French commentators have gleefully pointed out, for less than four hundred. An Englishman may be pardoned if he feels some interest in the date from which the count begins. If it is to be reckoned from the defeat of the Armada in 1588 we have already exhausted the three hundred years and have entered the period of the 'more' – how much more the Prophet neglected to specify. Perhaps, when the American programme of naval expansion has been completed, the famous 'pempotam' will pass imperceptibly from the hands of the British fleet into those of the combined and allied navies of Britain and the United States. It would, at any rate, be agreeable to think so.

The foregoing are the most satisfactory of those quatrains which Nostradamus devoted to the history of England and the most sceptical reader will be compelled to admit that two lines among them,

Senat de Londres mettront à mort leur Roy:

[1]. Mr Alexander Fraser who has, with extraordinary devotion, put the whole of the present volume into Braille, makes the interesting suggestion that '*les Lusitains*' may mean the passengers in the *Lusitania* sunk at a period when we were beginning to lose our supremacy at sea and when unprecedented numbers of soldiers were being transferred over the ocean during the First World War.

and

> *Le grand empire sera par Angleterre . . .*

are, in their way, sufficiently remarkable. The quatrains that follow are given rather as curiosities than as proofs of the Prophet's powers. The following quatrain has been held to refer to Elizabeth:

> *La dechassée au regne tournera,*
> *Ses ennemis trouvez des conjurez;*
> *Plusque jamais son temps triomphera,*
> *Trois et septante, la mort, trop asseurez.*   (VI, 74)

The rejected one shall come to the throne; her enemies will be found to be conspirators; more than ever shall her period be triumphant.

So far, so good, the difficulty begins with the last line. Ward proposes the insertion of a comma between *trois* and *et septante* (*septante*, of course, is the old form of *soixante-dix*) and interprets: 'At seventy she shall go assuredly to death, in the third year of the century'. It is true that Nostradamus often drops the thousands and hundreds from a date and that *trois* might therefore mean 1603 which was the year of Elizabeth's death. As she was born on September 7th, 1533, and died on March 24th she was actually sixty-nine and six months, or in her seventieth year.

The raid of Essex and Raleigh on Cadiz in 1596 is thought to be glanced at in the following:

> *Devant le lac ou plus cher fut getté*
> *De sept mois, et son ost desconfit*
> *Seront Hispans par Albanois gastez,*
> *Par delay perte en donnant le conflict.*   (VIII, 94)

Albanois cannot mean Albanians of whom Nostradamus had assuredly never heard. It stands for Albanies or men of Albion, and the quatrain might be translated: Before the lake, where much treasure was stranded, after a seven months' voyage, and the host discomfited, the Spaniards shall be worsted by the English, by time lost before giving battle.

'The bay and harbour of Cadiz may very well be called a lake, being twelve miles one way, and at least six the other, whilst the entrance to it from Rota to the Castle of St Sebastian is a good six miles. When Essex got possession of the Castle of Puntales, he commanded the whole town and harbour. The idea of *lake* is actually expressed in the very name of Cadiz, which is derived from the Punic word *Gaddir*, an *enclosed place*.' (Ward.)

The English expedition destroyed there thirteen warships and forty huge galleons, part of the great 'silver fleet' from South America, which had got stranded in the harbour. 'Had the Spaniards been alert, they might have unloaded the treasure-ships, and so saved the cargoes. If they had attacked the English at once instead of awaiting the onset, they might have beaten them off, or at least have kept them out of the harbour. But they were so supine that the Duke of Medina had at last to fire the ships to prevent their capture.' (Ward.)

The language of Nostradamus is sometimes curiously exact even when dealing with frontiers and political arrangements which were not in existence during his lifetime. Thus he could write:

> *La grande Bretaigne comprinse d'Angleterre,*
> *Viendra par eaux si haut à inonder . . .* (III, 70)

The Scottish and English crowns were united in 1603 on the accession of James I and VI. He assumed the title of 'King of Great Britain' on October 24th, 1604. Bacon tells us that, in the lifetime of Elizabeth, he had often heard the rhyme

> When hempe is sponne,
> England's done.

'Hempe' stands for Henry, Edward, Mary and Philip, and Elizabeth, 'which' says Bacon, 'thanks be to God, is verified only in the change of name; for that the King's style is now no more of England but of Britain.' Nostradamus reflects this change with almost pedantic accuracy.

'Great Britain, comprising England,' says the prophet, 'will suffer a great flood'. Was there in fact a flood about this time when England was first comprised in the larger unity of Great Britain? There was. It occurred in January, 1607, when the sea broke down the dykes in Somerset and inundated a stretch of country thirty miles long and six miles wide. Bristol and its neighbourhood suffered severely, and there was a similar, although not so disastrous, inundation on the coast of Norfolk.[1]

Both 'D.D.' and Ward attribute to the time of Charles I a quatrain which to the present writer seems to belong to a later period:

> *Soubs le terroir du rond globe lunaire,*
> *Lors que sera dominateur Mercure*
> *L'isle d'Escosse fera un luminaire,*
> *Qui les Anglois mettra à déconfiture.* (v, 93)

In this sublunary world, when Mercury shall be lord of the ascendant, the island of Scotland will produce a luminary prince who will put the English to discomfiture.

Who is the 'luminary' in question? Possibly the Young Pretender. 'Discomfiture' is however too strong a word seeing that the Prince was defeated, but he got as far as Derby and certainly gave the English a bad fright.

We have already dealt with several quatrains referring to Cromwell. The following is also considered to apply to him:

> *Esleu sera Renard, ne sonnant mot,*
> *Faisant le saint public, vivant pain d'orge,*
> *Tyrannizer après tant à un cop,*
> *Mettant à pied des plus grands sur la gorge.* (VIII, 41)

Renard (who, like Brer Rabbit, 'ain't saying nuffin') will be elected; playing the saint in public, living on barley bread, in order to tyrannize after a while (*après temps* instead of *après tant*) by a coup (d'état), placing his foot on the neck of the greatest.

---

1. Garencières was successful in finding a detailed account of this flood in a Latin work entitled *Rerum in Galliâ, Belgiâ, Hispaniâ, Angliâ, etc., gestarum anno* 1607, *à Nicolao Gotardo Artus Dantisco*, VII, Book 2.

The only difficulty would seem to be the strange phrase 'living on barley bread'. Ward's suggestion that it has reference to the phrase *faire ses orges*, to enrich oneself unscrupulously at the expense of others, is unconvincing. There is a certain attraction in his second proposal that 'it might even mean that he got his bread by barley, or John Barleycorn, from the Huntingdon brewery'. The phrase may merely imply that he was moderate in diet.

Another Cromwellian quatrain is not without interest.

> *Pour ne vouloir consentir au divorce,*
> *Qui puis après sera cogneu indigne,*
> *Le Roy des isles sera chassé par force:*
> *Mis à son lieu qui de Roy n'aura signe.* (x, 22)

For not wishing to agree to the divorce of his Crown . . . the King of the Islands will be dethroned by force, and one put in his place who will have none of the insignia of kingship.

The construction of the second line presents some difficulty. Ward translates: 'which would afterwards have been regarded as an unworthy action', but this is not very satisfactory. The whole passage seems to mean that Charles was dethroned because he would not divest himself of the prerogatives of the Crown, which afterwards was itself trampled underfoot or looked upon as of no account. But, however, this may be, the quatrain indicates quite clearly that a King of the Isles is to be succeeded by one who will have no visible sign of kingship, and this in itself is sufficiently remarkable.

In the year following the execution of the King, Cromwell was appointed commander-in-chief of the Commonwealth forces, in order that he might lead an army against the Scots. He entered Scotland with sixteen thousand men on July 22nd, 1650, found David Leslie, the Scottish general, entrenched in a strong position near Edinburgh and spent a month trying to lure him out. On August 30th it was decided to retreat to Dunbar and await reinforcements. Leslie pursued and seized the passes beyond Dunbar and the hills behind it. Cromwell's situation looked desperate, when on the evening of September 2nd the Scots began to move down from the hill to the narrow space at its foot with the intention of attacking. Cromwell attacked first, fell on the exposed flank of the Scottish army with overwhelming force, and snatched a decisive victory. Edinburgh, Leith and the eastern portion of the Lowlands passed into his hands.

This battle of Dunbar is described with some particularity in a very curious verse:

> *La bande foible la terre occupera,*
> *Ceux du haut lieu feront horribles cris:*
> *Le gros trouppeau d'estre coin troublera,*
> *Tombe pres Dinebro descouvers les escrits.* (VIII, 56)

The quatrain might have remained uninterpreted for ever but for the word Dinebro. This is a very transparent anagram for Edinbro and gives the clue to an interpretation which fits the Battle of Dunbar in all its details.

The weak band (or the smaller army) shall possess the field. Those from the Highlands (!) will utter horrible cries. The large force will be cornered and find its tomb near Edinburgh, even the papers of the Scots falling into the victor's hands. The phrase *estre coin*, to be cornered, in a corner, is particularly interesting because the Scots had boasted before the battle that they 'had Cromwell in a pound'. We know, from a quatrain which will be quoted later, that the phrase '*Le sang du juste*', the Just Man's blood, was used by Nostradamus in reference to the execution of Charles I. The same phrase occurs again in a most peculiar quatrain:

> *Le sang du Juste par Taurer la daurade,*
> *Pour se venger contre les Saturnins*
> *Au Nouveau lac plongeront la maynade,*
> *Puis marcheront contre les Albanins.* (VIII, 40)

What, in the name of both the Major and the Minor Prophets, can Taurer la daurade mean?

The mysterious 'D.D.', pursuing his researches in the early years of the eighteenth century, has an elaborate commentary on the subject which, whatever the reader may think of it, is worth quoting for its learning and ingenuity.

NOSTRADAMUS AND THE HISTORY OF ENGLAND 131

'Some people stick to the Church of *England* discipline, even to a superstition, and to their last breath. These people had the nickname of *Tories* cast on them by the Cromwellites; which is as much as to say some have the law of the Church put upon them, from the Hebrew *Torah*, which signifies the *law*, or the *law of the Church of God*. Perhaps did Cromwell himself, or some of his confident advocates and ministers, designedly invent that cursed name; as it is likely from what happened in the year 1651, when the Parliament ordered the law-books to be translated out of *Latin* into *English* wherein the lawyers took a great deal of freedom by using the *verbalia passiva* very frequently, and almost on all occasions, according to their own fancy and pleasure. As, for instance, Apellans and Apellatus, they made an *Apealer* and an *Apealee;* the *Arrestans* and *Arrestatus* the *Challenger* and the *Challengee;* as likewise the *Warranter* and the *Warrantee;* the *Voucher* and the *Vouchee;* the *Leaser* and the *Leasee;* in which manner they used likewise the terms of *Torer* and *Toree;* a *Torer*, in the first place – that is, a promoter of the Common Prayer and Church of England service; and an imposer of human traditions, instead of God's law; and, in the second place, a *Toree;* that is, one that submits and suffereth such laws to be imposed upon him. Which *nomina verbalia passiva*, so much in vogue amongst the English lawyers, are not at all English but mere French, and the *Participium Passivum* itself; and more proper to the neat *French* than the corrupted *Provincial Dialect;* which last our Nostradamus very often mixes with his style; wherein they commonly used to say, *Les confirmads, les restads, les escilads*, instead of *les confimez, les restez, les exilez*, etc. And according to this *Dialect* one must say, LES TORADS, instead of LES TOREZ, and thus does our Poet.'

If we accept 'D.D.'s' amendment of the first line to '*par Tore et les Torads*' the quatrain may therefore be interpreted:

The blood of the righteous man, for Torah and Torees' sake [that is, for the sake of the Law of the Church and the Tories who supported it] cries for vengeance against the Saturnine rebels. The maenad (that is the country which is already drunk with blood) will be plunged by them into a new blood-bath, and they will march against the English, or men of Albion (*Albanins* being the same as *Albanois* in VIII, 94). In other words a new army will be raised by the adherents of the young Charles, become King by the execution of his father, and this army will march into England to be disastrously defeated at the Battle of Worcester. If this seems too fanciful the reader is reminded that all the quatrains of this group are put forward merely as curiosities, which title, at least, can scarcely be denied them.

The flight of Charles after the battle is referred to in the following:

> Regne en querelle aux frères divisé,
> Prendre les armes et le nom Britannique:
> Titre Anglican sera tard avisé
> Surprins de nuict mener à l'air Gallique.   (VIII, 58)

The Kingdom being in a state of civil war, brother contending with brother for the arms and name of Britain, the King (he who holds the Anglican title) advised too late, will be surprised and forced by night to seek the air of France. When Charles at last made up his mind (remarks Ward) to visit Scotland and fight for his crown, it was already too late. After the Battle of Worcester he managed to escape from the city under cover of night and at last after flying from place to place for weeks succeeded in getting ship to Dieppe and rejoined his mother safely at St Germain on October 20th, 1651.

Nostradamus reverts once more to the same topic, a little more vaguely:

> Sur la minuict conducteur de l'armée
> Se sauvera, subit esvanouy,
> Sept ans après, la fame non blasmée;
> A son retour ne dira onc ouy.   (X, 4)

Ward's translation could hardly be bettered: 'Upon the stroke of midnight, the leader of the army (King Charles II) shall save himself (by flight), and suddenly evanish. For seven years longer that is, to a day, till the death of Cromwell, his reputation will survive unchallenged; at his Restoration no one will say anything but yes.'

Cromwell died in 1658 on his *Fortunate Day*, September 3rd, the day on which he gained the victories of Dunbar and Worcester. The universal acclaim which greeted Charles on his return in 1660 is well expressed by Nostradamus' final line.

We must now deal with two very striking quatrains.

> *Le sang du juste à Londre fera faute,*
> *Brulez par foudres de vingt trois les six;*
> *La dame antique cherra de place haute,*
> *De mesme secte plusieurs seront occis.* (II, 51)
>
> *La grand peste de cité maritime*
> *Ne cessera que mort ne soit vengée*
> *Du juste sang par pris damné sans crime,*
> *De la grand dame par feincte n'outragée.* (II, 53)

These are very remarkable verses of something more than curiosity value. They are linked, not only by their proximity in the text but by the references to the 'blood of the Just', one mentions a fire and one a plague, and the first of these gives a date, albeit in an ambiguous form. Nostradamus, as we have seen, always misses out the hundreds, and if *vingt trois les six* does not mean anything as it stands, *trois-vingt et six* might mean a great deal, since it was in 1666 that London burned.

La dame antique is supposed to be St Paul's Cathedral, built on the site of a temple of Diana. The translation of the quatrains should therefore read:

The blood of the Just shall be required of London, burned by fire (literally fireballs) in thrice twenty and six: the old cathedral shall fall from its high place, and many (edifices) of the same sect shall be destroyed.

The great Plague of the maritime city shall not cease till Death is avenged for the blood of the Just taken and condemned for no crime and the great cathedral outraged by feigning Saints.

Nostradamus, with his monarchical instincts, regarded both the Great Plague and the Fire of London as the vengeance of Heaven for the execution of Charles I. Between the two quatrains is another (II, 52), much less explicit which seems to deal with a naval war. It is enough perhaps to note that in 1665 and 1666 England was engaged in such a war with the United Provinces.

Even the enemies of Nostradamus have sometimes admitted that he predicted 'the Revolution of 1688 with tolerable clearness'.[1] The following is the quatrain in question:

> *Trente de Londres secret conjureront,*
> *Contre leur Roy, sur le pont l'entreprise:*
> *Luy satalites la mort degousteront,*
> *Un Roy esleut blonde, natif de Frize.* (IV, 89)

Thirty of London shall conspire in secret against their King; upon the bridge the plot shall be devised. His satellites shall taste of death. A fair-haired King shall be elected native of Friesland.

There are serious difficulties here. William of Orange was born at The Hague, which is not in what is now called Friesland. Still, as Friesland is part of Holland and Holland as a separate country did not exist when Nostradamus wrote, we may here, perhaps, allow him to score the point. But, so far as is known, William III was not blond. The truth is of course difficult to determine because, at least in later life, he wore a periwig, like almost all his contemporaries. Then, if there is any significance in the number of conspirators, it has not yet come to light; and what can be the meaning of 'on the bridge'? Garencières says roundly that the plotters used to meet at the 'Bear at the Bridge foot', this being a celebrated inn on the south side of London Bridge, demolished in 1761. But as he thinks the whole conspiracy directed against Charles I, his testimony is not of much value. A final point: some editions print *là mort* instead of *la mort*, which might mean that the rebellious adherents of James II tasted death on the bridge, that is, that their severed heads were exposed there on spikes, as was the custom.

A more convincing quatrain is the following:

> *La Sœur aisnée de l'Isle Britannique*
> *Quinze ans devant le frère aura naissance,*
> *Par son promis, moyennant verrifique,*
> *Succedera au Regne de Balance.* (IV, 96)

---

1. *Quarterly Review*, XXVI, 189.

A modern astrologer makes the following comment:[1] 'This is an uncommonly neat description of the *marriage* of Mary the Second of England and its effects on the Succession.

'The "Balance" is the French name of the Sign Libra (♎); and Libra on its material side is universally allowed by astrologers to connote marriage, partnerships, and public enemies.

'(1) Mary was *married* to her cousin William of Orange when she was fifteen (November 4th, 1677).

'(2) As a Dutchman he represented the *public enemy*.

'(3) The reign of William and Mary is the only instance in English history – at least, since the Conquest – of a *partnership* in the Crown.

'I should be inclined to translate the quatrain therefore:

'The Elder Sister of the British Isle will succeed to the Throne, the Succession being confirmed by (*moyenant verrifique*) her marriage vows (*promis . . . de Balance*) made when she was fifteen years old and before the birth of her brother.'

The next quatrain to be considered is one of those which are perhaps the more convincing in that they refer in detail to some event not very important in itself. During the War of the Spanish Succession, the Duke of Marlborough and Prince Eugène were encamped near Arras. During the night there came to them the Cardinal de Bouillon, Grand Almoner of France, who had fallen into disgrace at court and, being related to Prince Eugene, took this opportunity of making his escape. Marlborough sent out a strong convoy to meet him, to prevent his falling into the hands of the French scouts from Ypres.

All this is very unimportant; the strange thing is that Nostradamus seems to have known all about it.

> *Le grand Prélat Celtique à Roy suspect,*
> *De nuict par cours sortira hors de regne:*
> *Par Duc fertile à son grand Roy Bretaine,*
> *Bisance a Cypres et Tunes insuspect.* (VI, 53)

---

1. Miss Alice E. Leaver, Honorary Member of the Astrological Lodge of London, in a letter to the present writer.

The great French prelate (Celtique in Nostradamus always means French) suspected by the King, shall post with haste by night out of the realm, by aid of the Duke fertile [in conquests] to his great King[dom] of Britain, through Bisance, Ypres and Béthune undiscovered.

This is 'D.D.'s' interpretation and is not unconvincing, although one must confess to a certain scepticism concerning the last line. It seems so much more likely to mean 'Byzantium, Cyprus and Tunis'. Concerning the epithet *'fertile'*, 'D.D.' makes the following rather quaint comment:

'The Daemons speak all sorts of languages, but Nostradamus did not understand the English, whence it came that at the hearing of the name of Marlborough, he started, and thought "Qu'est-ce que Marl?" Thereupon, it was inspired to him, "C'est une terre fertile et graisse", whereby he is ascribing to him both *Nomen* and *Omen* at once: the Duke, by whose indefatigable zeal and unconquerable valour the Kingdom of Great Britain should be fertile in conquests'. With this almost contemporary note we may leave it.

Many commentators on Nostradamus have had a political motive in their writing. 'D.D.' is no exception, his object being to prove that Nostradamus had foreseen the Hanoverian Succession. He relies principally upon two quatrains, of which the first runs thus:

> *Après viendra des extrèmes contrées,*
> *Prince Germain, dessus le throsne doré;*
> *La servitude et eaux rencontrées,*
> *La dame serve, son temps plus n'adoré.*   (II, 87)

He interprets: Afterwards shall come, from a distant land, a German prince upon the gilded throne. The slavery and waters shall meet (!). The lady a serf, her time no more adored.

Hanover however can scarcely, without straining language, be referred to as one of the *extrèmes contrées*. The third line seems to have no meaning and the Protestant prejudices of 'D.D.' (he was probably an Anglican clergyman and Doctor of Divinity) prevented him from interpreting the final line. In Nostradamus *La Dame* nearly always stands for Mother Church and the quite appropriate meaning would then be that as the accession of George I defeated the hopes of the Papists, Catholicism was by this enslaved and in *his* time no more adored.

Hopefully our courtier-commentator leaps upon the next quatrain in his list, a quatrain which certainly seems to promise smooth things:

> *Le regne humain d'Anglique geniture*
> *Fera son regne paix union tenir:*
> *Captive guerre demy de sa closture,*
> *Longtemps la paix leur fera maintenir.* (x, 42)

The humane throne of English geniture will have as its object the maintenance of peace and union. War will be captive or at least confined to half its usual bounds. Peace will be secured to the country for a long time. Under Walpole, the chief minister of the early Georges, England certainly enjoyed a long peace.

There is one more quatrain which certainly has something to do with England, for the word *Londre* occurs in the second line.

> *Dedans la terre du grand temple celique*
> *Nepveu à Londre par paix feincte meutry:*
> *La barque alors deviendra scismatique,*
> *Liberté feincte sera au corn' et cry.* (vi, 22)

The indefatigable 'D.D.' tries to see a reference to the murder of Darnley. '*Nepveu*', in Nostradamus, usually means Napoleon III. '*La barque*' is almost certainly the papacy. The verse is offered, without prejudice, to the ingenuity of budding historians, amateur detectives and the solvers of crossword puzzles. The present author is unable to see any meaning in it at all. And this, so far as he is aware, completes the tale of references to English history in the works of the Prophet.

CHAPTER SIX

Nostradamus and the French Revolution

IT is not necessary to be a Frenchman in order to agree that the French Revolution was one of the major events of human history, and (if there is anything in prophecy at all) it would be strange if some hint of its coming had not been vouchsafed to prophets of previous ages. Nor is this hope disappointed. Disregarding attempts to interpret Biblical texts in this sense, and to press into service the Prophet Ezekiel and the Book of Revelation, we may yet find some foreshadowings of the great events which are, to say the least, sufficiently curious.

In the *Imago Mundi* of Pierre d'Ailly, a manuscript dated 1414 reposing in the Library of Douai,[1] it is stated that 'numerous great and astonishing alterations and transformations of the world, particularly as concerns the laws and the religious sects, will take place in the year 1789'. As the present author has not seen the manuscript in question and as the book was apparently never printed, perhaps it would be safer not to rely upon this prophecy.

We are, however, on surer ground with another example. Pierre Turrel of Autun was born in the second half of the fifteenth century and died before 1531, for his work which was published in that year refers to him as *feu maistre Turrel*. Master Turrel was not only an astrologer and prophet but one of the greatest mathematicians of his time. He became Rector of the college of Dijon and was the teacher of the famous Pierre Castellan, Grand-Almoner of France and one of the most distinguished Orientalists of the sixteenth century. So successful in his own lifetime were the predictions made by Turrel, by the aid of his astrological calculations, that he was accused of sorcery before the Parliament of

1. Baron de Novaye. Demain ...? Paris, 1905.

Dijon, but was acquitted after an eloquent defence by his pupil Castellan. Turrel says:

'Let us leave speaking of things accomplished, or which have been accomplished, which almost all men know, unless they are ignorant, and let us speak of... the marvellous conjunction which astrologers say occurs about the year one thousand seven hundred eighty and nine, with ten revolutions of Saturn, and moreover twenty-five years later will be the fourth and last station of the altitudinary firmament. All these things considered and calculated, the astrologers conclude that if the world lasts until then (which is known to God) very great and remarkable changes and alterations will be in the world, especially concerning sects and laws.'[1]

It will be seen that Turrel not only gives the date 1789 for the beginning of the upheaval, but indicates that it will reach its term twenty-five years afterwards, that is in 1814, the year of Napoleon's abdication.

This is so astonishing that the reader may be pardoned for wondering if the passage be not a forgery. It is said to occur in the work by Turrel entitled '*Le Période, c'est-à-dire la fin du monde; contenant la disposition des chouses terrestres par la vertu et influence des corps celestes*'. It is a book excessively rare seeing that it is to be found neither in the Library of the Arsenal, the *Bibliothèque Mazarine*, nor the *Bibliothèque Nationale*. It is, however, mentioned in the catalogue of the library of St Geneviève in Paris, the contents of which were dispersed at the Revolution. Bareste, who gives the impression of being a scholarly and conscientious person, professes to have had a copy in his hand,[2] and to have read the passage in question.

---

1. '*Or laissons à tant à plus parler des chouses faictes, et que ont faict, que quasi tous hommes sçavent, s'ilz ne sont ignorants, et parlons de la huictième maxime, et merueilleuse coniunction que les astrologues disent estre faicte environ les ans de Nostre Seigneur mil sept cens octante et neuf, avec dix revolutions saturnelles; et oultre vingt-cinq ans aprés sera la quatrième et dernière station de l'altitudinaire firmament. Toutes ces chouses considérées et calculées, concluent les astrologues que si le monde iusques-là dure, (qu'est à Dieu tant congneu) de tres-grandes et admirables mutations et alterations seront au monde: mesmement des sectes et des loix.*'

2. '*Si nous n'avions en ce moment ce vieux livre entre les mains nous ne voudrions pas croire à la prophétie qu'il renferme.*' Eugène Bareste: *Nostradamus*, Paris, 1840, p. 198.

He even gives a description of the wood-engraved vignette on the title page.

Fortunately, however, we are not dependent on the word of Bareste (for the present author would readily admit that once people become interested in prophecy they will stop at nothing) for the passage in question was plagiarized in a work published at Lyons in 1550. This is *Le Livre de l'estat et mutations des temps*, by Richard Roussat, canon of Langres, a copy of which is in the *Bibliothèque Nationale*. Roussat reproduces the passage *in extenso*, and almost in the same words, without any acknowledgement of its origin. On another page of the same treatise he remarks:

> 'Now I say that we are at the moment and we approach the future renovation of the world about two hundred and forty-three years, according to the general computation of the historiographers counting from the date of the compilation of the present treatise.'[1]

If we add 243 to the date of publication 1550 we arrive at 1793, but the dedication is dated 1549, which gives us 1792, the year of the inauguration of the revolutionary calendar.

As if all this were not enough there is a passage in the *Liber Mirabilis* of 1524, founded on a set of Latin distichs said to have been written by Jean Muller in 1476, a passage which may be translated as follows:

> 'When a thousand years have been accomplished after the Virgin gave birth, and when seven hundred years more have passed, the eighty-eighth year will be very astonishing and will bring in its train sad destinies ... all the empires of the universe will be overthrown, and everywhere there will be a great mourning.'[2]

Well, Jean Muller was a year out, but in view of the fact

---

1. 'Maintenant, ie dis que nous sommes en l'instant et approchons de la future renouation du monde enuiron deux cens quarante trois ans, selon la commune supputations des historiographes, en prenant à la datte de la compilation de ce present traicté.' p. 86.

2. 'Après mille ans accompli depuis l'enfantement de la Vierge, et que sept cents ans se seront encore écoulés, la quatre-vingt huitième amnée sera bien étonnante et entrainera avec elle de tristes destinées ... tous les empires de l'univers seront bouleversés, et de toutes partes il y aura un grand deuil.'

that he wrote in the fifteenth century he may perhaps be forgiven for giving the date of the French Revolution as 1788 instead of 1789. But it is time to return to Nostradamus. What has *he* to say concerning these matters?

The most interesting passages are to be found in the 'Epistle to César' (his son) which he inserted, as preface, in the first edition of the *Centuries*, and in the 'Epistle to Henri II' printed in the second edition. He refers to something which he calls '*le Commun Advenement*' which might be translated 'Advent of the Commons' or 'Rise of the Third Estate', an event which Nostradamus, as a good Royalist, regarded with undisguised horror. He declares that it will take place early in the seventh millennium, which sounds vague indeed until we realize that the prophet was founding his calculations on the system founded on the Vulgate of St Jerome and declared canonical by the Council of Trent. He says elsewhere, more precisely, that 4173 years and eight months '*more or less*' elapsed between the Creation and the birth of Christ, so that in his view the eighth millennium would begin in the year 1757, and the French Revolution might be considered (since we are dealing with millennia) as happening early in this period. He adds that at this time the adversaries of Jesus Christ and his Church will begin to 'pullulate', which was certainly true enough in the second half of the eighteenth century.

There follows a passage of astrological calculation of impenetrable complexity, and it is difficult to know what year he means when he says

'*et cômencant icelle année sera faicte plus grande persecution à l'Eglise Chrestienne que n'a esté faicte en Afrique, et durera ceste-icy iusques à l'an mil sept cens nonante deux, que l'on cuydera estre une renovation de siècle.*' (Epistle to Henri II, paragraph 89.)

In a certain year therefore there will begin a persecution of the Church as terrible as that of the Vandals in Africa in the sixth century (which is presumably what he has in mind) and this persecution will last until the year 1792, which will be thought to be a renovation of the century. As we have already noticed the year 1792 was marked by the inauguration of the revolutionary calendar. By writing '*cuydera estre*' he seems to imply that he knew it would not last.

We know that Nostradamus had read the works of Roussat not only by his use of the phrase '*renovation de siècle*' which is an echo of Roussat's '*renovation du monde*' but by a still more explicit passage:

> *Chef d'Aries, Jupiter et Saturne,*
> *Dieu eternel quelles mutations* ... (I, 51)

which is a versification of Roussat's '*En après la très fameuse approximation et union de Saturn et de Jupiter qui se fera près de la teste d'Ariès, l'an de Nostre Seigneur mil sept cens et deux ... grandes altérations et mutations.*' It is not very plain why the year 1702 should be singled out as a year of great changes. Nostradamus, more wisely, gives no date in this connexion. Elsewhere, as we have seen, he mentions 'mil sept cens nonante deux', i.e. 1792.

But why should he say that the persecution of the clergy would *end* in 1792? Because, reply the commentators with perhaps too legalistic an ingenuity, in that year the Church in France ceased to exist as a Church, a law of August 26th expelling all priests who refused to submit to the Civil Constitution of the Clergy. In a passage of his Epistle to Henri II Nostradamus foretells that '*la persécution des gens ecclésiastiques durera onze ans quelques peu moins*' – will last a little less than eleven years. If we count from the Civil Constitution (July 12th, 1790) to the Concordat (July 15th, 1801) that gives us eleven years *plus* three days. The three days are on the wrong side of the account, or seem so until we remember that, in 1792, nine days were chopped off the calendar; so Nostradamus was right after all.

In a yet more curious passage he declares that all the realms of Christendom, and the lands of the Infidels too, will tremble for a space of twenty-five years – once more the twenty-five years from the Revolution to the abdication of Napoleon – and that there will be grievous wars, cities and castles destroyed, women violated, children dashed against the walls, and so many evils committed by the power of Satan that almost the whole world will be made desolate. And before these things *certain strange birds will cry in the air, 'To-day! To-day!'* and after some time will disappear. Are the strange birds the Imperial eagles? But these considerations must be left to the next chapter.

The revolutionary upheaval was foreseen by Nostradamus not only in its broad outline but in some of its most curious particulars, as in the quatrain in which he mentions the 'Whites' and the 'Reds':

> *Quand la lictière du tourbillon versée,*
> *Et seront faces de leur manteaux couvers,*
> *La republique par gens nouveaux vexée,*
> *Lors blancs et rouges jugeront à l'envers.* (1, 3)

When the dregs of the [revolutionary] torrent shall have mounted to the surface, and their faces shall be covered by their cloaks (i.e. concealing their aims beneath a cloak of legality) the Republic shall be vexed by parvenus, and 'Whites' and 'Reds' shall be equally mistaken in their judgements.

In times of revolution, the Church is always one of the first and principal sufferers:

> *Las! qu'on verra grand peuple tourmenté,*
> *Et la loy saincte en totale ruine,*
> *Par autres loix toute la Chrestienité,*
> *Quand d'or d'argent trouvé nouvelle mine.* (1, 53)

Alas! that one shall see a great people tormented, and the holy law in total ruin, everything Christian regulated by new laws, when gold and silver find a new mine. The final line refers to the decree of the National Assembly of December 19th, 1789, which created an issue of four hundred million *assignats* – a new currency based on the goods of the clergy.

Three days later a further decree changed the ancient provincial division of France into *départements* with new names. Nostradamus notes:

> *Faux exposer viendra topographie,*
> *Seront les cruches des monumens ouvertes,*
> *Pulluler secte, saincte philosophie,*
> *Pour blanches noires, & pour antiques vertes.* (VII, 14)

Topography shall come to be arbitrarily changed; the urns of the monuments shall be opened (i.e. the sepulchres of the Kings of France at St Denis shall be violated and their ashes flung to the winds), anti-Christian sects will pullulate, and Philosophy (the philosophy of Voltaire) will usurp the place of Religion. Black will pass for white and novelties (green things) will prevail against the old traditions.

The fate of the clergy troubled Nostradamus very much. The suppression of the ecclesiastical costume is glanced at in the lines:

> *Yeux clos ouverts d'antique fantaisie,*
> *L'habit des seuls seront mis à neant....* (II, 12)

The eyes of the people being closed to Christianity but open to antique paganism, the priests' habit will be abolished. Nostradamus, on several occasions, refers to priests as '*les seuls*', i.e. those who live alone, or celibate. In another quatrain he prophesies the abolition of the monasteries:

> *En bref seront de retour sacrifices,*
> *Contrevenans seront mis à martyr,*
> *Plus ne seront moines, abbez, ne novices,*
> *Le miel sera beaucoup plus cher que cire.* (I, 14)

There will shortly be a return of persecution, and the clergy will be called upon for the greatest sacrifices. Those who resist will be martyred. There will be no more monks, abbés or novices and (since no more candles will be needed for the churches) honey will be much dearer than wax.

Lest we should think that these prophecies concern any other country than France, there is another quatrain which takes up the theme of the foregoing, and mentions Paris:

> *D'esprit de regne munismes descriés,*
> *Et seront peuples esmeus contre leur Roy:*
> *Paix, sainct nouveau, sainctes loix empirées,*
> *Rapis onc fut en si très dur arroy.* (VI, 23)

The ancient traditions which serve as ramparts (Latin, *munimen*) shall be decried, and the people shall be moved against their King. There will be a momentary truce, and a new sanctity (i.e. a Church controlled by the State) but the result will be that the holy laws go from bad to worse. Never was Paris (of which Rapis is the perfect anagram) in such a critical situation.

Some commentators think that the third line should be interpreted differently. The 'peace' in question is the Concordat concluded by Napoleon, and the 'new saint' is St Napoleon (the Christian martyr under Diocletian, whose feast day is August 15th) included in the calendar by Pius VII in order to please the Emperor. But this is perhaps to push ingenuity too far.

We now come to an event which is not only one of the most dramatic episodes in French history but is of particular interest to students of Nostradamus, for it is described in one of his most explicit quatrains – the Flight to Varennes. Had the enterprise succeeded the whole course of the Revolution might have been changed; had it never been attempted Louis might have kept the confidence of the people and his head. But he tried and failed, and the route to Varennes led both him and Marie Antoinette to the scaffold.

On April 18th, 1792, the King, then at the Tuileries, wished to go to St Cloud. It was Palm Sunday, and the royal party, with the bishops and courtiers, were already installed in the carriages and were ready to set off. The crowd prevented them, the King insisted, and the tocsin began to sound from the belfry of St Roch.

The King leaned out of his carriage and was met by a cry from thousands of throats: 'No! No! The King is trying to run away.'

Louis made the moving reply: 'My children, I love you too much to leave you.' To which the crowd replied, 'We too love you, but we love *you alone*.'

The Queen, so pointedly excepted, shrank back in her seat weeping and trembling. There was no help for it. The carriage turned back and Louis realized that he was a captive.

Henceforward escape became his sole preoccupation, in so far as such a word can be used of the timid and vacillating King.

It would have been easy for him to escape by himself. He was an excellent horseman and he could easily have slipped out of the Tuileries disguised as a courier and placed himself at the head of his troops assembled near the frontier. But the Queen had made him promise not to go without her and the children, and to this he agreed, although the difficulties of the enterprise were thus multiplied a hundredfold.

Preparations for the flight were actively pushed forward, but with an ineptitude and a refusal to face the plain facts of the case which make one wonder whether Fate itself was not resolved upon the destruction of Louis and his family. The King ordered a large berline (a kind of private stage coach) to be secretly prepared. M. de Bouillé, in whose hands were the arrangements for the flight, suggested that two English *diligences* would be much less likely to attract attention. M. de Bouillé was overruled. The King proposed to avoid Rheims and to pass through Varennes. M. de Bouillé pointed out that there was no regular relay on that route, and that it would be necessary to place one there specially and so give rise to suspicion. The King persisted in preferring the road through Varennes.

The date of departure was fixed for June 11th then changed to June 19th. It was of the utmost importance that no further change should be made, for everything depended on an exact time-table. Bouillé was in command of all the troops on the eastern frontier, and he arranged for detachments to be placed at various points of the route. M. de Choiseul was to have men and fresh horses ready at Varennes. Everything was prepared.

Suddenly the King decided to postpone the departure for twenty-four hours. He had remembered that he would draw his pay (the new quarter's civil list) on the morning of the 20th and it seemed to his economical soul foolish to leave without it. A natural reaction perhaps, but it disorganized the whole scheme.

Three men were to travel with the royal party as coachman and footmen. It would have been easy to give them some inconspicuous costume; they were instead clothed in the livery of the Prince de Condé who was already an *emigré*, and whose servants were therefore particularly open to suspicion. Instead of employing men who knew the way, they seem to have chosen them at hazard. One of them did not even know Paris, with consequences which very nearly proved fatal at the very beginning of the enterprise.

The Queen, instead of contenting herself with a simple toilet box, had one specially made for travelling, and half the jewellers of Paris were called in to make it sufficiently splendid. The King was to pass as the intendant or *valet de chambre* of the Queen who in turn was supposed to be a certain Madame de Korff. But instead of following, as an intendant would, in another vehicle, he was placed in the principal seat face to face with his supposed mistress. Instead of having two, or even four horses, they had six, although that number was a privilege of royalty. Pistols and blunderbusses were stowed away in the luggage and the footmen provided only with small hunting knives. Instead of taking M. d'Agout, a resolute man who knew the route and had been specially recommended to the King, they took the governess of the royal children, because her rank entitled her to precedence over M. d'Agout. M. de Choiseul, who was to leave twelve hours before the King, was burdened with the Queen's hairdresser whom she could not bear to leave behind.

The King's costume was surprisingly sensible. He wore a grey coat and breeches, a satin vest, grey stockings, buckled shoes and a small three-cornered hat. The Queen was dressed in a white gown, which was not unreasonable in view of her supposed rank as baronne. The Dauphin was put into girl's clothes. He resisted strongly, as any boy would, and was only quieted by being told that he was going to play in a comedy. What a comedy!

That they ever got out of the Tuileries at all is a miracle. The great berline was waiting at the Barrière de Clichy, and it was necessary to reach it separately. The Queen and her attendant got lost; they had to ask the way and were almost run over by the carriage of Lafayette, the very man who had promised the Assembly that the Royal Family would *not* escape. However, escape they did, for a time.

All went well as far as Bondy. There was an early nineteenth century play called *The Forest of Bondy*; it is mentioned here for reasons which will appear shortly. At Montmirail the axle (soupente) broke and two hours were lost in repairing it. Then another half-hour was lost because the King insisted on climbing a little hill which took his fancy. At Chalons Louis showed himself at the window and was recognized by several bystanders. Two of the horses fell down and one of the postillions was hurt, fortunately only slightly. Then suddenly, as they were leaving Chalons, a mysterious horseman who has never been identified, shouted in at the carriage: 'Your measures are badly conceived. You will be arrested.'

When they arrived at Pont-de-Somme-Vesle there was no sign of the soldiers who should have been awaiting them. They *had* been there, but owing to the delay in the arrival of the berline and the menacing attitude of the peasants, they had retired, thinking it better that the King should find no troops than that he should find them engaged in a scuffle with the local inhabitants. He found indeed the place deserted, relayed and departed for Sainte-Menehould. But the Queen had already uttered the prophetic words: 'We are lost!'

At Sainte-Menehould the King was recognized again, this time by Drouet the postmaster, that is the official in charge of the relays of horses. Now Drouet was an ex-deputy of the Federation. He was not able to prevent the departure of the royal carriages, but he revealed his suspicions to the municipality and was authorized by them to start in pursuit.

When the royal party arrived at Varennes it was already dark. It had been arranged that the relay of horses should be placed at a farm on the near side of the little town. By error, or fatality, it was placed on the far side, and while time was wasted looking for it Drouet arrived. He acted quickly, blocked the bridge which led out of the town by overturning upon it a cart of furniture which happened to be near, then knocked up the *procureur* of the commune, a grocer and chandler whose name was Sauce.

When Louis arrived in the centre of the town he found the whole place in an uproar. His horses' heads were seized and Sauce demanded his passports. Though false, they were in order, for they had been signed by the King himself. But now the tocsin began to sound, the whole countryside had been aroused by the news of the King's flight and Sauce thought it best to invite the whole party into his own home to spend the night.

There were troops on the other side of the bridge. A handful of resolute men could have rescued the King, but the officers could not be certain of their men and the attitude of the citizens was menacing. The King consented to stay. Before morning a messenger arrived from the National Assembly ordering the return of the King to Paris. The attempt to escape had failed. Louis and Marie Antoinette went back to their death.

Such was the famous Flight de Varennes, and it leads us to perhaps the most remarkable quatrain in the whole of the *Centuries*, remarkable not only for its general accuracy, but for the details which are included. It is as if Nostradamus had seen these events pass before his eyes, *some two hundred and thirty years* before they happened.

It will be admitted that the little town of Varennes has only come into the limelight of history on one occasion, and is perhaps unlikely ever to do so again. The quatrain which mentions Varennes is concerned with a nocturnal flight through a forest. Here it is:

> *De nuict viendra par la forest de Reines,*
> *Deux pars, vaultorte, Herne la pierre blanche,*
> *Le moyne noir en gris dedans Varennes:*
> *Esleu Cap. cause tempeste, feu, sang, tranche.* (IX, 20)

By night will come into Varennes through the forest [of

Reines] two married persons (we shall see in another quatrain the husband alone referred to as '*le part solus mary*'), by a circuitous route (from *vaulx*, a valley and *torte*, tortuous), Herne, the white stone, and the monk in grey, the Elected Capet; and the result will be tempest, and fire and blood and *tranche* (*trancher*, to cut, to slice). We have already seen *Cap* used for Capet. Nostradamus always did so, and here makes his intention clearer by the full stop. But why the 'Elected Capet'? Because Louis XVI was the first King of France to hold his position not by Divine Right but by the will of a Constituent Assembly. And he is flying through the forest by night, this elected king who is also a monk, or monkish by temperament (Louis was never an ardent lover and for the first part of his married life was actually impotent), and he is dressed in grey (which we have seen to be the case) and the end of his adventure will be the *tranche* of the guillotine.

The Higher Criticism and the commentators themselves have several things to add. First there is no '*forest de Reines*'. The name is unknown to the map-readers, and some have suggested that '*forest*' is really *fores*, a door in Latin, and refers to the door in the Queen's apartments from which she escaped. '*Herne*,' on the other hand is supposed to be an anagram for Reine (the rules of anagram-making allowing for the change or suppression of a letter) and *noir* is the anagram of *roi*. *Le moyne noir*, the monkish king.

In the eyes of the sceptic such ingenuities probably detract from the effect of the quatrain. It is sufficiently remarkable already with its combination of Varennes, night, circuitous route, Elected Capet dressed in grey, and *tranche*. *La pierre blanche*, the white stone, is a poetical description of Marie Antoinette. We know that she was dressed in white from the memoirs of Bouillé himself, but the phrase may have a double meaning. Madame Campan relates in her *Mémoires* that she visited the Queen on the return from Varennes, and found to her horror that her hair had turned white. She had been as it were frozen into stone with anxiety and sorrow, and in her own words, the hairs of her head were *blanchis par la douleur*. There is a further possibility. One of the main causes of the Queen's excessive unpopularity was the famous 'Affair of the Diamond Necklace'. Is it fanciful to suggest that Nostradamus was hinting at this when he spoke of 'la pierre blanche?'[1]

We have seen that the unfortunate royal party passed the night at the house of one Sauce, chandler and *procureur-syndic* of the commune. He is sometimes called Sausse, but Dumas the elder, who in 1855 took the trouble to retrace the route to Varennes and found some people living who had witnessed the King's arrest, is positive that the name was Sauce. The Sauces had been chandlers and *marchands-épiciers* in the place from father to son, and in the sixteenth century the name would have been spelt Saulce. This brings us to the second most astonishing quatrain in the *Centuries*:

> *Le part solus mary sera mitré*
> *Retour: conflict passera sur le thuille*
> *Par cinq cens: un trahyr sera tittré*
> *Narbon: & Saulce par coutaux avons d'huille.* (IX, 34)

The husband alone will be *mitred*. Return. A conflict will pass over the tiles by five hundred; a traitor will be titled Narbonne and from Saulce we have oil in quarts. It is thought that *coutaux* should be *quartauts*, and some editions print this, and interpret the phrase as meaning 'oil sold retail'. Sauce, the real historical Sauce, certainly did so. There is treason about and perhaps Sauce is involved in it [2] (he was awarded 20,000 *livres* by the National Assembly for having prevented the flight of the King) and 'Narbon' is also involved. Now the Comte de Narbonne was war minister of Louis XVI and deep in intrigues with the revolutionaries. The rest of the quatrain is even more interesting.

The husband by himself (some read *marri*, afflicted) will be *mitred*. This is a very strange word, but the facts are these. After Louis's return, the Tuileries were, on June 20th, 1792,

1. I owe this suggestion to Dr Letitia Fairfield.
2. This is, of course, the Royalist view. From any other Sauce was merely doing his duty as *procureur* of the commune.

invaded by the mob who compelled the King to assume the red cap of Liberty, the Phrygian cap which is so strangely like a mitre, or at least sufficiently like a mitre to suggest the word to a sixteenth-century Catholic peering more than two hundred years into the future.

On August 7th, the mob returned, led by the Marseilles contingent under Barbarossa (in Thiers' *History of the French Revolution* we learn that they numbered *five hundred*) and once more invaded the Tuileries.

> *Retour: conflict passera sur la thuille.*

In the time of Nostradamus the palace of the Tuileries was new, and the memory was still recent of the tile furnaces on the site of which it had been built and from which it derived its name. It will be admitted that, if all these things are coincidences, they are, in this quatrain, falling pretty thick.

When the insurrection of August 14th, 1792, put the King's life in danger, he took refuge with his family in the Legislative Assembly. It was decided to confine them in the Temple, in the tower situated opposite the old palace of the Templars. The little Dauphin was allowed to play in the garden within the enclosure of the walls. Nostradamus comments:

> *Roy et son cour au lieu de langue halbe,*
> *Dedans le temple vis à vis du palais,*
> *Dans le jardin Duc de Mantor et d'Albe . . .* (IX, 22)

King and his court in the place of much speaking (*halbe* for *hable: hâbler*, to talk much); within the Temple opposite the palace; in the garden the Duc of Mantor and of Albe.

Now the Dauphin was Duke of Normandy, and his father often called him 'mon petit Normand', 'Mantor' is the anagram of Normant (omitting one 'n' in accordance with the usual practice of those tiresome people the anagram-makers). Albon is in Dauphiné from which issued that race of Dauphins who yielded their estates to France on condition that the eldest son of the royal house should henceforward bear the title of Dauphin. There is nothing in this perverted

THE FRENCH REVOLUTION

ingenuity which is foreign to the tortuous sixteenth-century mind of the Prophet, but if the reader is unable to accept the anagrams he may still find the quatrain singularly exact. '*Roy et son cour . . . dedans le temple*' is alone enough to strike the imagination. The thought of Louis XVI in the Temple seems to have haunted Nostradamus. He returns to it in the quatrain which follows the one above quoted:

> *Puisnay jouant au fresch dessoubs la tonne,*
> *Le haut du toict du milieu sur la teste,*
> *Le pere Roy au temple . . .* (IX, 23)

The younger child (i.e. younger than his sister Marie-Therèse, afterwards Duchesse d'Angoulême) playing *al fresco* underneath the tower (*tonne* for *tour*), the highest middle point of the roof above his head, his father the King in the Temple. . . . The detail of the description suggests that Nostradamus had had an actual vision of the young prince playing in the courtyard while his father looked down upon him from the window of his prison.

The placid and good-natured King who even on the day of his execution ate heartily and gave no sign of distress, does not seem to have realized the fate which threatened himself and his family. The temper of the populace was rising and was fanned into flame by a host of newspapers, pamphlets, satires and political songs.

> *De gent esclave chansons, chants & requestes,*
> *Captifs par Princes & Seigneur aux prisons,*
> *A l'advenir par idiots sans testes,*
> *Seront receus par divines oraisons.* (I, 14)

The songs and demands of the servile populace, while (*par* for *per, pendant*) King and Princes are captive in prison, shall be received as divine oracles by idiots who have lost their heads. The sympathies of Nostradamus, as we have frequently had occasion to remark, were staunchly royalist.

The King was lost. He had been doomed to the scaffold by the fatal journey to Varennes. The 'Elected Capet' was not to be allowed to escape.

> *Mort conspirée viendra en plain effect,*
> *Charge donnée & voyage de mort:*
> *Esleu, crée, receu par siens, deffait.*
> *Sang d'innocent devant soy par remort.* (VIII, 87)

The conspiracy against the life of the King will come to its full effect; the charge laid upon him (as a constitutional king) and his attempted flight (*voyage de mort*) will cause his ruin. He will be overthrown (*deffait*) by those of his own people who have elected, created, and received him as King. His innocent blood will be before the eyes of the French people as a perpetual remorse.

The flight of a Bourbon is mentioned in another quatrain not included in the earlier editions, but which appears in the version published at Leyden by Pierre Leffen in 1650. Its authenticity is not therefore absolute, but it is still a hundred and forty years before the French Revolution, and the pun in the first line is very typical of Nostradamus.

> *Alors qu'un bour. sera fort bon,*
> *Portant en soy les marques de justice,*
> *De son sang lors portant son nom,*
> *Par fuite injuste recevra son supplice.* (VII, 44)

When a Bourbon shall be really *bon*, bearing in his own person the marks of Justice, he will be unjustly (Latin *injuste*) condemned to death by reason of his flight. The construction of the third line is obscure. Some commentators read '*long nom*' instead of '*son nom*', Louis being the sixteenth of his name to sit on the throne of France.

Linked with this is another quatrain:

> *Le trop bon temps, trop de bonté royale,*
> *Fais & deffais, prompt, subit, negligence,*
> *Legier croira faux d'espouse loyalle,*
> *Luy mis à mort par sa benevolence.* (X, 43)

This is interpreted as follows: Louis (was Nostradamus punning, as usual, on the resemblance between Louis and Luy?) will be put to death by reason of his good nature, his irresolution, the instability of his character, his negligence and the

THE FRENCH REVOLUTION 155

lightness with which he suspected his loyal spouse. The third line is supposed to hint at the famous 'Affair of the Diamond Necklace' in which Marie Antoinette was suspected, wrongly, of being involved. The actual execution of the King is treated in one of the most mysterious of the quatrains – mysterious by reason of the wealth of its recondite allusions.

> *Par grand discord la trombe tremblera,*
> *Accord rompu, dressant la teste au ciel,*
> *Bouche sanglante dans le sang nagera,*
> *Au sol la face oingte de laict et miel.* (I, 57)

The discord caused by the Revolution will be like a whirlwind. The agreement (the constitution decreed by the National Assembly and accepted by Louis XVI) will be broken. '*Dressant la teste au ciel*' would be appropriate enough for the behaviour of the King on the scaffold, but it is also an historical fact that during his last moments Louis was actually reciting the verse of the third Psalm: '*Domine gloria mea et exaltans caput meum*'. The bleeding mouth will swim in blood – blood gushes from the mouth of the decapitated. The face anointed with milk and honey (i.e. at the Coronation) lies on the ground. The Office of St Agnes contains the words: *Mel* (honey) *et lac* (milk) *ex ore ejus* (mouth) *suscepi, et sanguis* (blood) *ejus ornavit genas* (face) *meas*, and it would almost seem as if Nostradamus had had these words in mind when composing his quatrain, but whether that be so or not the fact remains that Louis XVI was executed on January 21st, which is the feast of St Agnes.

Even the details of the disposal of the body seem to have been foreseen. In another quatrain we read:

> *Prince de beauté tant venuste,*
> *Au chef menée, le second faict, trahy.*
> *La cité au glaive de poudre face aduste,*
> *Par trop grand meutre le chef du Roy hay.* (VI, 92)

The prince of remarkable beauty (Louis XVI was extremely handsome in his youth) will see intrigues (*menées*) directed against his person, he will be deposed to the second rank (as a constitutional king), and betrayed. *La cité au glaive* is a magnificent phrase for Paris dominated by the guillotine, but it pales in interest before the rest of the line, for *poudre face aduste* (Latin, *fax*, a torch, and *adustus* consumed) means consumed with a powder that burns. In order that there might be no relics of this '*trop grand meutre*', the body and the hated head (*chef du Roy hay*) were put, immediately after the execution, into a wicker basket and carried to the cemetery of the Madeleine, where they were thrown into a deep pit, and *covered with quicklime*.

The efforts of the moderate Revolutionaries to prevent the execution of the King had been unsuccessful, and the struggle between them and the extremists of the 'Mountain' took on a new intensity and virulence. Nostradamus refers to the Republicans as 'Saturnins' and now the Revolution, like Saturn, was devouring its own children. The following quatrain is remarkable, although the accepted interpretation of the first line leaves something to be desired:

> *A soustenir la grand cappe troublée,*
> *Pour l'esclaircir les rouges marcheront:*
> *De mort famille sera presque accablée,*
> *Les rouges rouges le rouge assommeront.* (VIII, 19)

In considering this we must remember that Nostradamus always means Capet when he speaks of 'cappe', or 'cap', and also that he writes in his usual telegraphese. The 'Reds' will therefore march (ostensibly) to support the King but really to thin the ranks of his followers. The rest is plain sailing. The family of Louis XVI was indeed nearly wiped out, and the last line is one of the most dramatically appropriate in the whole of the *Centuries*. The progress of the Revolution, the extremists of the 'Mountain' destroying the more moderate *Girondins*, could not be better expressed. *Les rouges rouges le rouge assommeront* – the red 'Reds' will annihilate that which is merely 'red'! What better name than '*rouge rouge*' could be found for Robespierre?

Some think that he is glanced at also in the line:

> *Le tiers premier pis que ne fut Neron....* (IX, 17)

the first personage of the Third Estate will be worse than Nero. But other commentators believe that it merely means 'the Third Estate having made itself the First'. There is another reference to the Third Estate in the remarkable quatrain:

> *Barbare empire par le tiers usurpé,*
> *La plus grand part de son sang mettra à mort,*
> *Par mort senile, par luy le quart frappé,*
> *Pour peur que sang par le sang ne soit mort.* (III, 59)

The government being barbarous, once the Third Estate had usurped power, will put to death innumerable victims of which the greater part will be of its own blood. The third line is obscure, but the fourth is an admirable figure of the reason for the Terror – for fear that the reign of blood should be overthrown by those (i.e. the *emigrés*) who were willing to wade through blood and invade their country in order to put an end to the Revolution.

Another reference to the new Nero is to be found in the fifty-third quatrain of the ninth *Centurie*, but it would be tedious to multiply instances. If we accept the linking together of these verses and their connexion with the *commun advenement*, we must admit that Nostradamus foresaw with singular clarity the revolutionary excesses and stated quite plainly when they would take place.

In the months following the execution of the King the Terror was in full career and claimed thousands of victims. Menaced by civil war at home – the Royalist rising in La Vendée – and by the danger of foreign invasion, the Government plunged into a savage repression:

> *Des innocens le sang de veufve et vierge,*
> *Tant de maux faicts par moyen ce grand Roge,*
> *Saincts simulacres trempez en ardent cierge,*
> *De frayeur crainte ne verra nul que boge.* (VIII, 80)

The typography is not impeccable: *nul que boge* is plainly *nul qui bouge*, and this justifies us in accepting the obvious reading *Rouge* for Roge. The quatrain might be translated: The blood of innocent children, of widows, of virgins! So many evils wrought by means of this great Red Revolution; the holy images steeped in burning wax (an excellent image for the destruction of churches); through fear and terror none will dare to move.

Nowhere were these horrors worse than at Nantes, where the principal inhabitants with those of the neighbouring districts had in June 1793 constituted themselves as a 'Central Assembly of resistance to oppression'. They decreed that the National 'Convention not being free, it is the duty of all citizens to restore it to freedom'. This local counter-revolution brought swift vengeance upon its authors. Thousands were guillotined; many others were bound and placed in boats which were then taken to the middle of the Loire and scuttled, the occupants being drowned. These are the famous '*Noyades de Nantes*'. Nostradamus writes:

> *Des principaux de cité rebellée,*
> *Qui tiendront pour liberté ravoir,*
> *Destrancher masses, infelice meslée,*
> *Crys, hurlemens à Nantes piteux voir.* (v, 33)

We are plainly concerned with atrocities at Nantes. Of the principal citizens of the rebellious city who tried to recover Liberty, many beheaded [1] (literally chopped up), unhappy *melée*, cries, shrieks at Nantes, piteous to see.

The phrase *infelice meslée* is interesting. Did Nostradamus foresee the full horror of the *noyades*, when men and women were stripped naked and bound together, face to face, before being towed out and drowned in the river?

Louis XVI had been executed in January 1793; the execution of the Queen did not take place until the following October. The King had been condemned by the Convention, itself erected, *ad hoc*, into a supreme court of Justice. The trial of the Queen on the other hand was referred to the newly created revolutionary tribunal served by a jury selected by lot. The jury, it is hardly necessary to remark,

[1]. The earliest editions have '*Destrancher masles ...*' The reading *masses* occurs first in the edition published at Rouen in 1691.

was an institution imported from England. It was foreign to French procedure and was of course utterly unknown in France at the time of Nostradamus. Yet he seems to make the very distinction we have been discussing in the first two lines of one of his quatrains:

> *Le regne prins le Roy convicra,*
> *La dame prinse à mort jurés a sort.*

The government (*le regne*), usurping the privileges of royalty, will convict the captive King; the captive Queen will be condemned to death by jurors chosen by lot. Does this seem too fantastic? Let us examine the remaining lines of the quatrain:

> *Le vie à Royne fils on desniera,*
> *Et la pellix au fort de la consort.* (IX, 77)

Life will be denied to the Queen's son. The fate of the unfortunate Dauphin is still wrapped in mystery, but whether he died in prison or was merely reported to have done so, the line would be equally applicable. The last line is the most astonishing of all, for *pellex* is the Latin for a courtesan. The exact construction is a matter of dispute, but it is possible that *fort* should be *sort* (an easy typographical error when the long s was still in use), and Nostradamus delighted in the kind of play upon words which would be constituted by the phrase '*sort de la consort*'. The courtesan who shared the fate of the consort was, it is perhaps needless to add, Madame Du Barry. So that we have in one quatrain mention of four personages, a King, a Queen, a Queen's son and a courtesan, and their predicted fate exactly fits that of Louis XVI, Marie Antoinette, the Dauphin, and Madame Du Barry.

There is another quatrain concerning Marie Antoinette which is valuable not only for its own sake but as an answer to those who hold what may be called the Theory of Probabilities concerning Nostradamus. According to this theory it is only necessary to prophesy enough, to publish a sufficiently large number of verses, for some of them to find their mark. Ingenious commentators, it is believed, will always be able to twist historical events to fit. Let us examine the quatrain in question in the light of this theory.

It runs as follows:

> La Royne Ergaste voyant sa fille blesme
> Par un regret dans l'estomach enclos:
> Cris lamentables seront lors d'Angolesme,
> Et au germain mariage forclos. (x, 17)

First as to the meaning of *Ergaste*.[1] The Latin word *ergastulum* means a prison for refractory slaves. *La Royne Ergaste* is therefore a prisoner constrained to labour. In the Temple Marie Antoinette was compelled to mend her own garments, but, apart from that consideration, the phrase can only mean the captive Queen, and captive queens are not so very common in history. The captive Queen in question has a daughter with her, pale with sorrow, and in the next line we have the word *d'Angolesme*, and something in that following concerning an unsuccessful marriage.

Now the facts are these. Madame Royale, daughter of Marie Antoinette, had been betrothed in 1787, at the age of nine, to Louis Antoine de Bourbon, duc d'Angoulême, her cousin-german. The marriage was not celebrated until 1799. The young princess, imprisoned in the Temple, was much distraught by the sorrows of her family and in particular by the execution of the King, her father, and it is thought that the emotions which she there underwent were the cause that her marriage remained childless. Does '*l'estomach enclos*' mean 'the sealed womb'?

It seems impossible that Nostradamus should have foreseen all this, and yet what theory of coincidences will cover the facts? Is it conceivable that the Prophet of Salon, considering the probabilities of what might happen to the French Royal House, should have brought into one quatrain, by mere chance, a captive Queen, a distressed daughter, an Angoulême, a cousin-german and an unsuc-

---

1. The edition of 1566 has *Estrange*, which would equally well apply to the Austrian Marie Antoinette, but of course without the convincing particularity of *Ergaste*.

cessful marriage? It is easier to believe in his gift of prophecy.

Another reference to the Duchesse d'Angoulême is sometimes seen in one of the *Sixains* published in the early years of the seventeenth century:

> *Un peu devant ou après très-grand' Dame,*
> *Son ame au ciel, & son corps soubs la lame,*
> *De plusieurs gens regretté sera,*
> *Tous ses parents seront en grand' tristesse,*
> *Pleurs & souspirs d'une Dame en jeunesse,*
> *Et à deux Grands la deuil delaissera.* (Sixain, 55)

This falls into the category of these verses which are not necessarily convincing in themselves, but which, when placed beside others of a more definite character, have an illustrative and cumulative value. It is sufficient to note that *Dame* in Nostradamus nearly always means a royal lady, and that *Grand* means a male member of the royal house. The royal lady whose soul mounts to heaven while her body suffers 'under the knife', is therefore supposed to be Madame Elizabeth, sister of Louis XVI, guillotined some seven months after the execution of Marie-Antoinette. The '*Dame en jeunesse*' is the young Duchesse d'Angoulême, her companion in captivity; and the 'two Great Ones' are the surviving brothers of Louis XVI, the Comte de Provence, afterwards Louis XVIII, and the Comte d'Artois, afterwards Charles X.

The elder branch of the House of Bourbon, cut off from direct succession by the death of the Queen, will yet give two Kings to the throne of France. Under the cover of a strange allegory Nostradamus hints at this:

> *Tranché le ventre naistra avec deux testes,*
> *Et quatre bras: quelques ans entiers vivra*
> *Jour qui Alquiloye celebrera ses festes.* . . . (I, 58)

By a stroke of the knife (as it were, by a Caesarian operation) a creature will be born with two heads and four arms and will live in safety for several years during the time in which the Law of the Eagle will celebrate its festivals.

The two heads are those two who will be crowned: Louis XVIII and Charles X. The four arms are those four who will not be crowned: the Dauphin, who is said to have died in the Temple on June 8th, 1795, the Duc de Berry, assassinated on January 13th, 1820, and the Dukes of Angoulême and Bordeaux, exiled on August 16th, 1830. They will live safely through the period when Napoleon rules in France. *Alquiloye celebrera ses festes* is truly magnificent.

After the death of Marie Antoinette the Terror continued with ever increasing violence. Not only the moderates but many of those who had voted for the execution of the King found their way to the scaffold.

> *Le juste à tort à mort on viendra mettre,*
> *Publiquement et du milieu esteint,*
> *Si grande peste en ce lieu viendra naistre*
> *Que les jugeans fuyr seront contraints.* (IX, 11)

The Just will wrongfully be put to death, publicly and in a *place where the fires are extinct*. Such a great pestilence will be born in this place that the judges themselves will be constrained to fly.

The sense is plain enough. It was indeed as if the guillotine bred a pestilence, as if Louis's death spread by contagion. But what does Nostradamus mean by *milieu esteint*, the place where the fires are extinct?

In his time, as we have frequently had occasion to remark, the site of the Palace of the Tuileries and the adjoining land was occupied by tile-furnaces. Nostradamus must have seen them during his visit to Paris in 1556, and as he paced over the ground which was afterwards to be the Place de la Concorde he saw, in his mind's eye, that the fires of the furnaces had been extinguished, and that where they had glowed now stood a strange machine – two upright posts and between them a diagonal knife which fell, and rose, and fell again, monotonous as death and fatal as a pestilence. So strange a phrase thrown out, as it were, by hazard, is somehow more convincing than many a plainer statement of the *Centuries*.

THE FRENCH REVOLUTION

As the summer of 1794 wore on even Paris grew tired of the endless slaughter. Beneath the surface the revolt against Robespierre grew steadily. Parties came together, even the revolutionary '*sections*' combined against him.

> *Contre les rouges sectes se banderont,*
> *Feu, eau, fer, corde par paix se minera,*
> *Au point mourir ceux qui machineront,*
> *Fors un que monde sur tout ruynera.* (IX, 51)

Against the Reds the sections shall combine. Peace will come and put an end to Fire (the burning of churches and chateaux), Water (such horrors as the Noyades of Nantes), Iron (the knife of the guillotine) and Rope ('*Les aristocrates à la lanterne*'), to such a point that those who engineered these things shall die, except One who will spread ruin throughout the world. The One in question is, of course, Napoleon. It is often forgotten how revolutionary he had been in his early years.

When the news of the fall of Robespierre became public Paris went mad with joy. The Directoire replaced the Commune, to be followed by the Consulate and the Empire. But the peace which the end of the Terror seemed to promise was illusory. France was to see many years of war and many changes of rulers:

> *Tant d'ans en Gaule les guerres dureront,*
> *Outre la course du Castulon monarque;*
> *Victoire incerte trois grands couronneront:*
> *Aigle, Coq-lune, Lyon soleil en marque.* (I, 31)

So many years in Gaul the wars will last, after the passage of the Castulon Monarque; uncertain victory will crown three Great Ones who have as their symbols the Eagle, the Cock-Moon and the Lion-Sun.

The Castulon Monarque is the Goddess of Liberty clothed in the *castula*, the tunic of the Roman virgins. It is curious that sculptors have persistently depicted her in this very garment. The Lion-Sun is the legitimate line of Christian royalty, the Cock-Moon the House of Orleans, whose policy was as changing as the moon and whose symbol was the Gallic Cock. The Eagle needs no comment.

And now the day of the Eagle, the *Alquiloye* which Nostradamus had foreseen, was rapidly approaching. The *Centuries* contain so many allusions to the career of Napoleon that they demand a chapter to themselves.

CHAPTER SEVEN

Nostradamus and Napoleon I

THE French Revolution looms very large in the *Centuries*. It is not perhaps surprising that the career of Napoleon occupies an even larger place. Napoleon was just the kind of fatidic figure to appeal to the Prophet, and indeed a prophet would hardly be worth the name who, concerning himself with French history, should fail to foresee the rise of Bonaparte. But there is foreseeing and foreseeing, and the reader who has followed the argument thus far will feel that he has a right to expect not only a general outline but a wealth of detail concerning the achievements of the Man of Destiny. He will not be disappointed.

Nostradamus begins at the beginning:

> *Un Empereur naistra pres d'Italie,*
> *Qui à l'Empire sera vendu bien cher:*
> *Diront avec quels gens il se ralie,*
> *Qu'on trouvera moins prince que boucher.* (I, 60)

An Emperor will be born near Italy who will cost the Empire dear; when it is seen with what people he allies himself he will be found less like a prince than a butcher. The last line recalls the estimate of Cromwell – *Plus Macelin que Roy*, more like a butcher than a king. There is indeed a curious parallelism in the mind of the Prophet between the two men, as we shall see more clearly when considering another quatrain. The lines quoted above, of course, might refer to one of the Holy Roman Emperors. They *might*, although it is difficult to think of one. They certainly fit Napoleon. And more is to follow:

> *Du plus profond de l'Occident d'Europe,*
> *De pauvres gens un jeune enfant naistra,*
> *Qui par sa langue seduira grande troupe,*
> *Son bruit au regne d'Orient plus croistra.* (III, 35)

In the extreme west of Europe a child will be born of poor parents who will seduce by his speech a great army; his renown will grow greater in the Kingdom of the East. Napoleon was born on August 15th, 1769, in Corsica which is not in the *extreme* west of Europe, although it might seem so by contrast with 'the Kingdom of the East'. The effectiveness of his proclamations to his troops is well known. The reference in the last line is to the campaign in Egypt which so much increased his growing fame.

If this is still not quite satisfactory, we are given a hint of his name:

> *D'un nom farouche tel proferé sera,*
> *Que les trois seurs auront fato le nom:*
> *Puis grand peuple par langue & faict duira,*
> *Plus que nul autre aura bruit & renom.* (1, 76)

The vocable of his name will be as terrible as that which the Three Fates (*les trois sœurs*) received from Destiny (*fato*, from *fatum*, Latin, Destiny). He will lead (*duira* from *duco, ducere*) a great people by his words and his deeds; more than any other he will have fame and renown.

The second part is plain sailing, but why a *nom farouche*? Was the astounding Nostradamus really thinking of that Angel of the Abyss in the Apocalypse, the Destroyer, whom the Jews called Abaddon and the Greeks Apollyon?

Le Pelletier even goes further and suggests $N\acute{\eta} - \alpha\pi o\lambda\lambda\acute{v}\omega\nu$ Verily-the-Exterminator, and to support his claim points out that the η is not arbitrary and is in fact found sculptured on the base of the column in the Place Vendôme:

NEAPOLIO. IMP. AUG.
MONUMENTUM. BELLI. GERMANICI.
ANNO MDCCCV.

Certainly it is just the kind of play upon words in which Nostradamus would have delighted if he could have foreseen – but we are catching ourselves out in an absurdity. Who knows what he could not foresee? He was certainly much preoccupied with the question of the Great Man's name.

> *Du nom qui oncques ne fust au roy gaulois*
> *Jamais ne fut un foudre si craintif.*
> *Tremblant l'Italie, l'Espagne et les Anglois,*
> *De femme estrange grandement attentif.* (IV, 54)

Of a name which no King of France had before him never was a thunderbolt so fearful,[1] causing to tremble, Italy, Spain and the English. He will be greatly attentive to a foreign woman.

No ruler of France had borne a new name since Francis I, before Nostradamus was born. Napoleon was the first to do so. The second and third lines explain themselves and the 'foreign woman' can be either the creole Josephine, the Austrian Marie Louise, or the Polish Marie Walewska.

We have seen the tricks which Nostradamus liked to play with names and also his delight in nicknames. He has a nickname for Napoleon; he calls him Teste Raze – Shavenhead, the man whose hair was so short by comparison with that of the Kings of the *Ancien Régime*.

> *De la cité marine & tributaire*
> *La teste raze prendra la satrapie:*
> *Chasser sordide qui puis sera contraire;*
> *Par quatorze ans tiendra la tyrannie.* (VII, 13)

The man with short hair will assume power (*la satrapie*) in the marine city, tributary of the enemy. He will chase away the mercenary who afterwards (*puis* for *depuis*) will be against him and he will hold absolute power for fourteen years.

Bonaparte recaptured Toulon from the English in December, 1793; it was his earliest success as a commander and after it his reputation and his power grew steadily. The *sordides* in question may be either these same English (a pre-echo if the phrase be not an absurdity of Napoleon's 'Nation of Shopkeepers') or else the members of the Directory, who

---

1. Some French critics have objected that *craintif* means 'afraid', and not 'to be feared', but this is pedantry indeed. English makes exactly the same transposition when it speaks of a 'fearful' thunderbolt. It is not the thunderbolt which is full of fear but those who see it coming.

were certainly mercenary enough. He held absolute power from the '*Coup d'Etat of* 18 *Brumaire*', 1799, to his abdication in 1814 – fourteen years.

In 1795 the star of Napoleon had risen, but it still glimmered at the horizon. In the year following the recapture of Toulon he set out on that Italian campaign which gave his contemporaries their first taste of his qualities as a general.

> *Terre Italique près des monts tremblera* ... (I, 93)

The Italian territory near the mountains (i.e. Lombardy) will tremble. At Milan Bonaparte addressed to his troops one of his first proclamations. The Austrians retired without defending the city and the French entered in triumph.

> *Avant l'assaut l'oraison prononcée,*
> *Milan prins d'Aigle par embusches deceus,*
> *Muraille antique par canons enfoncée,*
> *Par feu et sang à mercy peu receus.* (III, 37)

Before the assault the oration will be pronounced; Milan deceived by ambushes, taken by the Eagle; the ancient wall broken down by cannon in the midst of fire and blood, few will receive mercy.

The second part of the quatrain is thought to refer to Pavia, the inhabitants of which rose against the French. The wall was pierced by a bombardment and the city given over to fire and slaughter.

At Villa-Nova Bonaparte became anxious. The Directoire at home left him without orders and without support. In order to save his army he was compelled to fight at Arcola, joining himself in the hand-to-hand struggle on the bridge. He took Mantua, but treated its defender with generosity. Nostradamus comments:

> *A Cité neufve pensif pour condamner,*
> *L'oisel de proye au ciel se vient offrir,*
> *Après victoire à captif pardonner,*
> *Cremone et Mantoue grands maux aura à souffrir.* (I, 24)

At Villa-Nova (the new city) Bonaparte's thought condemns those who have placed him in extremity. The bird of prey

NOSTRADAMUS AND NAPOLEON I

offers itself to heaven (by risking its own life). After the victory the captive is pardoned. Cremona and Mantua (i.e. the north of Italy) suffer much in these campaigns.

L'oisel de proye is interesting. In another quatrain Nostradamus calls Bonaparte 'the son of the falcon' (*fils de l'aisnier*). 'Young eagle' seems to have been the idea in his mind, in these days before Bonaparte had reached his full stature.

His boundless ambition, unsatisfied by his Italian conquests, turned its eyes eastward, to Egypt, and the Directoire, partly perhaps to get rid of a general whose growing stature had begun to alarm them, agreed to the fitting out of an expedition against that country. That Nostradamus was aware of the order of these events seems to be shown by the following:

> *Grand Po grand mal pour Gaulois recevra,*
> *Vaine terreur au maritin Lyon,*
> *Peuple infiny par la mer passera*
> *Sans eschapper le quart d'un million.* (II, 94)

The great river Po (i.e. the north of Italy) will receive great harm for (the ambition of) a warrior of Gaul. Vain terror to the maritime Lion. A large number of men will pass by sea, and a quarter of a million of these will never return (will be without escape).

Bonaparte set sail for Egypt with a large army. The second line may mean that his preparations caused vain terror to the English (the maritime Lion) or else that the presence of the British fleet in the Gulf of Lions caused terror to Bonaparte – vain terror because it did not succeed in stopping him.

The first act of the French expedition was to seize Malta, then held by the Knights of Rhodes.

> *Proche de Malthe, Herodde prinse vive,*
> *Et Romain sceptre sera par Coq frappé.* (v, 14)

Near the time (*proche*) when the Roman sceptre shall be smitten by the Cock, Malta will be taken.

By the Treaty of Tolentino (in February of the previous

year) the Pope had ceded part of the States of the Church to France. 'Herodde' needs some explanation. Is it a portmanteau word composed of heroes and Rhodes? *'Vive'* would seem to imply that Malta was captured suddenly, or without much bloodshed.

The British, however, were hot on Bonaparte's trail, and their ships coming from the Adriatic entirely destroyed the French fleet at the Battle of Aboukir.

> *Naufrage à classe près l'onde Hadriatique,*
> *La terre esmeuë sur l'air en terre mis,*
> *Egypt tremble augment Mahometique,*
> *L'Heraut rendre à crier est commis.* (II, 86)

The meaning is not as clear as it might be but the sense seems to be as follows: Shipwreck to the fleet near the Adriatic wave; the earth is convulsed in the air and thrown to earth again; tremble Egypt; the power of Mahomet grows; the herald is sent to demand surrender.

The second line is explained by Elisée du Vignois, who says that 'the disembarked French army was terrified to learn that the admiral's vessel had been blown up and that its fragments strewed the shore.' The herald mentioned in the last line is the one sent to demand the surrender of Acre. This was refused and Bonaparte was compelled to raise the siege.

The ill-success of the expedition was plain to Nostradamus:

> *Si France passes outre mer Lygustique,*
> *Tu te verras en isles et mers enclos,*
> *Mahomet contraire, plus mer Hadriatique,*
> *Chevaux et d'asnes tu rongeras les os.* (III, 23)

France, if you pass the Gulf of Genoa (*Lygusticum mare*) you will find yourself besieged in the islands and on the seas. Mahomet will be against you and even more the Adriatic sea (i.e. the British fleet mentioned in the previous quatrain) and you will be driven to gnaw the bones of horses and asses.

The French, having set out on the Egyptian expedition, found the Turks against them and the British fleet. They were besieged in Malta and at Alexandria and suffered cruelly from hunger.

Still addressing France, Nostradamus warns her never to undertake such an expedition again:

> *De l'entreprinse grande confusion,*
> *Perte de gens thresor innumerable,*
> *Tu n'y dois faire encore extension,*
> *France à mon dire fais que sois recordable.* (III, 24)

From this enterprise will come great confusion with loss of men and countless treasure; you should not attempt such expansion there again. France! see that you remember my words.

It may be objected that there is no proof that this quatrain refers to the expedition to Egypt, but it follows the one above quoted, and seems to be linked with it. It is perhaps worth including as a curiosity. The quatrain concerning the return of Bonaparte is a little more definite:

> *Le chef qu'aura conduit peuple infiny*
> *Loing de son ciel, de mœurs et langue estrange,*
> *Cinq mil en Crete et Thessalie finy,*
> *Le chef fuyant sauvé en marine grange.* (I, 98)

The chief who shall have conducted a large army (*peuple infiny* links the quatrain with II, 94, quoted above: *Peuple infiny par mer passera*) far from the skies of home in a land of strange manners and language, shall have in the end five thousand in Crete and Thessaly. He himself shall be saved by flight in a 'marine grange'.

The final phrase is very clumsy and seems dictated by the rhyme. A marine grange or barn is of course a wooden ship. Bonaparte succeeded in eluding the British fleet and landing in France. His army, reduced to five thousand men, was left in the hands of the Turks, masters of Crete and Thessaly (where there had just been a massacre of the French). The British consented to transport these men back to France.

Such was the famous Expedition to Egypt, and the strange thing is that instead of shattering Bonaparte's reputation for ever it actually seemed to enhance it. During his absence the Directoire had fallen into considerable discredit and he saw that the time had come to seize power for himself. He did so by the '*Coup d'Etat of* 18 *Brumaire*' (November 9th, 1799).

We now come to a very odd quatrain. It is written not in French but in Provençal, a language which was probably spoken by Nostradamus in his daily intercourse with the people of Salon.

> *Lou grand eyssame se lèvera d'abelhos,*
> *Que non sauran don te siegen venguddos.*
> *De nuech l'embousq lou gach dessous las treilhos,*
> *Ciutad trahido per cinq lengos non nudos.* (IV, 26)

There will arise a great swarm of bees and no one will know from whence they come. The ambush will be set during the night; the Jay will instal himself in the trellises, and the City will be betrayed by five tongues not naked.

An impenetrable allegory? But let us examine it a little more closely. There will arise a great swarm of bees. If you go to Fontainebleau, or walk through the rooms of Malmaison decorated by Napoleon, you will see it still, that swarm of bees, settled thickly on carpet and wall-hanging and covering even the silk backs of the chairs. Bees were the Napoleonic emblem; they stand also here for the swarm of his relatives which arrived no one knew whence, and settled all over Europe. The ambush is the *coup d'état* of 18 Brumaire, prepared during the previous night. It succeeded, Napoleon took up his quarters in the Tuileries, and, like the jay in the fable who decked himself in the peacock's feathers, was thus invested with some of the splendour of the old Kings of France. *Treilhos* is the anagram of Tholries, a pun on Tuileries. How Nostradamus must have chuckled as he thought that out, and how the modern commentator must wish that he hadn't! The five 'tongues' are the five talkers or politicians who delivered Pàris to Napoleon, and they are not naked because they wore their robes as members of the Directory.

Having seized power, as above related, he forced the

NOSTRADAMUS AND NAPOLEON I 173

Great St Bernard pass into Italy and made himself all-powerful there also. Nostradamus comments:

> *L'Oriental sortira de son siege,*
> *Passer les monts Appenons, voir la Gaule,*
> *Transpercera le ciel, les eaux et neige,*
> *Et un chacun frappera de sa gaule.* (II, 29)

The Man of the East will leave his place (the one assigned to him by the Directory in the hope of getting rid of him, and where he had had to submit to a siege by the English) to pass by Italy (the Apennines) and see France again. He will pierce heaven, the water, and the snows (by crossing the Alps) and will smite everyone with the point of the spear (gaule). By itself the quatrain would be unconvincing, but it serves to fill out the picture which Nostradamus is painting of Bonaparte's progress towards Empire.

> *De soldat simple parviendra en empire,*
> *De robbe courte parviendra à la longue:*
> *Vaillant aux armes, en Eglise, où plus pyre,*
> *Vexer les prestres comme l'eau fait l'esponge.* (VIII, 57)

From being just a soldier he attained to the Empire, from the short robe (the Consular robe was short) he attained to the long (the Imperial mantle was long).[1] Valiant in arms, in ecclesiastical matters he was not so successful and he vexed the clergy by alternately elevating them and depressing them (as water swells up a sponge and then leaves it limp and flabby).[2]

Napoleon proclaimed himself Emperor on May 18th, 1804. France was soon to discover his insatiable appetite for conquest:

---

1. The reader may be reminded that in the time of Nostradamus the short robe meant the military profession and the long that of the maker and interpreter of laws; hence, from soldier to law-giver.
2. Some commentators suggest that *vexer* is from the Latin *vexare*, to lift up, to swell, but this seems to rob the line of half its meaning. The simpler explanation, as so often, is the better.

Par teste raze viendra bien mal eslire
Plus que sa charge ne porte passera.
Si grand fureur et rage fera dire
Qu'a feu et sang tout sexe tranchera. (v, 60)

In Shaven-head France will come to see that she has made a very bad choice; she will be saddled with a burden (*charge*) beyond her power to carry. He will be animated with such a warlike fury as to make men say that one sex (the whole male population of Europe) would be, by blood and fire, cut off. Comment is needless.

Napoleon himself took a considerable interest in prophecy. He consulted soothsayers in Egypt and some commentators profess to believe that he was acquainted with the 'Prophecy of Olivarius' and the so-called *Prophétie d'Orval*, both of which have been rashly attributed to Nostradamus. They are, in all probability, post-Napoleonic forgeries and we need not here be concerned with them further.[1] But of the prophecies of Nostradamus himself he was certainly aware and if he had not been they would have been brought to his notice by a flattering piece of propaganda issued in Paris in 1806.

This was '*Nouvelles Considérations puisées dans la Clairvoyance Instinctive de l'Homme, sur les Oracles, les Sibylles et les Prophéties, et particulièrement sur Nostradamus Par Théodore Bouys, Ancien professeur à l'école centrale du départment de la Nièvre, et avant la révolution, président de l'élection de Nevers.*'

The author professed to reveal to his readers the marvels of Magnetism and the instinctive clairvoyance procured by *somnambulisme magnétique*, that instinctive clairvoyance which he declares made known to Nostradamus 'the brilliant destinies of Napoleon the Great, which are to enjoy a long and happy reign, to bring lasting peace to the Continent, to be one day as redoubtable on the sea as he is on land, and to conquer England in order to give to all nations the Freedom of the Seas.'

About an eighth of the work only is devoted to Nostradamus, the rest being concerned with other prophecies, and

1. See Appendix.

with considerations on the 'voices' of Joan of Arc and of 'magnetism' in general, but his remarks on the Prophet of Salon gain a certain piquancy by his own strong Bonapartist opinions and the period at which he wrote. His handling is scholarly and not too credulous, and he makes the suggestion (interesting in a schoolmaster of the period) that it is the vice of modern education to prevent the development of certain instinctive faculties which are common enough among less civilized people. He cites the famous quatrain concerning the Flight to Varennes, and adds: 'I owe the explanation of this quatrain, and many others, to an inhabitant of Nevers who has composed a long and interesting commentary on Nostradamus. M. de Vaudeuil, son of the former president of the *parlement* of Toulouse, communicated several to me and I have taken a dozen or more from the old commentators. Without the reading of the work of M. Mxxx which he was good enough to give to his friends, I would never have understood more than five or six quatrains. I would never have thought of opening Nostradamus. All that is found of interest (in my own work) I owe to the private conversations I have had with my compatriot, my old study-companion, who before the revolution had become *promoteur* of the archbishopric of Paris and is now manager and owner of a porcelain factory.'

The long and interesting commentary by the mysterious Mxxx, inhabitant of Nevers, seems never to have been published, and research has so far failed to establish his identity, but the passage is of value as showing the interest in Nostradamus at the time, and the fact that contemporaries saw in the events of the French Revolution the fulfilment of some of his prophecies.

After dealing with various quatrains concerning Louis XVI Bouys turns to the 'Predictions of Nostradamus on Napoleon, Emperor of the French, of which some, already accomplished, are a presumption and indeed ought to be an assurance that the remainder will be accomplished also.'

He cites several verses, including:

Heureux au règne de France, heureux de vie . . . (x, 16)

which is now usually referred to Louis XVIII, as it gives him a chance to praise Napoleon for his love of peace (!), and then turns to what is for him the burning question of the moment, the projected invasion of England. Nostradamus had written:

> *Dedans Boulogne voudra laver ses fautes;*
> *Il ne pourra au temple du soleil.*
> *Il volera faisant choses si hautes,*
> *Qu'en hierarchie n'en fut onc un pareil.* (VIII, 53)

Bouys remarks: 'This quatrain is without doubt one of the most powerful of those written by Nostradamus concerning the Emperor Napoleon. What other prince, in fact, could come to Boulogne to expiate the fault of having been too confident, of having presumed too much on the loyalty of his enemies and their fidelity in the execution of treaties? (The reference is of course to the Peace of Amiens.) What other prince could not succeed in the Temple of the Sun, in Egypt, and yet flies so high that none in all the hierarchy of princes can be considered his equal? Now, he makes formidable preparations at Boulogne and we shall see in the following quatrains that this enterprise will have the greatest success and that the Emperor Napoleon will end by making the conquest of England.' The two quatrains in question are these, and in view of what actually happened, are not without interest:

> *De l'aquilon les efforts seront grands,*
> *Sur l'océan sera la porte ouverte:*
> *Tremblera Londres par voile découverte*
> *Le régne en l'isle sera réintegrant.* (II, 68)

> *La forteresse auprès de la Tamise,*
> *Cherra pour lors le roi dedans serré:*
> *Auprès du pont sera vu en chemise,*
> *Un devant mort, puis dans le fort barré.* (VIII, 37)

We have seen that the first of these, which Bouys quotes incorrectly, reversing the third and fourth lines, can with more likelihood be referred to the expedition of James II to Ireland, aided by the French fleet. The second has never been explained, and may be left to the ingenuity of the reader.

The optimism of the worthy schoolmaster was unjustified, as another quatrain might have told him if he noticed it and had been able to interpret it before the event. It was concerned with nothing less than the Battle of Trafalgar.

> *Entre deux mers dressera promontoire,*
> *Qui puis mourra par le mors du cheval,*
> *Le sien Neptune pliera voile noire,*
> *Par Calpre et classe auprès de Rocheval.* (I, 77)

There is a promontory between two seas; there is one who will die afterwards by the bridle of a horse, and Neptune, for his own, will unfurl the black sail; in the strait of Calpe, when his fleet is near Cape Roche.

Now it would be absurd to pretend that Bouys or any one else could interpret this beforehand. It is none the less extremely curious, for the French admiral Villeneuve was later strangled by the Emperor's Mamelukes whose custom it was to use for such a purpose the bridle of a horse. The other admiral, Neptune's own, the great Nelson himself, fell, as the world knows, in the glorious action and his body was brought back to England, the ship bearing a black sail in sign of mourning. Calpre is the classical Calpe, one of the Pillars of Hercules which we call Gibraltar, and the battle was fought between this and Cape Roche. Trafalgar is itself a promontory between two seas.

Again Nostradamus writes:

> *Après combat et bataille navale,*
> *Le grand Neptune à son plus haut beffroy,*
> *Rouge adversaire de peur viendra pasle,*
> *Mettant le grand Ocean en effroy.* (III, 1)

After the combat and the naval battle, great Neptune (England) will be raised as on a pinnacle. The Red adversary (Napoleon, in the eyes of the Prophet, never ceased to be the revolutionary, the *Rouge*) will grow pale with fear, putting the ocean in a panic. The last line presumably refers to his attempt to institute a blockade against England which, like his naval operations, was a failure.

The fact that we know these things, and know that both Bouys and Napoleon were doomed to disappointment, gives added point to the second half of the Boulogne quatrain. For the Emperor, seeing that the invasion of England was hopeless, wheeled his army about, swept through Europe like a whirlwind and coming up with the two other Emperors, of Austria and Russia, beyond Vienna, won over their combined forces the glorious victory of Austerlitz. 'He will fly so high and do such deeds that in the hierarchy of rulers none will be found his equal.' The abrupt change from failure to triumph staggered Europe and is reflected in the very construction of the prophetic quatrain.

Nostradamus was not a Bonapartist – if the superficial absurdity of the remark may be pardoned – but he regarded Napoleon with a kind of reluctant admiration, rather like that felt by the nineteenth-century French Royalists, and like many of these the Prophet seems to have believed that the Emperor's final misfortunes were a judgement upon him for his treatment of the clergy and, in particular, for his persecution of the Pope.

Nostradamus took considerable interest in the welfare of the Papacy and it is not therefore surprising to find that he devotes several quatrains to its fortunes during the French Revolution and the Empire. In an obscure but extremely interesting quatrain he had written:

> *Istra de mont Gaulfier & Aventin,*
> *Qui par le trou advertira l'armée*
> *Entre deux rocs sera prins le butin,*
> *De SEXT. mansol faillir la renommée.* (v, 57)

Let us take the last two lines first. Between two rocks shall the booty be taken and the renown of *Sext. Mansol* shall fail. Who is *Sext. Mansol? Man. sol.* stands for *manens solus*, the man who lives alone, who has made a vow of celibacy. In other places Nostradamus refers to priests as *les seuls*. Sext. stands for sextus, and the priest, *par excellence*, who is also *sextus*, is Pius VI, the *Pastor peregrinus* of the prophecy of Malachy and the only Pontiff to bear that number since the composition of the *Centuries*. By the Treaty of Tolentino of February 19th, 1797, the Pope was deprived of Avignon and of the Romagna and other lands in Italy, the two rocks, as it were, on which his power reposed.

The first two lines of the quatrain are even more curious. The exact construction is difficult to make out, but the words *mont Gaulfier* leap to the attention. For the brothers Montgolfier had invented the air balloon in 1783, and at the Battle of Fleurus in 1794 an attempt was made to use it for military reconnaissance, by suspending, *beneath the hole*,[1] a man in a basket to act as observer (*advertira l'armée*). The result of the battle left Rome (Mount Aventine) open to the French. Whether this interpretation be accepted or not, it seems plain that Nostradamus had 'received' the word Montgolfier (or Mont Gaulfier) two hundred years before the brothers had ever been heard of, and that he had some notion of the construction of their apparatus and some idea of its possibilities in war. Let us return to the relations between the Papacy and Revolutionary France.

> *Tout à l'entour de la grande cité*
> *Seront soldats logés par champs & villes:*
> *Donner l'assaut Paris Rome incité*
> *Sur le pont lors sera faicte grand pille.* (v, 30)

All around the great city shall soldiers be lodged in fields and towns. Paris being incited to assault Rome, great pillage will be made on the Sovereign Pontiff.

The death of the French general Duphot in a riot gave General Berthier, whose troops surrounded the city, an excuse for an assault on Rome. The Pope was pillaged, being dispossessed of his estates and imprisoned in his palace. He was later taken as a captive to Valence, where he died.

> *Pol mensole mourra trois lieues du Rosne . . .* (VIII, 46)

[1]. It is perhaps unnecessary to remind the reader that the Montgolfier balloon was open at the bottom, a fire being placed there in order to heat the air in the interior of the balloon and so cause it to rise.

The Great Celibate (*pol.* from the Greek πολύς, much, *mensole* being the same as *mansol* in the quatrain quoted above) will die three leagues from the Rhone. Valence is in fact on that river which, not far away, at Lyons, is joined by the Saône. Hence Nostradamus writes, with reference to the same event:

> *Romain Pontife garde de t'approcher*
> *De la cité que deux fleuves arrouse.*
> *Ton sang viendra auprès de là cracher,*
> *Toy et les tiens quand fleurira la rose.* (II, 97)

Roman Pontiff, beware of approaching the city (i.e. Lyons) which is bathed by two rivers. You and yours (will be there) when the rose is in bloom.

Pius VI died after violent vomiting on August 29th, 1799. He was accompanied to Valence by thirty-two priests, prisoners like himself, and the reference to the rose may mean that these events took place in the summer. Some commentators see a symbolical meaning, the white lily of legitimacy having given place to the revolutionary red of the rose.

After the death of Pius VI, the cardinals, dispersed by the Revolution, managed, amid many difficulties, to hold a conclave in Venice and elected a new Pope who was known as Pius VII. Meanwhile, Bonaparte had become First Consul.

These events were, in the mind of Nostradamus, closely intertwined.

> *Par l'univers sera faict un monarque*
> *Qu'en paix et vie ne sera longuement,*
> *Lors se prendra la piscature barque,*
> *Sera regie au plus grand detriment.* (I, 4)

A universal monarch will be set up who will not live long in peace; then one will take control of the Fisherman's Boat, and it will be governed to its greatest detriment. The Fisherman's Boat is, of course, the Barque of Peter, the Papacy, the prestige of which suffered by the weakness of the Pope's

NOSTRADAMUS AND NAPOLEON I

attitude towards Napoleon. Pius VII came to France for the first time to crown Napoleon Emperor and the second time as his prisoner. The Rapacious Eagle (the *aquila rapax* of the prophecy of Malachy) had him firmly in his claws, and he was only released by the abdication at Fontainebleau. Nostradamus comments:

> *En naviguant captif prins grand Pontife,*
> *Grand après faillir les clercs tumultuez :*
> *Second esleu absent son bien debiffe,*
> *Son favory bastard à mort tué.* (v, 15)

While navigating his Boat the great Pontiff will be taken, and made prisoner. The clergy will be thrown into a tumult. He, the second elected one to be absent from Rome (the first being Pius VI) will dissipate his goods. The illegitimate monarch whom he had favoured by consenting to crown him will be deprived of [political] life.

The States of the Church were incorporated in the Empire in 1809, but the judgement of God was not long to be delayed:

> *Terroir Romain qu'interpretoit Augure,*
> *Par gent Gauloise par trop sera vexée,*
> *Mais nation Celtique craindra l'heure,*
> *Boreas classe trop loing l'avoir poussée.* (II, 99)

The Roman territory governed by him who interprets as Augur (i.e. the successor of the Pontifex Maximus of pagan Rome) will be much troubled by the Gaulish people. But this nation when it has pushed too far (into Russia) shall fear the hour of Boreas, the cold north wind, and its fleet, i.e. the fleet of England (*classe* from the Latin *classis*).

The punishment (to continue this ecclesiastical and apocalyptic interpretation of his history) will be hastened by Napoleon's wickedness in divorcing his first wife, or in terms of the popular legend, Napoleon never had any luck after his abandonment of Josephine.

> *Le divin mal surprendra le grand Prince,*
> *Un peu devant aura femme espousée,*
> *Son appuy et credit à un coup viendra mince,*
> *Conseil mourra pour la teste rasée.* (I, 88)

The punishment of God will fall upon the great Prince; a little before he will have married a wife. The support of his allies and his credit at home will suddenly become very small and Shaven-head will have no good counsel to turn to. If we admit (as we must) that Shaven-head means Napoleon, the quatrain is among the most explicit.

To punish his faithless ally the Emperor Alexander, Napoleon undertook the Campaign of Russia. With an immense army he reached Moscow, the Russians retreating before him. With the old city in flames he was compelled to retreat, and his great plan for a new Roman Empire embracing the whole of Europe (he had just created his infant son King of Rome) crumbled into ruin.

> *Amas s'approche venant d'Esclavonie,*
> *L'Olestant vieux cité ruynera,*
> *Fort désolée verra sa Romanie,*
> *Puis la grande flamme esteindre ne sçaura.* (IV, 82)

A great mass of men will be seen coming from the Land of the Slavs (the broken mass of the *Grande Armée* in retreat from Moscow). *L'Olestant*, the Destroyer, will ruin the old city, and he will not know how to put out the great flame. He will see his Roman dream vanish away.

Romanie should not, of course, be confused with Rumania which did not exist at the time. In another quatrain (VIII, 60) Napoleon is referred to as

> *Premier en Gaule, premier en Romanie,*

that is, 'first in France and in the lands of Rome'. *Olestant* is a harking back to the previous word-play on the Greek root for 'destroy'. Once more we have a quatrain obscure, and even misleading, when taken by itself, but adding to the cumulative effect.

The ill-success of the *Grande Armée* in Russia showed Europe that Napoleon was not invincible. The nations began to rise against him once more, and the Eagle found itself, as it were, surrounded by other birds of prey ready to devour it.

> *L'aigle poussée entour de pavillons,*
> *Par autres oyseaux d'entour sera chassée....*

The eagle pushed back into his own territory (surrounded by his banners) will be pursued by other birds around, that is by the eagles of Russia, Austria, and Prussia. The sound of military music on her own frontiers will bring France to her senses.

> *Quand bruit des cymbres tube & sonnaillons*
> *Rendront le sens de la dame insensée.* (II, 44)

From the south came Wellington, having fought his way through Spain to be welcomed at Bordeaux as a friend rather than a conqueror.

> *Par la Guyenne infinité d'Anglois*
> *Occuperont par nom Anglaquitaine....* (IX, 6)

Across Guyenne an infinite number of English soldiers will occupy the old English province of Aquitaine, thus baptizing it anew (a Nostradamian joke!) with the name of Anglaquitaine.

France is assailed from both sides:

> *Tous ceux de Iler seront dans la Moselle,*
> *Mettant à mort tous ceux de Loyre et Seine,*
> *Le cours marin viendra près d'haute velle,*
> *Quand l'Espagnol ouvrira toute veine.* (I, 89)

Those of the Iller (a tributary of the Danube, that is the Austrians) will advance up the valley of the Moselle, slaying the French (those of the Loire and the Seine). The marine torrent (i.e. the English) will come near the high valley (i.e. will pierce the Pyrenees) when the Spaniard shall open every vein. The last line seems to mean that the reconquest of Spain by Wellington opened the road to France. Some commentators have thought that in the strange phrase 'haute velle', the Prophet was groping towards the very name of Wellington, but this supposition is quite unnecessary for the explanation of the quatrain.

> *Les cinq estranges entrez dedans le temple,*
> *Leur sang viendra la terre prophaner,*
> *Aux Tholosains sera bien dur example....* (III, 45)

The Five Strangers (i.e. England, Austria, Prussia, Russia and Spain) will enter the temple (i.e. invade the sacred soil of France). Their blood will profane the earth. Nostradamus seems to have heard far in the future the faint strains of the Marseillaise:

> *Qu'un sang impur*
> *Abreuve nos sillons!*

The people of Toulouse will be made a hard example. When the bloody battle of Toulouse was fought by Wellington the war was already over but the combatants did not know it.

Napoleon's desperate situation gave him the opportunity of testing the loyalty of those to whom he had given thrones. One of the bitterest blows was the defection of Murat, King of Naples and the Emperor's brother-in-law. Nostradamus knew all about this too:

> *Gaulois qu'empire par guerre occupera,*
> *Par son beau frere mineur sera trahy;*
> *Par cheval rude voltigeant trainera,*
> *Du fait le frere long temps sera hay.* (x, 34)

The Gaul who by war will gain an Empire, will be betrayed by his youngest brother-in-law; on horseback this hard-riding cavalier will carry all before him; on account of this (treason) the brother will long be hated.

The phrase: '*son beau frere mineur*' should be noted; Murat was in fact the husband of Napoleon's youngest sister. He was also the most dashing cavalry leader in the whole army. His popularity never recovered from his act of betrayal, and Napoleon refused his proffered help at the Battle of Waterloo.

In the spring of 1814 the Allies advanced on Paris:

> *Comme un gryphon viendra le Roy d'Europe,*
> *Accompagné de ceux d'Aquilon,*
> *De rouges et blancs conduira grand troupe,*
> *Et iront contre le Roy de Babylon.* (x, 86)

Like a gryphon will come the King of Europe, accompanied by those of the North; he will conduct a great army of the reds and the whites and they will go up against the King of Babylon.

The 'King of Europe' means either the King who is recognized by the whole of Europe, or the legitimate King of the noblest throne in Europe. Paris is called Babylon in several quatrains and the King of Babylon is Napoleon. These symbolisms detract from the effect of the quatrain and it would not have been quoted here but for its third line. The great army of 'reds' and 'whites' are the English and the Austrians whose tunics were respectively red and white.

The rapacious monarch whose power had sprung from the Revolution was now tracked to his lair:

> *Avec le noir Rapax et sanguinaire,*
> *Yssu du peaultre de l'inhumain Neron*
> *Emmy deux fleuves.* . . . (IX, 76)

In the *Centuries*, as we have seen, '*noir*' always means *roi* or monarch. The adjective Rapax is interesting. In the prophecy of Malachy, Napoleon, the persecutor of Pius VII, is called *Aquila Rapax*, the greedy eagle. *Peaultre* means rudder, hence government, and 'the inhuman Nero' is of course the Revolution already referred to as acting '*pis que ne fit Neron*'. *Emmy deux fleuves*, between two streams, means Paris, between Seine and Marne, sometimes called by Nostradamus Babylon or Mesopotamia, which likewise, as its name indicates, lay between two streams, the Euphrates and the Tigris: '*Neufve Babylone, cité libre, assise dans une autre exigue Mesopotamie*', as he calls the French capital in his Epistle to Henri II. Nostradamus loved these learned circumlocutions.

For a time Napoleon hoped to be able to keep by intrigue the throne he had not been able to preserve by force of arms. The Emperor Alexander was willing to listen but Napoleon had an implacable enemy in Talleyrand:

> *De leur senat sacriste fait boiteux,*
> *Fera scavoir aux ennemis l'affaire.* (II, 76)

The senator who is also a priest and lame will reveal the affair to his enemies.

Napoleon went into exile on the Island of Elba, but as every schoolboy knows, the deliberations of the Congress of Vienna, which was to settle the peace of Europe for ever, were interrupted by his unwelcome return. To this world-shattering event the Prophet devoted several quatrains. We shall quote no more than two of them, and unfortunately they are even more than usually marked by that pedantic punning in which Nostradamus took such delight. We must remind ourselves that this learned paronomasia was considered in the sixteenth century to be the very flower of scholarship; and was not thought out of place even on the most serious occasions. In the single phrase which Clément Marot sent to Francis I to console him for the death of his mother there are no less than six puns. The characters of Shakespeare pun when their hearts are breaking –

'Old Gaunt indeed and gaunt in being old.'

The indulgence of the reader is asked for the inclusion of quatrains which, in spite of their conceits, are of considerable interest. The impatient sceptic is advised to skip them altogether. The first reads as follows:

> *Grand Roy viendra prendre port près de Nisse,*
> *Le grand empire de la mort si en fera,*
> *Aux antipolles posera son genisse,*
> *Par mer la Pille tout esvanouyra.* (x, 87)

The Great King will come to port near Nice (city of Niké, Goddess of Victory) but [in spite of that] he will make of his great empire an empire of Death. He will set up his household gods (or his root; some commentators read *genii Lares*, some *genitus*) towards the opposite pole (but probably with a punning reference also to Antibes, which the Ancients called Antipolis, the place 'opposite the city' of Nice). The nation above all others given to piracy and pillage (Nostradamus hints elsewhere that this was his opinion of the English) will cause all Napoleon's power to vanish into the sea, by banish-

NOSTRADAMUS AND NAPOLEON I

ing him to St Helena, which being south of the Equator, may be said to lie towards the other pole (*aux antipolles*).

What a farrago! It is like a telegram sent by a miser enamoured of puns and who had had the disadvantage of a classical education. But tiresome as it is, it is not *meaningless*. In fact it has far too much meaning, and it fits the facts of Napoleon's return.

Here is the second quatrain:

> *Au peuple ingrat faictes les remonstrances,*
> *Par lors l'armée se saisira d'Antibe,*
> *Dans l'arc Monech seront les doleances.*
> *Et a Frejus l'un l'autre prendra ribe.* (x, 23)

Remonstrances will be made to the ungrateful People (Louis XVIII issued a proclamation urging fidelity to the new régime which had given them peace; but the only place where the army was faithful to him was Antibes where it seized the town and shut the gates against Napoleon). In the seat of sovereignty there will be lamentation (*arché*, sovereignty and *moné*, dwelling, but with a punning reference to Arké and Monoiké, the ancient names of Hyères and Monaco). And at Fréjus one and the other shall take ship. Louis himself had previously embarked at Fréjus when leaving France; Napoleon embarked there for Elba, and he landed again at Golfe Juan, which is between Fréjus and Antibes, and, of course, near Nice. All these places were well known to Nostradamus himself; during his wanderings in Provence he must have passed through all of them, meditating as he did so on the meaning of their corrupted but still classical names, and seeing in his mind's eye a stout little man in a uniform of a very un-sixteenth-century cut, making a final grasp at a shadowy empire.

And now, leaving aside a dozen quatrains the inclusion of which would have served only to weary and confuse the reader, we come to the Battle of Waterloo.

It is a curious fact that, on those rare occasions when the rebus-verse of Nostradamus rises into poetry, it is inspired by one of the major historical events. He writes:

> *Au mois troisiesme se levant le Soleil,*
> *Sanglier, Leopard, au champ de Mars, pour combattre,*
> *Leopard laissé au ciel estend son œil,*
> *Un Aigle autour du Soleil voit s'esbattre.* (I, 23)

It is such a good stanza that one is tempted to try to translate it into English verse:

> The Hundred Days are past! the hour is nigh,
> Leopard and Boar allied – the fight's begun.
> The Leopard, lonely, lifts an anxious eye –
> An Eagle's wings are blotting out the sun.

Or more literally: At the third month, the sun rising, the Wild Boar and the Leopard are ready to fight on the field of battle. The Leopard, left to himself, lifts his eye to heaven [for help] but sees only a battling eagle against the sun.

The Leopard is, of course, England; the Boar is the brave and headstrong Blücher. But Blücher had been beaten back at Ligny and the junction of the British and Prussians had not taken place when Wellington decided to stand at Waterloo. It was June 18th, 1815, three months, or rather a Hundred Days, after Napoleon's return. All day long his troops battered the English squares while Wellington cast anxious eyes to the horizon hoping for the arrival of his ally to turn the French flank. Up the slope came the flower of Napoleon's army, the Imperial eagles flying. It is astonishing to note that as Wellington faced south he saw them against the sun as Nostradamus had foretold. Then, when the day was nearly over and the British still unbroken, Napoleon saw on his right a cloud of dust. 'It is Grouchy', he cried. But it was not Grouchy. It was Blücher.

> *Prest a combattre fera defection,*
> *Chef adversaire obtiendra la victoire,*
> *L'arriere garde fera defension,*
> *Les defaillans mort au blanc territoire.* (IV, 75)

He who was ready to fight (Grouchy) will not be present at the battle. The hostile chief (Wellington) will gain the victory. The Imperial Guard, usually kept in reserve in the rear, will make a great defence (*La garde meurt mais ne se rende pas*) and those who fail (that is, the Napoleonic troops) will be either physically or politically dead in a territory which has become once more white, by the restoration of the Bourbons. Paris, says a contemporary, looked as if there had been a fall of snow, there were so many white cockades.

So Napoleon disappeared once more, this time into an exile from which there was no return. And again Nostradamus rises to the occasion.

> *Le grand Empire sera tost translaté*
> *En petit lieu qui bien tost viendra croistre,*
> *Lieu bien infime d'exigue comté*
> *Où au milieu viendra poser son sceptre.* (1, 32)

The commentators here have missed their opportunity. Elisée du Vignois merely remarks: 'Napoleon was sent to the Island of Elba, a little country smaller than some counties, the name of which was soon to become celebrated by the treaty which recognized him as its monarch.' But Nostradamus saw more clearly than that. He saw the great Empire shrink to a little space (the Island of Elba); he saw it grow again (the Hundred Days), and he saw it shrink once more to nothing but a tiny rock in the middle of the ocean, where at last Napoleon would lay down his sceptre.

So we take leave of Shaven-head, the man with the terrible name of the Destroyer, the Emperor who was born near Italy, the soldier who failed in the Temple of the Sun, the King of Babylon, the fearful Thunderbolt – for all these names does Nostradamus give him. So vanished also the great Swarm of Bees.

CHAPTER EIGHT

The Restoration that was and the Restoration that wasn't

To the 'Teste Raze' succeeded the 'Chevelu', the man with long hair, a most appropriate epithet for Louis XVIII who wore his own hair loose about his shoulders.

> *Les longs cheveux de la Gaule Celtique,*
> *Accompagnés d'estranges nations....* (III, 83)

The long hair of Old France, accompanied by foreign nations (the Allies who had replaced him on the throne). He is also

> *Le bon vieillard tout vif ensevely....* (III, 72)

the good old man buried while still quite alive. In this semi-humorous phrase Nostradamus hints that Louis, exhumed, as it were, to take his place on the throne, was hastily buried once more on the return of Napoleon from Elba. However, he was not dead yet,

> *L'ensevely sortira du tombeau....* (VII, 24)

(the buried one will emerge from his tomb) and after Waterloo he reigned in peace for the rest of his life. The Prophet also calls him '*Sang Mathieu Roy*', the King of the blood of Æmathien and

> *Prince Germain dessus le throsne doré....* (II, 87)[1]

that is 'The prince descended from the old line of the Frankish kings on the gilded throne', and, with the same idea in mind, '*Le blond au nez forche*,' the blond King with the hooked nose. One cannot help feeling that Nostradamus

1. The early eighteenth-century commentator 'D.D.' referred this quatrain to the accession of George I of England.

TWO RESTORATIONS

regarded Louis XVIII with that mixture of affection and contempt which is, after all, the judgement of history.

> *Heureux au regne de France, heureux de vie,*
> *Ignorant sang, mort, fureur & rapine,*
> *Par nom flatteur sera mis en envie:*
> *Roy desrobé, trop de foye en cuisine.* (x, 16)

Happily re-established on the throne of France, happy in his life (in that he did not perish on the scaffold like Louis XVI, nor was he chased from the throne like his brother and successor Charles X, and that, moreover, during his reign France was at peace); he will be given a flattering name implying desire (he was in fact known as 'Le Désiré', his Restoration having been so long hoped for); a King who was more interested in cookery than in affairs of state. The gluttony of Louis was proverbial and resulted in his becoming excessively fat. It is possible that Nostradamus is here punning on the double meaning of *foye*, and we may perhaps remind ourselves without frivolity that the French answer to the question 'Is Life worth living?' is '*Question de foi(e)*' – 'It depends on the liver', or 'It is a matter of faith.'

Meanwhile Napoleon was still languishing in the captivity of St Helena:

> *Cent fois mourra le tyran inhumain;*
> *Mis à son lieu sçavant & debonnaire,*
> *Tout le Senat sera dessous sa main,*
> *Fasché sera par malin temeraire.* (x, 90)

The inhuman tyrant will die a hundred deaths; put in his place is one cultivated and debonair (*sçavant & debonnaire* could hardly be bettered as a description of Louis XVIII); both houses of parliament (*tout le Senat*) constituted by the Charter of 1815 will profess an absolute devotion to his person (will be under his hand); he will be troubled by an audacious and wicked man.

The final sentence is very interesting. The last few years of the good-natured King were clouded by a family tragedy, the assassination of his nephew the Duc de Berry, heir to the throne after Charles X. To Nostradamus the succession to the French throne and the fate of the legitimate heir was always a matter of supreme importance, and this may explain his pre-occupation with an event which, to English readers at least, means very little. Apart from the reference above he gives it the honour of two special quatrains:

> *Chef de Fossan aura gorge couppée*
> *Par le ducteur du limier et levrier:*
> *Le faict patré par ceux du mont Tarpée,*
> *Saturne en Leo 13. de Fevrier.* (III, 96)

Now the Duc de Berry was the son of the Comte d'Artois (the future Charles X) and Marie-Thérèse of Savoy, whose father Victor Amadeus III was King of Sardinia; Fossano is a town in the Kingdom of Sardinia. The Chief of Fossan will have his throat cut by the man in charge of the bloodhounds and the greyhounds. The deed will be committed (Latin, *patratus*) by those of the Tarpeian Rock (i.e. by Republican criminals, since it was the custom of Republican Rome to hurl its criminals from the summit of the Tarpeian Rock), Saturn being in relation to Leo, on February 13th.

Now for the historical facts. As the Duc de Berry was leaving the Opera on the evening of February 13th, 1820, he was attacked and stabbed ('throat cut' is therefore rather figurative than exact) by one Louvel, an employé of the royal stables, who had been instigated to the deed by the Republicans. According to the astrologers Saturn rules Aquarius, the opposite sign to Leo, opposition being a maleficent aspect. This would seem to imply that judicial astrology played some part at least in the predictions of Nostradamus.

In the other relevant quatrain he writes:

> *Lune obscurcie aux profondes tenebres,*
> *Son frere passe de couleur ferrugine:*
> *Le grand, caché long temps sous les tenebres,*
> *Tiendra le fer dans la plaie sanguine.* (1, 84)

This careless stanza, with its repetition of '*tenebres*,' has been interpreted as follows:

While the Comte d'Artois, as an émigré and, as it were, like a moon obscured, escaped the Revolution, his elder brother (Louis XVI) died (*trépassait*) by the guillotine (*couleur ferrugine* means blood-red). The great one (the son of the Comte d'Artois) hidden in exile for so long, will hold the steel in the bloody wound.

The exciting line is the last one. Picture the Duke, a dark top-hatted silhouette, emerging from the brilliant interior of the Opera into the fitful lantern light of the porch. A man pushes his way through the crowd and, lurching forward, plunges a knife into his body. The Comte de Choiseul catches him as he falls and hears him say, 'I am murdered. *I am holding the hilt of the dagger.*'

And someone else heard it too, a bearded figure lurking in the shadow, and the light from the guttering lamp fell for an instant upon the face *of a man who wasn't there*. For he had died more than two hundred and fifty years before.

And if the quatrain does not really refer to the Duc de Berry at all, the reader will probably regret it as much as anybody.

The assassination of the Duke was a terrible blow to the Legitimists. They knew that behind the throne stood the menacing if portly figure of the Duke of Orleans, representative of that branch of the Royal Family of France which welcomed and thrived upon the disasters of the elder line. The Duke of Orleans' father, Philippe Egalité, had even voted for the death of Louis XVI, an act of treachery which had not saved his own head from the guillotine. The House of Orleans represented an alternative line of kings and was only awaiting its opportunity.

Then a miracle happened. Seven months after the death of her husband the Duchesse de Berry was brought to bed of a son.

> *L'arbre qu'estoit par long temps mort seché,*
> *Dans un nuict viendra à reverdir:*
> *Cron. Roy malade, Prince pied estaché,*
> *Criant d'ennemis fera voile bondir.* (III, 91)

The tree, long dry and dead, will grow green again in a

night (September 29th, 1820), the King who is then born will be for a time (Greek χρόνον, for a time) sickly, and will suffer damage to his foot. *Criant d'ennemis* is a phrase which has given some trouble to the commentators. The present author suggests *Craint*, and the reading: Fear of his enemies will cause him to hoist sail (i.e. go into exile).

The Duke of Bordeaux, as he was called before being better known as the Comte de Chambord, fell from his horse at Kirchberg in Austria on July 28th, 1841, after the exile of his family, and limped slightly for the rest of his life. This is one of those minor but characteristic details which Nostradamus invariably fixed upon to distinguish his characters. He calls him, in different places, and in different languages, the Lame Man – in French, *Le Boiteux*, in Provençal, *Rouc*, in Latin Claude (from *claudus*) and in Greek, Ascans (from σκάζων).

In 1820 his exile was still ten years in the future, but the threat of it hung over him from the beginning. On the very night of his birth the Duke of Orleans made his way to the Tuileries, to the very bedside of the Duchesse de Berry, and contested the legitimacy of her son.

> *Un serpent veu proche du lict royal,*
> *Sera par dame nuict chiens n'abayeront:*
> *Lors naistre en France un Prince tant royal,*
> *Du ciel venu tous les Princes verront.* (IV, 93)

A snake will be seen by the Lady (*Dame*, as we have noticed before, always means a Royal Lady in Nostradamus), will be seen by night near the royal bed. The dogs will not bark (because the Duke of Orleans, as a Prince of the Blood, had the right of entry) when there is born in France a Prince so royal that all the Princes [of Europe] will see in him, as it were, a gift from Heaven. The baby prince was indeed accepted as such and called '*Dieudonné*' and '*L'Enfant du miracle*'.

These events have, perhaps, but little interest for the English reader, but they loom very large in the work of the French commentators who, almost without exception, belong to the ultra-legitimist wing of political opinion. Even for the English reader, however, the quatrain is sufficiently curious, and it is perhaps worth while to pursue the career of the Comte de Chambord a little further before reverting to the usurpation of the Duke of Orleans and the main stream of French history. It is certainly difficult to escape from the conviction that Nostradamus knew a great deal about him.

> *Long temps au ciel sera veu gris oyseau,*
> *Aupres de Dole et de Toscane terre,*
> *Tenant au bec un verdoyant rameau,*
> *Mourra tost grand et finera la guerre.* (I, 100)

Long time will there be seen in the sky near 'Dole' and the territory of Tuscany, a grey bird carrying in his beak a flowering branch. His greatness will die [too] soon, and he will end the war.

The reference to the flowering branch links this stanza with the quatrain quoted above (III, 91) and with the one to be quoted below. At his birth the Comte de Chambord was hailed as the dove (the grey bird) returning to the Ark with the branch in its beak. In exile he lived for a considerable time in Venice, which is near Dolo, and at Modena, near Tuscany, where he was kindly received by the reigning Duke Francis IV, and married his daughter Marie Louise in 1846. He died, as the last line indicates, without regaining the throne of France, and before his death received the Comte de Paris, the Pretender of the Orleans branch, also in exile, and thus put an end to the struggle between the rival claimants.

His marriage is glanced at in the following quatrain so similar in style and imagery:

> *Du vray rameau de fleur de lys issu*
> *Mis & logé heritier d'Hetrurie,*
> *Son sang antique de longue main tissu,*
> *Fera Florence florir en l'armoirie.* (V, 39)

Issued from the true branch of the Fleur-de-lys, placed and lodged by the heir of Etruria, his ancient lineage, the product of long years (a web of long weaving) will cause Florence to flower in armorial bearings.

Modena is believed to have been founded by the Etruscans. The House of Modena was of common origin with that of Florence and was so closely allied to it by innumerable intermarriages that they formed (says Le Pelletier) one single family. The arms of Florence display the fleur-de-lys, so that a marriage with the French Royal House would double these emblems and make Florence '*florir en l'armoirie*'.

The Ducal House, however, like that of the Comte de Chambord himself, were destined to flourish in nothing else. It is time to return to the Revolution of 1830 and the accession of Louis-Philippe.

Nostradamus, true to his passion for nicknames, calls Louis-Philippe *Le Macedon*, the Macedonian. Philip of Macedon, father of Alexander the Great, usurped the crown from his nephew, Amyntas III, son of Perdiccas III, Philip's brother. Louis-Philippe usurped the crown from his nephew so that the nickname is therefore doubly appropriate. It is thought that when, with further allusion to classical history, he refers to Sparta in the following quatrain, he does so because Sparta had two kings at once, and so did Paris during the '*Révolution de Juillet*'.

> *Celuy qu'en Sparte Claude ne peut regner,*
> *Il fera tant par voye seductive,*
> *Que de court, long le fera araigner,*
> *Que contre Roy fera sa perspective.* (VI, 84)

He who arranges that in Sparta the Lame Man cannot reign will do so much by way of seduction. In the third line some editions read '*attaigner*' and the line would then mean that Louis-Philippe, whose loyalty was doubtful at the Restoration and even before, had waited a long time to attain his ends, but had long cherished views (*perspective*) and intentions hostile to the King. The following quatrain speaks more clearly, mentions the word Orleans and puns upon it:

> *Par avarice, par force & violence*
> *Viendra vexer les siens chef d'Orleans,*

TWO RESTORATIONS

Près Sainct Memire assaut & resistance
Mort dans sa tente, diront qu'il dort leans. (VIII, 42)

By his avarice and his abuse of power Louis-Philippe will discontent his subjects or his own supporters. There will be assault and resistance near St Memire. Orleans will lie low in his tent, so that it will be said that he is asleep in it – *léans* an old French word meaning 'inside it'. The actual combat took place in and around the Church of St Merri, so that Nostradamus was only half successful in 'getting' the name. The pun on Orleans would be tiresome in a historian. It is stupefying in Nostradamus, seeing that when he wrote the whole idea of 'Orleans' would have been completely incomprehensible. Gaston d'Orleans, the founder of the House, was the brother of Louis XIII.

The 'false sleep' of Louis-Philippe is mentioned once more in the following:

Plus ne sera le Grand en faux sommeil,
L'inquietude viendra prendre repos:
Dresser phalange d'or, azur & vermeil,
Subiuguer Afrique, la ronger iusques os. (V, 69)

The Great One will be no longer in pretended sleep, for inquietude will take its rest. The flag of gold, blue and red will be unfurled and he will subjugate Africa, gnawing it to the bone. Louis-Philippe, unlike the legitimate Bourbons, accepted the revolutionary tricolour. Nostradamus gets one of the colours wrong; he says 'gold' instead of 'white' or, in heraldic language 'or' instead of 'argent', but as the very existence of the flag was more than two hundred years in the future, the old eyes of the Prophet may perhaps be pardoned for being slightly colour-blind. The last line is astonishing enough, for the accession of Louis-Philippe, the acceptance of the red-white-and-blue and the French conquest of Algeria all took place in the same year, 1830.

Just as if to show that he knew all about it, Nostradamus gives us another quatrain, summing up the whole of the reign:

> *Sept ans sera Philipp. fortune prospere:*
> *Rabaissera des Arabes l'effort;*
> *Puis son midi perplex, rebors affaire,*
> *Jeune Ognion abismera son fort.* (IX, 89)

Fortune will be favourable to Louis-Philippe during the first seven years of his reign (from 1830 to 1838); he will overcome the Arabs. The middle of his reign will be troubled by a difficult affair (between 1838 and 1840 he could not make up his mind what action to take with regard to the 'Oriental Question' and he ended by allowing his ally Mohammed Ali to be driven out of Syria, against the feeling of the nation). The young Ognion will undermine his power.

Ognion or rather Ogmion is the Celtic Hercules which appeared both in 1792 and 1848 on the Republican five-franc pieces. If one accepts these interpretations at all one can only be astonished by their detail. It is as if Nostradamus had actually travelled into the future, mixed with the revolutionary crowd and had the pieces of money in his hand. '*Jeune Ognion*' presumably means the *new* Republic (that of 1848) as opposed to the old Republic of 1792.

The last years of the reign of Louis-Philippe (like those of Louis XVIII) were saddened by the death of the heir to the throne.

> *L'aisné Royal sur coursier voligeant,*
> *Picquer viendra si rudement courir,*
> *Gueulle, lipée, pied dans l'estrein pleignant,*
> *Trainé, tiré, horriblement mourir.* (VIII, 38)

The 'Royal Eldest' flying on a courser, will ride furiously; mouth torn, foot caught in the stirrup, or step, dragged, pulled, to die horribly.

It should be said at once that Louis-Philippe's eldest son was not flung from his horse, but he was killed none the less when the horses of his carriage bolted, on July 13th, 1842. He tried to jump to safety, but his foot caught in the step of the vehicle, and he fell backwards, his head hitting the ground. In the sixteenth century, of course, a young Prince would not have ridden in a carriage but on horseback.

TWO RESTORATIONS

Meanwhile Louis-Philippe had attempted to revive his waning popularity by bringing from St Helena the ashes of Napoleon, and enshrining them in the Invalides.

> *Du Triumuir seront trouvez les os,*
> *Cherchant profond tresor aenigmatique,*
> *Ceux d'alentour ne seront en repos.*
> *Ce concaver marbre et plomb metallique.* (v, 7)

The bones of the Triumvir will be found, seeking for an enigmatic treasure; those around will not be peaceful while hollowing the marble and the metal, lead.

At the *Coup d'état de 18 Brumaire*, the five members of the *Directoire* were reduced to three, including Napoleon with the title of First Consul. He was really therefore, in the antique sense, a Triumvir. The enigmatic treasure which Louis-Philippe sought was the secret of the Emperor's abiding popularity, which he hoped to transfer to himself. His action, on the contrary, had the effect of encouraging the Bonapartists who claimed a part in the work of hollowing the tomb. Inside the tomb itself the remains of Napoleon are enclosed in a leaden coffin.

The reign of Louis-Philippe was nearing its close.

> *Après le siege tenu dix-sept ans,*
> *Cinq changeront en tel revolu terme:*
> *Puis sera l'un esleu de mesme temps,*
> *Qui des Romains ne sera trop conforme.* (v, 92)

After the throne has been held for seventeen years (from August 9th, 1830, to February 24th, 1848), five will change in the same period of time. (The five in question were the remaining princes of the House of Orleans, the Comte de Paris, the Duc de Nemours, the Prince de Joinville, the Duc de Montpensier and the Duke d'Aumale.) Then, at the same time, one will be elected (Louis Napoleon) whose policy will not be too closely conformed to that of the Romans.

Le Pelletier, writing in 1866, remarks at this point: 'I do not permit myself here – or elsewhere – to judge the politics of His Majesty the Emperor; I merely state, following

Nostradamus, a palpable fact; the Roman revolutionaries think that the French Government has been too accommodating in its dealings with the Holy See, while the Catholics think, on the contrary, that he has not supported it with all the energy of which he is capable.' The reference, of course, is to the Italian Revolution and the Temporal Power, but these matters must be left until later. It is sufficient to remark here upon the extraordinary exactitude of the quatrain quoted above: A King who reigns for seventeen years (Louis-Philippe was the only King to do so since the publication of the *Centuries*) followed by someone who 'shall be elected' (by the plebiscite which installed Louis-Napoleon).

But we are hurrying on a little too fast. Louis-Napoleon had already made an abortive attempt at insurrection by a landing at Boulogne with a handful of followers. When this failed he was imprisoned by Louis-Philippe's government in the fortress of Ham. On May 6th, 1846, he escaped, and after that his rise was rapid. Nostradamus has an interesting comment on these events:

> *Au deserteur de la grande forteresse,*
> *Après qu'aura son lieu abandonné,*
> *Son adversaire fera si grand proüesse*
> *L'empereur tost mort sera condamné.* (IV, 65)

When he [i.e. Louis-Philippe] shall have abandoned his place to the deserter of the great fortress, his adversary [i.e. Louis-Napoleon] will display such great prowess that the Emperor shall be considered as dead too soon.

The last line is congested but the meaning of the whole is clear. Louis-Philippe, too soon convinced that the Imperial ambitions of the nephew of Napoleon have been scotched, will have to abandon his throne to him who has escaped from Ham.

In another quatrain the Prophet writes:

> *A la main gauche viendra changer le sceptre,*
> *De Roy viendra Empereur pacifique.* (V, 6)

The sceptre will change hands in a somewhat underhand fashion. After the King will come a peaceful Emperor.

'Pacifique' may be ironical, since one of Napoleon III's first statements on coming to power was '*L'Empire, c'est la paix!*' 'Underhand' is scarcely an exaggeration for the methods by which Louis-Napoleon diverted the Revolution of 1848 to his own profit.

We have seen that in Nostradamus 'Tiers' means the Third Estate, or the French people under a revolutionary government when the other two Estates may be said to cease to function. The National Assembly of 1848 was just as much a revolutionary body as its predecessor in 1792, but it was much less violent and much less powerful. Nostradamus seems to have foreseen this.

> *Tiers doigt du pied au premier semblera*
> *A un nouveau monarque de bas haut:*
> *Qui Pyse & Luques tyran occupera,*
> *Du precedent corriger le deffaut.* (IX, 5)

The Third Estate [established in power for a second time] will seem no more than the toe of the foot of its predecessor to the new monarch raised on high from below – in other words, Louis-Napoleon will find it easier to deal with the second Revolution than Napoleon I found it to deal with the first. Le Pelletier explains the third line (in somewhat farfetched fashion) by reminding us that in 1831 Louis-Napoleon had placed himself at the head of a band of Italian revolutionaries and attempted to seize Civita-Castellana. By thus directing the revolutionary movement in Tuscany he may be said, metaphorically, to have occupied Pisa and Lucca. The reader will scarcely find this explanation very convincing. The predecessor whose 'fault' (i.e. failure to attain power) was corrected by the new tyrant was, the same author suggests, Napoleon II, the Duc de Reichstadt.

Louis-Napoleon's first action was to offer himself as a candidate in the presidential election. To the surprise of the world he was elected.

> *Esleu sera Renard ne sonnant mot,*
> *Faisant le saint public, vivant pain d'orge,*

> *Tyranniser apres tant à un cop,*
> *Mettant à pied des plus grands sur la gorge.* (VIII, 41)

The Fox will be elected, the fox who like Brer Rabbit 'ain't sayin' nuffin'' – Napoleon III was later to be known as '*le taciturne*'. In public he will behave like a saint, and live extremely simply. But afterwards, by a *coup d'état*, he will exercise tyrannical power, placing his foot on the throats of the great.

But why, the reader may well ask, should all this be supposed to relate to Napoleon III? Has not this quatrain already been referred to Cromwell? Are we not being led into the dangerous road of arbitrary interpretations in which so many Nostradamian commentators have come to grief? It is difficult to answer in the negative with any confidence. Yet Nostradamus does seem to have known something of these events, for he returns again and again to the Elected One, whom he also calls the 'Nephew' on more than one occasion. Such a name must have been completely incomprehensible until three hundred years after he wrote; but, after all, there is a Nephew in French history, a Nephew *par excellence*, Louis-Napoleon the son of Louis, King of Holland, brother of Napoleon I. What has Nostradamus to say about the Nephew? What he has to say is singularly explicit:

> *Par le decide de deux choses bastards,*
> *Nepveu du sang occupera le regn....* (VIII, 43)

By the fall (Latin, *decidere*, to fall) of two illegitimate things the Nephew of the Blood will occupy the throne. *Le regne*, in Nostradamus, always means the government, the supreme power, as we have seen in previous quatrains. The two illegitimate things are the government of Louis-Philippe and the Second Republic. Nostradamus had a sixteenth-century distrust of limitations on the power of the monarch. To him they meant Huguenot intrigues and great nobles in revolt; and the constitutional monarchy of the Orleanists was therefore as repugnant to him as the Republic itself.

After the *coup d'état* of December 2nd, 1851, and the

plebiscite which, by more than seven million votes, gave him power for ten years, Louis-Napoleon lost little time in proclaiming himself Emperor of the French under the title of Napoleon III. All opposition was easily suppressed:

> *Cité livrée au premier cornet sonné.* (IV, 1)

The city of Paris delivered up to him at the first blast of the trumpet.

One of his first actions was to look about for a wife, but the Royal Families of Europe looked askance at the parvenu, and after several rebuffs he decided to marry Eugénie de Montijo on whom he had already cast eyes but who had informed him, in a famous phrase, that the road to her bedroom lay through a well-lighted church.

> *De terre foible et pauvre parentelle,*
> *Par bout et paix parviendra dans l'empire,*
> *Long temps regner une jeune femelle,*
> *Qu'oncques en regne n'en survint un si pire.* (III, 38)

A young female (the word *femelle* is somewhat contemptuous in French) of small estate and poor parentage will manage peacefully to arrive at the Imperial dignity (Eugénie and her mother played their cards with consummate skill) and will reign for a long time (actually eighteen years) with him who will be more disastrous for France than any that went before him.

Another quatrain, linked to this by the line

> *Onc Roy ne fut si pire en sa Province.* (x, 9)

glances at the birth of the Prince Imperial, son of a '*Castillon*' (that is, a Spaniard) *de fame infame* – raised to notoriety from a position of complete obscurity.

The baptism of the Prince Imperial has a quatrain all to itself, a quatrain so curious that it can scarcely be omitted in spite of its superficial difficulties.

> *Index et poulse parfondera le front,*
> *De Senegaglia le Comte à son fils propre,*
> *La Myrnamée par plusieurs de prin front. . . .* (x, 8)

The Count of Sinigaglia with thumb and index finger will moisten the forehead of his own son; the font (*myrnamée* is a word composed of the Greek words *murô*, to drip, and *nama*, fountain) will be held by many of the highest position.

Now, the Prince Imperial was baptized (the traditional gesture is with thumb and index finger joined) by Cardinal Patrizzi, as proxy for Pius IX whose godson the baby was. And Pius IX had been, before his elevation to the Papacy, Count of Sinigaglia! It is in trifles such as these that Nostradamus seems so often to astonish the reader.

The good relations, however, between Napoleon III and the Vatican did not last long. From the point of view of the latter, a sinister event occurred in 1856 when Cavour arrived in Paris to plead the cause of Italian unity.

> *Ambassadeur de la Toscane langue*
> *Avril et May Alpes et mer passer,*
> *Celuy de veau exposera harangue,*
> *Vie Gauloise ne venant effacer.* (VII, 20)

The ambassador of the Tuscan language passes the Alps and the sea to represent the Court of Piedmont, at the Congress of Paris, during April and May, 1856. He of the Calf will make a harangue in which he will declare that the presence of the Austrians in Italy is incompatible with the influence of France. 'He of the Calf' is a strange phrase, but stranger still is the explanation; for Cavour was the envoy of Turin, then the capital of Victor Emmanuel, later King of Italy, and Turin, Torino means the city of the bull (the Romans called it *Augusta Taurinorum*). Cavour is therefore the offspring of the bull, the calf! The explanation is none the less convincing for being more than a little absurd.

Napoleon had already been involved in the Italian revolutionary movement while still a young man. He had even been enrolled in the secret society of the Carbonari, and he now resolved, secretly at first, to attack the Austrians in Italy as his uncle had done before him and to make what profit he could for his own power. He could hardly do this without coming into conflict with the Papacy, and the commentators of Nostradamus (being nearly all Catholic Ultramontanes) are almost unanimous in believing that the disasters which finally fell upon him were the judgement of God for his oppression of the Pope.

Some of his revolutionary comrades, however, had already come to the conclusion that he was a traitor to their cause and four of them, led by the Count Orsini, resolved to assassinate him by means of bombs as he was leaving the *Opéra*. The attempt was made on January 14th, 1858, but although the portico of the building was damaged and several people killed, the Emperor himself was only slightly wounded. Pieri, the friend of Orsini, was arrested before the explosion occurred:

> *Jusques au fond le grand arq demoluë,*
> *Par chef captif l'ami anticipé.* . . . (v, 9)

The general sense is plain enough, and in the next quatrain the theme is continued:

> *Un chef Celtique dans le conflict blessé,*
> *Auprès de cave voyant siens mort abattre,*
> *De sang et playes et d'ennemis pressé,*
> *Et secours par incogneus de quatre.* (v, 10)

A French monarch (*celtique* in Nostradamus always means French) wounded in the conflict, seeing his subjects struck dead near the theatre (cave from the Latin *cavea*, the theatre) with blood and wounds, hustled by enemies, will be saved from the Four by unknown hands. The Four in question were Orsini, Pieri, Rudio and Gomez. The attempt threw France into a ferment, and although the Emperor's popularity was momentarily enhanced by it, he was severely shaken.

Into this picture moves the strange figure of the abbé Torné, or, as he liked to call himself in honour of Nostradamus' first disciple, Torné-Chavigny. We have already remarked upon the fascination which prophecies, and particularly the prophecies of Nostradamus, have exercised upon the French provincial clergy. What indeed more natural than that a lonely man, with a mind open to the miraculous and a passionate hope that the Monarchy would be restored in France, should devote his leisure to the interpretation of the Prophet of Salon? The abbé Torné was such a man.

When we first hear of him he is curé of La Clotte, a little village of Charente-Inférieure, in the diocese of Bordeaux. Elisée du Vignois, who speaks in notes to his own edition of Nostradamus as if he had known Torné personally, tells us that it was the attempt of Orsini to assassinate Napoleon III which first put the worthy curé on the right track of interpretation. But he must have studied the *Centuries* with great care before this, for already in 1858 (the year of Orsini's plot) his fame had spread and his activities had come to the notice of the authorities.

This is perhaps not so surprising as it might seem when we learn that Torné had already reached the conclusion that the reign of Napoleon III would shortly come to an end and that he would be succeeded by a legitimate King, the Henry V who was to deliver the country from all her troubles, and who has never ceased to excite the imagination of Catholic France. Torné made no secret of what he considered to be his discovery, and the news of it came to the ears of his ecclesiastical superior, Cardinal Donnet, Archbishop of Bordeaux. It is possible that the Imperial authorities had asked him to intervene, for Torné states quite plainly in his *Influence de Nostradamus dans le Gouvernement de la France* that 'in 1858 ... the Cardinal of Bordeaux, my metropolitan, asked me, on behalf of the Emperor, for the part of my manuscripts dealing with the life of Napoleon III in which I affirmed that Henry V would recover his throne.'

For the moment the matter went no further, but two years later a Bordeaux publisher brought out the first volume of the abbé's *L'Histoire prédite et jugée*, and the Imperial authorities, always touchy in matters of suspected treason or disloyalty to the régime, took immediate action. The volume was formally seized by M. Bleynie,[1] Procureur of Libourne

Nostradamus, who might well be supposed to take an

- 1. Torné himself spells the name Bleygnie.

interest in the fate of the most enthusiastic of his interpreters, seems to have foreseen all this three hundred years before it happened:

> *Du grand Prophete les lettres seront prinses,*
> *Entre les mains du tyran deviendront,*
> *Frauder son Roy seront ses entreprinses,*
> *Mais ses rapines bien tost le troubleront.* (II, 36)

The writings of the great Prophet will be confiscated and will come into the hands of the tyrant; to usurp the place of his king will be the object of his enterprises, but soon his spoliations will trouble him. Nostradamus returns to the same subject in another quatrain:

> *Dans la maison du traducteur de Bours,*
> *Seront les lettres trouvées sur la table,*
> *Borgne, roux, blanc, chenu, tiendra de court*
> *Qui changera au nouveau connestable.* (IX, 1)

The writings (Nostradamus uses the word *lettres* in the sixteenth-century sense) will be found upon the table in the house of the 'Translator of Bours'. Now *bours* or *bour* is an old word meaning a hole or a hollow, and *clot* has the same meaning. We should therefore, according to this interpretation, read 'The Translator (or the Interpreter) of La Clotte'. The Translator in question is blind in one eye, red-faced, and his few remaining hairs are white (*chenu* means bald). Elisée du Vignois seems to think that this description fits the abbé Torné, although he suggests that one-eyed may be intended in a metaphorical sense. Compared with the clear-sighted Nostradamus his interpreter was certainly 'one-eyed'. The 'New Constable' is supposed to be Marshal MacMahon, who after the fall of the Empire did occupy a place very similar to that of the *Connétables* of the sixteenth century, and the rest of the quatrain is said to indicate that in the time of MacMahon the abbé Torné would cut short his duties as a parish priest in order to devote himself entirely to the interpretation of Nostradamus.

Some commentators have seen a further reference to M.

Bleynie in the famous Latin quatrain in which Nostradamus warns off the ignorant and the barbarians:

> *Omnesque Astrologi, Blenni, Barbari procul sunto.* (VI, 100)

Blenni (from *blennus*, a fool). But in this perhaps it would be rash to follow them.

M. Bleynie, at any rate, having read the confiscated volume, thought it of sufficient importance to hand it over to M. de Vaugy, *sous-préfet* of Bayonne, who in turn brought it to the notice of the Emperor. Napoleon was visibly impressed. '*Ça épouvante et énerve l'imagination*', was his comment, but, probably thinking it beneath his dignity to take any action, he ordered M. Bleynie to restore the book to its author and to allow him in future full liberty of speaking, writing and publishing.

Between 1860 and 1862 the abbé Torné brought out the rest of his great work, and being something of an artist he illustrated his thesis by concocting a curious allegorical design, composed of his own picture, that of Nostradamus,[1] and the portraits of the Kings of France. In this he showed quite clearly the Comte de Chambord succeeding Napoleon III.

This was a direct challenge to the authorities, but no action was taken against the little Royalist priest. They may have hoped that his own actions would discredit him, except among a public as credulous as himself, for in the previous year (1861), not content with interpreting the *Centuries*, he had brought out a book entitled *L'Apocalypse interpretée par Nostradamus*, in which the Apostle of Patmos is made to speak in no uncertain terms concerning the approaching restoration of the Monarchy in France. Even the taciturn usurper must have smiled a little at this if it was ever brought to his notice. Torné had also convinced himself that the great series of paintings by Rubens in the Louvre concerning the life of Marie de Medici was full of occult allusions to the work of the Prophet of Salon. It was

---

1. Based on the engraved portrait in the edition of the *Centuries* brought out in 1697 by Jean Viret.

quite obvious that Nostradamus was driving the little man mad.

Napoleon, having made his preparations, suddenly announced to the stupefaction of Europe that his relations with Austria were not as happy as he could have wished. In the spring of 1859 a French army crossed the Alps.

> *Delà les Alpes grande armée passera,*
> *Un peu devant naistra monstre vapin:*
> *Prodigieux et subit tournera*
> *Le grand Toscan à son lieu plus propin.* (v, 20)

Beyond the Alps a great army will pass; a little before will be born an evil beast. In a strange and sudden manner it will come about that the Great Tuscan will return to his more native land.

The evil beast is the Italian Revolution. The two last are the most interesting lines, for one of the first results of the campaign of 1859 was to drive from Florence Leopold II, Grand Duke of Tuscany. As he was a Habsburg and retired to Austria, he is very aptly described as returning to his more native land (*propin* is from the Latin *propinquus*, related, parent, of the same nature).

As if to make it quite clear, Nostradamus added, in another quatrain:

> *Pleure Milan, pleure Luques, Florence,*
> *Que ton grand Duc sur le char montera,*
> *Changer le siege près Venise s'advance,*
> *Lorsque Colonne à Rome changera.* (x, 64)

Weep Milan, weep Lucca and Florence that your Grand Duke will mount the car [to depart]. The rest of the quatrain is difficult to translate literally, but the facts are these: Austria abandoned the province of Venetia to Napoleon III who turned it over to Victor Emmanuel. Florence became the latter's new capital until the time when the seat of government was transferred to Rome, the temporal power of the Pope having been brought to an end.

A great many quatrains in the *Centuries* are interpreted as referring to the Risorgimento and the Unification of Italy, but these events are little known to English readers and we will content ourselves with two further examples of the prevision of the Prophet.

> *Mars eslevé en son plus haut befroy*
> *Fera retraire les Allobrox de France,*
> *La gent Lombarde fera si grand effroy,*
> *A ceux de l'Aigle comprins sous la Balance.* (v, 42)

Mars (Napoleon III is called by this name in several quatrains) elevated to his highest point of power will accomplish the return of French Savoy (Allobrox, Allobroges, people of Savoy – Savoy, which had belonged to France under Napoleon I, was ceded once more on March 22nd, 1860). The people of Lombardy will cause great terror to those of the Eagle (i.e. the Austrians) who are in Italy. All astrologers are agreed that Italy has for its ruling sign the Balance.

> *Par Mars contraire sera le monarchie*
> *Du grand pescheur en trouble ruyneux,*
> *Jeune noir rouge prendra la hierarchie....* (vi, 25)

By the contrariety of Napoleon III in allying himself with Victor Emmanuel the monarchy of the Great Fisherman (i.e. the Papacy) will be in ruinous trouble. A young red King (*noir* for *roi* as so often in Nostradamus) will take over the government. Victor Emmanuel is red because he represents the Italian Revolution.

Meanwhile even the Pope had begun to be impressed by Nostradamus as interpreted by the Abbé Torné and took the latter sufficiently seriously to order from a bookseller at Nantes four copies of his complete works. Later the Interpreter visited Rome and had long interviews with Cardinal Antonelli and other eminent ecclesiastics. Even the Imperial officials, disturbed perhaps by the hectic brilliance of those last years of the sixties when it seemed to many that France was moving towards some kind of catastrophe, began to think there might be something in what the little priest said.

TWO RESTORATIONS

In 1867 two of them, M. de Vaugy (whom we have already met as *sous-préfet* of Bayonne and who had now become *préfet*) and his brother, the Director-General of Telegraphs, took it upon themselves to question Torné, not as government functionaries but as friends seeking enlightenment. They were particularly interested in a quatrain which might seem to concern their own district:

> *Entre Bayonne et saint Jean de Lux,*
> *Sera posé de Mars le promontoire,*
> *Aux Hanix d'Aquilon Nanar hostera lux,*
> *Puis suffoqué au lit sans adjutoire.* (VIII, 85)

We do not know whether the Abbé was able, in 1867, to interpret this as clearly as was afterwards done. But he knew who Mars was and the last line is plain enough. Later commentators have explained it as follows:

Between Bayonne and St Jean-de-Luz is the promontory of Biarritz where Napoleon III, like another Mars, loved to retire into the arms of Venus when the north wind ceased to blow (i.e. in the summer; *hanix* from the Greek *aniscus*, without force). The rest of the line is obscure, but Elisée du Vignois suggests: 'debauchery will blind him to the weakness of his condition and will ultimately lead to his death.' Actually he died after an operation for the stone, but his physical exhaustion may have been contributed to by his debaucheries so that when he fell into a syncope it was impossible to rouse him from it.

For the moment these premonitions were forgotten. Paris had never been gayer than it seemed in the summer of 1867. It was the year of the *Exposition Universelle*. All the charm, all the beauty of which France was capable was spread out for the gaze of the visitor. People came from all over the world; Hortense Schneider had four Kings in her dressing-room at once. Bismarck came and smiled grimly at the Parisians from the depths of his box at the *Opéra*. Nostradamus, too, and marvelled that the dark little Paris he had known three hundred years before had been transformed into such a city of light and splendour:

> *Où tout bon est, tout bien Soleil et Lune,*
> *Est abondant sa ruine s'approche.*
> *Du ciel s'avance vaner ta fortune,*
> *En mesme estat que la septiesme roche.* (v, 32)

Where everything seems good and all is well, gold and silver in abundance – her ruin approaches. Heaven sends one (it is an echo of Jeremiah li, verse 2 [1]) to fan thy fortune and to reduce thee to the same state of desolation as the seventh rock mentioned in the Apocalypse.

War between France and Prussia was declared on July 19th, 1870. On September 2nd, Napoleon capitulated at Sedan. We have already quoted the first two lines of the quatrain (VIII, 43) figuring his advent to power. We will now consider all four lines, for they are among the most remarkable in the works of Nostradamus.

> *Par le decide de deux choses bastards,*
> *Nepveu du sang occupera le regne:*
> *Dedans Lectoyre seront les coups de dards,*
> *Nepveu par peur pliera l'enseigne.* (VIII, 43)

The interpretation of the first two lines seemed obvious to a commentator like Anatole Le Pelletier, writing under the Second Empire (his edition of Nostradamus was published in 1867) but the remaining two lines – not unnaturally – puzzled him completely. He suggests that 'Lectoyre' may be Lectoure, a town in the *département* of Gers, but thinks it probable that the word had some other meaning only to be revealed after the event. He was plainly frightened of accepting the obvious intention of the last line, perhaps – since he was no Bonapartist – for fear of proceedings against him. He hedges, declaring that inversions of subject and object are familiar in all oracles, and permit us to transpose the active to the passive and vice-versa. Croesus, King of Lydia, was told by the oracle of Delphi that, in his proposed campaign, he would destroy a great empire. The oracle did not add that the empire in question would be his own. We

[1]. And will send unto Babylon fanners, that shall fan her, and shall empty her land.

can therefore believe, says Le Pelletier, that the Imperial Nephew will cause the ensign of his enemies to be furled, or hauled down, but adds, as in honesty bound, that the contrary might well be the case. The latter in fact was his obvious opinion, and his commentary is therefore of particular interest to those who have the advantage over him of knowing about the Battle of Sedan.

But what of the third line? Where or what is Lectoyre? Elisée du Vignois, writing in 1910, makes the ingenious, if not quite convincing, suggestion that it is a made-up word derived from the Latin *lecto*, a bed, and thinks that the '*coups de dards*' in question are the pains caused by the malady of the stone, from which Napoleon III was suffering on the field of battle, and which was the cause of his death shortly afterwards. Charles Nicoullaud, whose study of Nostradamus appeared in 1914, has the brilliant notion of treating the whole phrase '*dedans Lectoyre*' as an anagram and transforming it into '*Sedan le decroyt*', that is 'Sedan deposes him'. But this is altogether too clever. That Nostradamus used anagrams to conceal proper names is admitted by every one who has studied the subject, but there is obviously no limit to what you can do in this way with phrases and sentences. Has not some ingenious man discovered that the letters of the words *Révolution Française* can be rearranged to read

Un véto corse la finira!

Charles A. Ward made the interesting discovery that Blaew's map, printed in Amsterdam in 1620, shows the meadowland on the opposite side of the Meuse from Sedan inscribed with the names Grand Torcy and Petit Torcy. Now Lectoyre is the precise anagram, letter for letter, of Le Torcey. Even if this be nothing but a coincidence it is certainly a very happy one.

Certainly Nostradamus seems to have known more or less where the battle would take place, for in another quatrain he says:

> *Le grand Empire sera tost désolé,*
> *Et translaté près d'arduenne silve,*

> *Les deux bastards près l'aisné decollé,*
> *Et regnera Ænobard, nez de Milve.* (v, 45)

The great Empire will be soon desolated and translated (in the Shakespearean sense: 'Oh Bottom, how art thou translated!') near the Forest of the Ardennes. The Two Bastards (this alone is enough to link it to the quatrain quoted above) will be, like the Elder, deprived of their rule and there shall reign Aenobard, with the aquiline nose. Sedan is certainly the chief town of the arrondissement of the Ardennes. It has now witnessed two disastrous French defeats, in 1870 and in 1940. The whole district is covered with forest. But who is Aenobard?

To the Abbé Torné it seemed quite obvious that Aenobard was the Comte de Chambord, whose succession to the throne he had been prophesying for years. And now begins the strangest part of the strange story of the little priest. For if he was convinced, so were a great many other Frenchmen, and, fantastic as it may seem, this conviction of inevitability in their minds and his, very nearly brought the event about.

The war had yet to be fought to its disastrous conclusion, Paris had still to be besieged, and that Palace of the Tuileries which exercised Nostradamus's imagination so much burned by the Commune, Alsace and Lorraine surrendered to the Germans:

> *Des lieux plus bas du pays de Lorraine*
> *Seront les basses Allemaignes unis,*
> *Par ceux du siege Picards, Normans, du Maine,*
> *Et aux cantons se seront reunis.* (x, 51)

Lower Lorraine and the regions to the south (i.e. Alsace) will be united to lower Germany, with the consent of those besieged, Picards, Normans and men of Maine (i.e. the parts of France in German occupation), united, against the usual custom, in the chief towns of their cantons.

This is one of the quatrains which make the reader rub his eyes and wonder if it could really have been included in a book published in the sixteenth century. There is no doubt about it. It was.

And again:

> *Le Celtiq fleuve changera de rivage....*
> *Tout transmuë hormis le vieil langage....* (VI, 4)

The French stream will change its banks (i.e. the Rhine will no longer touch French territory); nothing will remain the same except the old language, which was, of course, German.

Soon after the suppression of the Commune, the Comte de Chambord returned to France and took up his residence in his chateau of Chambord. Then began endless negotiations. History seemed to be repeating itself with singular exactitude. Once more an Emperor had abdicated, once more three parties were contending for the throne: the Legitimists, the Orleanists, and the Bonapartists, who hoped to put forward the young Prince Imperial. The Legitimists were the most hopeful. Why should not Sedan, like Waterloo, be followed by a Restoration of the old line? For a time nothing seemed more likely; but the Comte de Chambord thought it better to retire to Belgium until the conflict had subsided. Years passed. Thiers fell in 1873, to be followed by Marshal MacMahon as President of the Republic. The Royalist hopes revived once more.

It all ended in a quarrel over a flag. The Comte de Chambord, true to the Bourbon tradition of learning nothing and forgetting nothing, insisted that his flag should be the white banner of the Ancien Régime with its three golden lilies. Tricolours appeared in answer all over Paris and MacMahon declared that he could not answer for public order if the white flag was flown in the capital. So the Restoration didn't happen. The Third Republic, conceived as a provisional government, staggered on for seventy years until it was fatally stricken on the field of a second Sedan, and the *Chef d'Etat* was no longer Marshal MacMahon but Marshal Pétain.

Some discredit fell upon the Abbé Torné, and, quite unjustly, upon Nostradamus too. For the Prophet, absurd as it may sound, seems to have foreseen the errors of his interpreter. 'Denys', he says, 'wets his pen' (Torné had now become curé of St Denis-du-Pin) 'and will not be silent'.

> *N'a sçeu secret, et à quoi tu t'amuses?*
> (Prés. XI, September)

He did not know the secret, and what are you laughing at?

But the little priest refused to admit himself beaten, and he now found that he was a person of some political consequence, important enough to be denounced in the speeches of Gambetta and encouraged of course by those Royalists who had not yet lost hope. He began to bring out a yearly almanack *Ce qui sera!* and in 1874 he abandoned his cure to devote himself entirely to this prophetic work. He interviewed Victor Hugo, he tackled Renan; he even in 1876 visited the Comte de Chambord at Goritz, and cherished the Pretender's last words as they parted: '*Au revoir en France*'. He claims to have swayed votes in the Senate, and perhaps he did. Certainly his vogue was tremendous.[1]

The following year was perhaps the apogee of the Abbé's influence. *Ce qui sera* (1878) was printed in large numbers. Copies were sent to Rome, to Frohsdorf (where the Comte de Chambord had his residence) and to the Elysée, and five hundred were distributed gratis 'to the cardinals, archbishops, and bishops of France, to the superiors of the great seminaries, to the curés of Paris, to members of the *Académie Française*, to the editors of leading newspapers both in the capital and in the provinces.' Some of the big shops bought thousands of copies which they distributed free to their clients.

He never seems to have made any money by his writings. Elisée du Vignois, who succeeded him as curé of St Denis-du-Pin and carried on his work of interpretation, declares, that he occupied a modest room in the Rue St Benoit in Paris, and afterwards a '*petit-rez-de-chaussée*' in the bookshop of Adrien Leclerc. Perhaps it was here that he inserted in his advertisements the touching plea: '*Ecrive à l'auteur, rue*

[1] '*L'abbé Torné-Chavigny a la vogue, on se l'arrache dans les salons politiques.*' *Moniteur Universel*, February 24th, 1876.

Cassette, 17, *Paris*'. He died in hospital on July 5th, 1880, without having seen his dream come true. The Comte de Chambord, the Grand Chyren of a mistaken interpretation, the Henri V that was not to be, followed him to the grave three years later, 'to celebrate' (in the words of Elisée du Vignois) 'before the Throne of the Lamb, the great festival of his ancestor St Louis, with all the Court of Heaven.'

CHAPTER NINE

To the End of the World

THE period of the Third Republic is not one which arouses much enthusiasm in the hearts of Frenchmen or very much interest in the minds of English readers. The only commentator of Nostradamus who has dealt with it in any detail is the indefatigable Elisée du Vignois, and one has the uncomfortable feeling when reading his interpretations that the material is being spread thinner and thinner and conviction attenuated to the point of vanishing altogether. The whole effort seems disproportionate, and we are unable to believe that the Prophet should devote nearly as many quatrains to the years between 1870 and 1910 (the date of du Vignois' book) as to the whole epic of the French Revolution and Napoleon. It is hard to think that the death of the Prince Imperial in Zululand is 'worth' eleven quatrains or even that eight or nine should be devoted to *l'Affaire Dreyfus*. Nor can we think that the visit of the Russian fleet to Toulon in 1893 deserves two, or that it was worth the Prophet's effort in peering into the future only to describe the *entrée* of M. Casimir-Périer into the Elysée or the *Accueil Glacial* of President Loubet, or a question asked by Jaurès in the Chamber of Deputies. We smile incredulously when we are told that the *Présages* XCII to CXL refer in order, month by month, to the events of the years 1891 to 1894. It is obvious that the commentator's preoccupation with contemporary politics has falsified his judgement.

None the less some of the quatrains in question are worth notice. One of the most convincing (or least unconvincing) of those supposed to refer to the Prince Imperial is the following:

> *L'enfant Royal contemnera la mere,*
> *Oeil, pieds blessez, rude, inobeissant,*

Nouvelle à dame estrange et bien amere,
Seront tuez des siens plus de cinq cens. (VII, 11)

The Royal Child, hard and disobedient, will refuse to listen to the entreaties of his mother. Very bitter news to the Lady who is a foreigner in the land where she now lives. There will be slain of his men more than five hundred. The Agence Havas put the number at 580, the commander-in-chief in his official despatch at 530.

Nostradamus does seem to have foreseen the accession and influence of Pope Leo XIII.

Apparoistra vers le Septentrion
Non loin de Cancer l'estoille chevelue. . . .
Mourra de Rome grand, la nuict disparue. (VI, 6)

The comet (the long-haired star – a beautiful phrase) will appear in the north. The Great One of Rome will die. Darkness will be dispelled (on account of the new 'light in heaven').

The Great One of Rome is supposed to be Pius IX, who died in February 1878. Cardinal Pecci, Archbishop of Perugia (which is to the north of Rome) was elected in his stead. Now, the curious thing is that in the prophecy of Malachy this Pope is given the motto *Lumen in coelo*, a light in heaven, and not only did he deserve this title by the brilliance of his intellect but his family arms show a comet. We have already noted the curious parallelism between certain phrases of Nostradamus and the Latin mottoes of Malachy, as, for example, *Aquila rapax* as applied to the Pope persecuted by Napoleon. We will return to this correspondence later in the chapter. What more, meanwhile, about the 'long-haired star'?

Durant l'estoille chevelue apparente,
Les trois grands princes seront faits ennemis,
Frappez du Ciel paix terre tremulente. . . . (II, 43)

During the appearance of the comet, the three great princes will be made enemies (of France); the world's trembling peace smitten by Heaven. This is referred to the

Triple Alliance of 1881 between Germany, Austria and the new Kingdom of Italy. Throughout its existence it was obviously directed against France, called into existence, as a counterpoise, the Triple Entente of France, Russia and Great Britain, and ultimately led to the World War of 1914–8.

As the nineteenth century drew to its close the rationalist and the materialist seemed to have established a permanent empire over thought. That Idea of Progress which Dr Inge has subjected to so destructive an analysis was part of the furniture of men's minds. But soon the world grew dark again, and portents and omens began to multiply.

It is in times when the air is heavy with the sense of impending disaster that men find their rationalism shaken and turn once more to the old superstitions which perhaps after all are not quite so completely superstitious as 'advanced' people used so think. To the facile optimism of the previous age succeeded a growing anxiety. It was plain, even to the least observant, that some catastrophe was about to happen, and men interested themselves as they have always done in similar circumstances in diviners and fortune-tellers of all kinds. It became almost a matter of course for newspapers with large circulations to devote some of their space every day to the predictions of astrologers. Many of them retained one on their staff among the dramatic, literary, and sporting critics. Within recent years the natural desire to peer into the future had become almost pathological in its intensity.

One of the results of this attitude was an increased interest in Nostradamus, and nowhere was this interest more marked than in France. The discredit into which he had unjustly fallen after 1870 was forgotten and a host of new commentators arose, unwarned by the fate of the Abbé Torné, and ready not only to interpret the past but to foretell the future by the aid of the *Centuries*. The fatuity of most of these works is only equalled by their self-assurance. In some of them England takes no part in the coming struggle at all, in others she betrays France. The loss of the Empire and the fall of the Monarchy is confidently predicted. France herself will be invaded, but nearly all agree that this time it will be by way of Switzerland.

This seems puzzling until we learn that Mélanie Calvat, the famous Shepherdess of La Salette, a mid nineteenth century ecstatic whose credit is still high among provincial French Catholics, prophesied as much in set terms. One can only wonder how much influence this belief had on the disastrous dispositions of the French General Staff in 1940.

It is impossible to dismiss such notions. Hitler is said to have taken the advice of his private astrologer before all his major decisions, and it is thought that he refrained from attacking England immediately after Dunkirk largely because this man informed him that the aspects were unfavourable. Still refusing to prophesy smooth things the astrologer was then dismissed. From the Court of Catherine de' Medici to the entourage of the Führer there was not so great a distance after all.

Warned by the examples of others one may well hesitate to venture into a bog where so many have been engulfed. Yet a study like the present one would obviously be incomplete unless some attempt were made to relate the quatrains of Nostradamus to contemporary events and even to those of the immediate future. It is idle to pretend that such identifications are very satisfactory. We search in vain for the unequivocal quatrain, such a gleam of light as illumined the execution of Charles I or the Flight to Varennes. It does not seem unreasonable to suppose, even granting Nostradamus' powers of seeing into the future, that, once the great crisis of the French Revolution was passed (for this, as we have seen, occupied the chief place in his thoughts) such powers should progressively diminish. Some of the quatrains which might seem to refer to the recent conflict and the events immediately preceding it are vague in the extreme. Even their literal translation is very difficult, and no one can pretend that there is any certainty in their interpretation.

The following, however, might very well stand for the monetary inflation which was so marked a feature of European finance during the nineteen-twenties:

> *Les similacres d'or et d'argent enflez,*
> *Qu'après le rapt lac au feu furent jettez,*
> *Au descouvert estaincts tous et troublez,*
> *Au marbre escripts, prescripts intergetez.* (VIII, 28)

There will be such an inflation of paper money (the counterfeits of gold and silver) that when the robbery is finished (when the milk has been skimmed) they will all be thrown into the fire. The exact sense of the last two lines is obscure; Dr Fontbrune [1] translates: exhausted and dissipated by the debt, all scrips and bonds will be wiped out.

The same ingenious author believed that Nostradamus not only foresaw the abdication of Edward VIII but thought the occasion of such importance that he devoted to it no less than three quatrains. None of the learned doctor's interpretations, however, carries much conviction, and one of them touches the ludicrous, when he suggests that 'Lonole' (which most commentators refer to Oliver Cromwell) is 'from the English Lonely (*loun 'lé*), he who seeks solitude'.

English idealists will perhaps be astonished that a Frenchman (of the Catholic Right, *bien entendu*) could think that the following was a forecast of the League of Nations:

> *Du lac Leman les sermons fascheront,*
> *Des jours seront reduits par des sepmaines,*
> *Puis moys, puis an, puis tous failliront,*
> *Les Magistras danneront leur loix vaines.* (I, 47)

It goes without saying that he provides no satisfactory explanation of the two middle lines.[2]

The seizure of power by General Franco and the civil war in Spain are thought by some to be reflected in the following:

---

1. Dr E. Fontbrune, *Les Prophéties de Maistre Michel Nostradamus*, 2nd Ed. Sarlat, 1939.
2. One of my correspondents, Mr James A. A. Porteous, rather happily suggests: 'Days pass into weeks, months, years; then the whole League system collapses.'

> *L'un des grands fuira aux Espagnes,*
> *Qu'en longue playe après viendra saigner,*
> *Passant copies par les hautes montaignes,*
> *Devastant tout, et puis en paix regner.* (III, 54)

One of the great ones will fly to Spain, which will afterwards bleed with a long wound, armies will pass by the high mountains, causing great destruction; then the great one will reign in peace.

An even more striking quatrain is the following:

> *De castel Franco sortira l'assemblée,*
> *L'ambassadeur non plaisant sera scisme;*
> *Ceux de Ribière seront en la meslée,*
> *Et au grand goulfre desnieront l'entrée.* (IX, 16)

Franco will drive the Parliament from Castile; this will not please the ambassador, who will break away. The supporters of Ribière (Primo de Rivera, who became Dictator of Spain in 1923) will be in the fight, and will prevent entry into the Great Gulf. Perhaps the Great Gulf is the abyss of Communism, from which Spain was saved, according to one point of view, by Franco's seizure of power. In any case, it is sufficiently remarkable to find the names Franco and 'Ribière' in the same quatrain.[1]

Frenchmen themselves admit with cynicism or indignation that the fall of France was due as much to the corruption within as to the foe without. And this time no Joan of Arc arose to deliver the country from its enemies:

> *La splendeur claire à pucelle joyeuse*
> *Ne luyra plus, long temps sera sans sel,*
> *Avec marchans, ruffiens, loups odieuse,*
> *Tout pesle mesle montre universel.* (X, 98)

The clear splendour which was revealed to the joyful virgin will shine no longer; the land will be long without wisdom (salt always stands for wisdom in Nostradamus); with merchants, ruffians, odious wolves, the whole scene will be one of universal confusion.

1. I am grateful to my correspondent, Mr W. G. Campbell, for pointing this out.

Hitler will do his best to undermine France before the battle begins:

> *L'oyseau de proye volant à la fenestre,*
> *Avant conflict faict aux François pareure:*
> *L'un bon prendra, l'un ambigue sinistre,*
> *La partie foible tiendra par bon augure.* (I, 34)

The bird of prey flying at the window will reveal itself to the French before the conflict is joined; one will accept it as good, another as sinister and treacherous; the small band (of actual traitors) will welcome it as a good omen. Although a quatrain like this is of no value or proof of the Prophet's powers, it awakens, none the less, a certain echo in the imagination.

France put all her trust in the Maginot Line but this did not avail to save her cities from destruction:

> *Pres du grand fleuve grand fosse terre egeste....*
> *La cité prinse, feu, sang cris conflict mettre....* (IV, 80)

Near the great stream (along the length of the Rhine), the excavated earth, a great trench; the city taken with fire, blood, cries and conflict.

Hitler's policy of 'protecting' nations which had nothing to fear from anyone but himself is happily described by Nostradamus in lines of epigrammatic terseness:

> *Un capitaine de la Grand Germanie*
> *Se viendra rendre par similé secours....* (IX, 90)

A leader of the Greater Reich will come to render help which is no help but only its counterfeit or, will cause to yield by offering 'protection'.

Thus will Germany enlarge her borders at her neighbours' expense:

> *Translatera en la grand Germanie,*
> *Brabant et Flandres, Gand, Bruges et Bolongne....* (V, 94)

He (Hitler) will include in the Greater Reich Brabant and Flanders, Ghent, Bruges, and even Boulogne.

> *Quand ceux d'Hainault, de Gand & de Bruxelles,*
> *Verront à Langres le siege devant mis:*
> *Derrier leur flancs seront guerres cruelles....* (II, 50)

When they of Hainault, Ghent, and Brussels shall see the siege set before Langres, behind their flanks will be cruel wars.

Harassed by the multitude of refugees the retreating armies will be mercilessly bombed, and driven back on Paris:

> *Les fugitifs, feu du ciel sus les picques,*
> *Conflict prochain des corbeaux, s'esbatans*
> *De terre on crie, ayde, secours celiques,*
> *Quand pres des murs seront les combatans.* (III, 7)

The fugitives, fire from heaven falling on their spears (the next conflict will be only one of crows over their dead bodies) will cry from earth to heaven for aid and succour, when the combatants will draw near the walls.

France is divided into two parts, and between these strife becomes so bitter that Paris (which Nostradamus so often compared with Mesopotamia) will cease to represent France:

> *Camp des deux parts conflict sera si aigre*
> *Mesopotamie defaillira en France.* (III, 99)

But these will-o'-the-wisp clues, lost and found again, become in the end more tiresome than impressive. Is there no definite name which might serve to relate the prophecies to the Second World War? The best we can offer are the so-called Hister quatrains. Like a telepathist or clairvoyant Nostradamus occasionally 'received' actual names, sometimes correctly, sometimes disguised, sometimes distorted. It is thought that Hister is the nearest he came to Hitler.[1] Le Pelletier, who of course knew nothing of Hitler, suggests two derivations for Hister, one from the Latin Ister, the Danube,

---

[1]. Mr Vincent Pautin suggests that the word 'Hister' written with the long S, as Nostradamus would have written it, would come even nearer to 'Hitler'.

and the other from the Etruscan *hister*, a comedian, an actor. May one suggest, without raising too broad a smile, that the Mountebank from the Danube was no bad name for Hitler? The first of the Hister quatrains runs as follows:

> *Bestes farouches de faim fleuves tranner;*
> *Plus part du champ encore Hister sera,*
> *En cage de fer le grand fera treisner,*
> *Quand rien enfant de Germain observera.* (II, 24)

Beasts mad with hunger will make the streams tremble (*iraner*, Provençal, to tremble); Hister will be in control of an ever growing territory; the great one will be dragged in a cage of iron, when the offspring of Germans observes no law of God or man.

The Battle of France resolved itself very largely into a battle of rivers which the German troops crossed tumultuously like beasts of prey maddened with hunger. If the 'great one' is identified with Pétain and the general sense admitted, the quatrain is not unremarkable.

The second follows a quatrain dealing in general terms with wars, incursions and mighty cities laid in ashes. It reads:

> *En lieu bien proche non esloigné de Venus.*
> *Les deux plus grands de l'Asie & d'Aphrique,*
> *Du Ryn & Hister qu'on dira sont venus,*
> *Cris pleurs à Malte & costé Ligustique.* (IV, 68)

In a place not far removed from Venus (the present author is unable to offer any explanation of this line [1]) the Two Greatest Ones of Asia and Africa will be said to come from the Rhine and Hitler; cries and tears at Malta and on the coast of Liguria.

If Mussolini might be called the greatest one in Africa and Japan the greatest one in Asia, then the second line refers to the Tripartite Pact. Both, says the third line, will make

[1] Mr W. Dawson Sadler, in a letter to the present author, makes the interesting suggestion that Venus should read Venice, the 'place near' being the Brenner Pass where the vital meeting of Hitler and Mussolini was held.

themselves Hitler's accomplice, and the fourth may be taken to refer to the bombing of Malta and the bombardment of Genoa.

Hitler's relations with Mussolini may be thought to be glanced at in the following:

> *La Liberté ne sera recouvrée,*
> *L'occupera noir, fier, vilain, inique,*
> *Quand la matière du pont sera ouvrée,*
> *D'Hister, Venise faschée la republique.* (v, 29)

Hitler first met Mussolini at Venice and although he then seemed much less important than the Italian dictator, the loss of Italian liberty may be dated from that day ('Liberty will not be recovered'). The control will be in the hands of a proud, wicked ruler of low origin, when *the Question of the Bridge shall be opened*. In Nostradamus the Pope as Pontifex Maximus is several times called '*le pont*', and the question of the Bridge is therefore the Concordat concluded between Mussolini and the Papacy in 1928. The Republic which is not pleased is presumably France.

The meeting at Venice which was ultimately to result in Italy being involved in Hitler's adventure, seems to have obsessed Nostradamus, for it is mentioned (if we can admit the reference) in two more quatrains:

> *Le grand naistra de Veronne et Vicence,*
> *Qui portera un surnom bien indigne,*
> *Qui a Venise voudra faire vengeance,*
> *Luy mesme prins homme de guet et fine.* (VIII, 33)

The great one will be born in the north of Italy, and will bear a very unworthy surname; at Venice he will desire vengeance but will be himself taken in a snare by a man clever at contriving ambushes.

Mussolini means the muslin maker. The vengeance which he desired was against those powers which frustrated his imperial aims and his dream of Mare Nostrum. And again:

> *Premier grand fruit le Prince de Pesquierre,*
> *Mais puis viendra bien et cruel malin,*
> *Dedans Venise perdra sa gloire fiere,*
> *Et mis à mal par plus joyne Celin.* (VIII, 31)

The first great prize that fell to him was the Prince of Peschiera. This would seem to refer to King Victor Emmanuel III who at Peschiera performed the one really kingly act of his reign. After Caporetto, he went to the front, took command in person, flatly rejected all proposals to fall back and proclaimed his resolve to stand and fight. The Council of War was held at Peschiera.[1] Then will come one very cruel and cunning, and he [Mussolini] will lose his proud glory in Venice and will be delivered over to evil by a younger Infidel. Celin or its other form Selyn is derived from the Greek for 'moon' and in Nostradamus means either Islam or apostasy in general.

Mussolini's first treachery was towards his socialist comrades of *Avanti*, the anti-war paper which he abandoned to found *Il Popolo d'Italia*. When he came into power he persecuted his former associates and sent the most important of them into exile.

> *Le Duc voudra les siens exterminer,*
> *Envoyera les plus forts lieux estranges,*
> *Par tyrannie Bize et Luc ruyner,*
> *Puis les Barbares sans vin feront vendanges.* (IX, 80)

The Duce will wish to exterminate his own comrades and will send the strongest of them out of the country, and by his tyranny will ruin Italy (the part for the whole). Then the Barbarians will make a vintage without wine – the vintage of blood – one of Nostradamus' happiest expressions.

A reference to the same events may perhaps be seen in the following:

> *Un Duc cupide son ennemy ensuivre,*
> *Dans entrera empeschant la phalange....* (IV, 51)

A greedy Duce following him who is really his enemy will take his place in the battle front, but will prove more a hindrance than a help.

Nostradamus from time to time seems to have had a

---

1. I am indebted for this suggestion to Mr J. J. Dwyer.

notion of some of the instruments of modern war. Some have seen in the following quatrain a reference to torpedoes:

> *Un peu apres non point longue intervalle,*
> *Par mer & terre sera faict grand tumulte:*
> *Beaucoup plus grande sera pugne navale;*
> *Feux, animaux, qui plus feront d'insulte.* (II, 40)

A little after a short interval [between two wars] a great tumult will arise by land and sea; the naval fight will be much greater [than it has ever been before]; fires and animals [? submarines] which will do great injury.

If the reader can accept this he will be willing to agree that when the Prophet speaks of grasshoppers (*'sauterelles'*) he means aeroplanes.

> *Les sauterelles terre & mer vent propice....* (III, 82)

Grasshoppers by land and sea, the wind being propitious. And again:

> *... si tant de sauterelles:*
> *Clarté solaire deviendra nubileuse,*
> *Ronger tout, grand peste venir d'elles.* (IV, 48)

So many grasshoppers that the light of the sun will be clouded, they will devour everything and bring a great pestilence.

It does seem as if Nostradamus had had some notion of bombs:

> *Sera laissé feu vif, mort caché,*
> *Dedans les globes horrible espouvantable.*
> *De nuict à classe cité en poudre lasché*
> *La cité à feu, l'ennemy favorable.* (V, 8)

There will be loosed living fire and death hidden in globes, horrible! frightful! By night hostile forces will reduce the city to powder, the fact that it is already on fire being favourable to the enemy. It almost seems as if the Prophet had had an inkling of the difference between incendiaries and H.E.s.

The periscopes of Hitler's submarine 'packs' in the North

Atlantic are happily hinted at in the third line of the following quatrain:

> *D'ou pensera faire venir famine,*
> *De la viendra le ressasiement,*
> *L'œil de la mer par avare canine*
> *Pour de l'un l'autre donra huyle, froment.* (IV, 15)

There where he thought to breed famine, from there will come supplies, for America will give to Britain oil and flour while the eye of the sea watches like a greedy dog.

The blockade and counter-blockade will thus turn in favour of Britain:

> *Ceux dans les isles de long temps assiegez,*
> *Prendront viguer force contre ennemis,*
> *Ceux par dehors morts de faim profligez,*
> *En plus grand faim que jamais seront mis.* (III, 71)

Those in the islands long besieged will take vigorous measures against their enemies; it is those outside who will die of hunger, so great a hunger as there has never been before.

The Second World War was the only one in which the countries mentioned in the following quatrain have been in alliance:

> *La gent de Dace, d'Angleterre, Polonne*
> *Et de Boësme feront nouvelle ligue,*
> *Pour passer outre d'Hercules la colonne,*
> *Barcins, Tyrrens dresser cruelle brigue.* (V, 51)

The people of the Balkans, England, Poland, and Czechoslovakia will make a new alliance, in order to keep open the Straits of Gibraltar; Spaniards and Italians (those of Barcelona and Tuscany) will hatch a cruel plot.

In another quatrain the Prophet says:

> *Vorneigne Dace et l'Isle Britannique,*
> *Par les unis freres seront vexées. . . .* (VI, 7)

Norway (Norvège), the Balkans and the Britannic Isle will be troubled by the alliance between the two dictators.

Hitler's *Drang nach Osten* may be reflected in the following if 'Nouvelle loy' may really be translated by his 'New Order':

> *Nouvelle loy terre neufve occuper,*
> *Vers la Syrie, Judée et Palestine,*
> *Le grand empire barbare corruer....* (III, 97)

The New Order will occupy new territory towards Syria, Judaea and Palestine; the great barbarian empire will fall in ruins.

On the other hand this may be a dream of a new Crusade against Islam, still an aspiration in sixteenth-century Europe, and, if one may judge from some of the more Ultramontane commentators, not wholly extinct in Catholic circles even to-day.

The two dictators will not hold out for long:

> *Les deux amis ne tiendront longuement....* (V, 78)

but will be put down from their seats, and the appointed time of the Man of Blood will be accomplished:

> *Un jour seront demis les deux grands maistres....*
> *Au sanguinaire le nombre racompté.* (II, 89)

Dr Fontbrune, whose major work on Nostradamus, published just before the last War, contained, with much rather wild speculation, some valuable hints, has recently come forward again with some new interpretations which are not without interest.[1] He suggests that the quatrain:

> *Le vieux mocqué ot privé de sa place,*
> *Par l'estranger qui le subornera,*
> *Mains de son fils mangées devant sa face,*
> *Les frères à Chartres, Orl. Roüan, trahira.* (IV, 61)

refers to Marshal Pétain. He was indeed known as '*Le Vieux*', and Dr Fontbrune interprets: *Le Vieux* will be mocked and deprived of his position as *Chef de l'État* by the enemy, who will pervert him, and betray him, the forces of his régime

1. In an article in *Ici Paris*, July 22nd, 1950.

(*mains de son fils*) destroyed before his eyes, while the brothers [in arms] reach Chartres, Orleans, and Rouen. It was, in fact, on August 19th, 1944, the day on which the Germans carried off Marshal Pétain to Sigmaringen, that three armies of the Allies reached, simultaneously, Chartres, Orleans, and Rouen.

Badoglio's attempt to bring the war to an end and Mussolini's violent reaction may be hinted at in the following quatrain:

> *Lorsque soldats furent seditieuse*
> *Contre leur chef feront de nuict fer luire,*
> *Ennemy d'Albe soit par main furieuse,*
> *Lors vexer Rome, et principaux seduire.* (VI, 68)

When soldiers are seditious against their chief and make their weapons shine by night the enemy of Albion will strive furiously, then will Rome be troubled and its principal citizens seduced from their allegiance.

Then the King of Italy will have his desire, by getting rid of Mussolini.

> *Roy trouvera ce qu'il désiroit tant,*
> *Quand le Prelat sera reprins à tort,*
> *Response au Duc le rendra mal content,*
> *Qui dans Milan mettra plusieurs à mort.* (VI, 31)

The King will find what he so much desired when the Prelate shall be wrongfully taken; the response received by the Duce will anger him, and in Milan he will put several to death. The execution of Ciano and others may seem to be glanced at in this. The second line is obscure, although some commentators have sought to link it with a quatrain which created considerable interest in the years just before the war because of its plain statement that the See of Rome would be transferred elsewhere by the power of three temporal rulers who were then supposed to be Hitler, Mussolini, and Franco:

> *Par la puissance de trois Roys temporels,*
> *En autre lieu sera mis le sainct Siège,*

Oü la substance de l'esprit corporel
Sera remis et receu pour vray siege. (VIII, 99)

By the power of three temporal Kings the Holy See will be transferred to another place where the substance of the Incarnate Spirit will be set up and received as the real Throne of Peter.

This event seems very unlikely now, but, as in most of the quatrains we have been considering we are moving in a world of pure conjecture. One can only envy those writers who are confident that the terrible events we have witnessed were but incidents leading up to the Second Coming of Christ and the End of the World. One would be able to follow them with a little less scepticism if the Restoration of the Bourbons was not somehow bound up with such transcendental events.

How far Nostradamus is involved in this curious notion it is difficult to say. As we peer darkly into the future, it becomes more and more difficult to separate the intentions of Nostradamus from the dreams of his interpreters. As we have seen, the Abbé Torné was mistaken in thinking that the fall of Napoleon III would be followed by the advent of the Grand Chyren, and also that the Prophet was aware of this misinterpretation. Elisée du Vignois, who continued Torné's work and brought out his vast and learned book in 1910,[1] knew that his predecessor had been mistaken, and that as the Comte de Chambord was already dead it was impossible that he should be the Henri V so long expected and so passionately longed for. He therefore transferred his apocalyptic loyalties to Henri Louis Charles de Bourbon, born at Lunel on November 27th, 1899, and thought he had found his justification in the phrase 'Grand Chyren Selin'. He placed his probable accession to the throne of France in the year 1917! So dangerous is it to interpret the Prophet in the light of a wish-fulfilment of one's own.

In the opinion of more sceptical commentators (who still

1. Elisée du Vignois, *Notre histoire racontée à l'avance par Nostradamus*, Paris, 1910.

believe in Nostradamus as a prophet) all the Grand Chyren quatrains refer, as explained in an earlier chapter, to Henri IV. In any case the direct line of the Bourbons is now extinct and if there be a 'Grand Chyren' or 'Grand Celtique' still to come he must be sought for elsewhere.

Not content with a Legitimist King, some of the commentators even postulate a Capet Pope, or in any case a close alliance between the French Monarchy and the See of Rome, an alliance (be it said, in passing) which was never very obvious in the days of the historical French Kings. Some of the quatrains of Nostradamus do seem to lend themselves as a basis for these fancies.

> *Le grand Celtique entrera dedans Rome,*
> *Menant amas d'exilez et bannis,*
> *Le grand pasteur mettra à mort tout homme*
> *Qui pour le coq étoient aux Alpes unis.* (VI, 28)

The Great Celtic will enter Rome at the head of a great company of the exiled and banished; the Great Pastor (with a singular lack of humanity) will put to death every man who has allied himself to Italy on behalf of the Cock.

The quatrains dealing with Antichrist and the end of the world present even greater difficulties to the mind which still clings to some rational view of History. The Prophet seems to imply that there will be three Antichrists. If Napoleon was one and Hitler was another the third is still to come:

> *L'Antechrist trois bientost annichilez,*
> *Vingt et sept ans sang durera sa guerre,*
> *Les heretiques morts, captifs, exilez,*
> *Sang, corps humain, eau rougie, gresler terre.* (VIII, 77)

The Third Antichrist will be soon annihilated; his war of blood will last twenty-seven years; heretics will be slain, enslaved or exiled; blood, human bodies, reddened water, hail upon the earth.

The prophet even dares to give a date:

> *L'an mil neuf cens nonante neuf sept mois,*
> *Du ciel viendra le grand Roy d'effrayeur. . . .* (X, 72)

In the year 1999 and seven months there will come from Heaven the great King of Terror.

In another quatrain the Prophet says:

> *Au revolu du grand nombre septiesme,*
> *Apparoistra au temps jeux d'Hecatombe,*
> *Non esloigné de grand d'aage milliesme,*
> *Que les entrez sortiront de leur tombe.* (x, 74)

When the wheel of Time shall have come to the Seventh Millennium there will begin the games of Death (*jeux d'Hecatombe*) not long from the great age of the Thousand Years when those who have entered the tomb will emerge from it.

It is no part of our purpose to plunge the reader into the complicated calculations of those who have endeavoured to predict the exact year of the end of the world. The collapse of the belief that only four thousand years passed between the Creation and the birth of Jesus Christ has rendered such a task meaningless. None the less it is interesting to try to understand what Nostradamus had in mind.

In another curious quatrain he says:

> *Vingt ans du regne de la Lune passez,*
> *Sept mil ans autre tiendra sa monarchie,*
> *Quand le Soleil prendra ses jours lassez,*
> *Lors accomplir et mine ma prophetie.* (1, 48)

When twenty years of the reign of the Moon shall be passed, another will resume his seven thousand year old reign; when the sun shall take up his days again then my prophecy will be accomplished.

The calculation of Roussat and others that the reign of the Moon will last from 1535 to 1889 seems to throw no light on this mystery. But the seven thousand years appear once more, and Nostradamus appears to connect them in some way with the end of his prophetic vision.

He accepted in fact the notion commonly held in the Middle Ages and later that the End of the World would come at the beginning of the Seventh Millennium. It derives from the pre-Christian Book of Enoch which was well known among the Jews of the first century and even influenced New Testament writers. It disappeared from the Canon, except among the Ethiopic and Slavonic Christians, about A.D. 300. In this work God tells Enoch that the duration of the world will be for a week of years, that is seven thousand, after which 'let there be at the beginning of the eighth thousand a time when there is no computation and no end; neither years nor months nor weeks nor days nor hours.'[1] There would seem to be an echo of this in Nostradamus' line:

Quand le Soleil prendra ses jours lassez.

It seems as if the Prophet counted 4,000 years before Christ, added 2,000 years (*L'an mil neuf cens nonante neuf sept mois*) to bring him to the commencement of the Seventh Millennium and then expected a further thousand years (the 'Millennium', usually so-called) before the final dissolution.

What does all this mean, except that he attempted to rationalize his own gleams of insight? When inspiration failed him he fell back upon the calculations of his conscious intelligence; in other words he tried to fit his visions into the scheme of world chronology common to the astrologers and theologians of his day.

The Christian world was thrown into a panic at the approach of the year A.D. 1000. When that fear, or hope, was proved to be groundless, the date of the Second Coming was transferred to the year 2000. The whole subject was complicated, as we have seen, by the necessity for finding in the scheme of the future some place for the allegories of the Book of Revelation. It is now usual to regard that work as an apocalyptic poem with a political bias against the Rome of the Caesars. But like all great works of art it transcends its occasion and becomes an allegory of human life itself. But this is far from saying that it can be safely used as a kind of transcendental almanack, a ready-reckoner of futurity, and few, except the incurably Fundamentalist, would make such a claim for it to-day.

1. Enoch xxx.

Perhaps it all depends on one's view of the meaning of History. At Oxford thirty years ago, it was fashionable to adopt an attitude of extreme scepticism to the suggestion that History teaches this or that. History teaches nothing, we were told, which can only mean that History has no meaning, that any pattern we fancy we see in it is a pattern imposed upon it by the incurably rationalizing tendencies of our own minds. This now seems, to the present writer at least, a strangely barren and perverse opinion. It is also a view which can only be held by isolation from the world in some academic ivory tower. If History has no meaning, it hardly seems worth while going on living. Yet what other theories of History are there?

There is what may be called the purely biological view of history. History is part of evolution. If the mammoth or the mastodon had found a chronicler, their battles in the Siberian wastes would now be the subject of history. Nations are like varieties of the animal kingdom; they evolve from small beginnings; they have their youth, their maturity, and their old age. This view was widely prevalent at the end of the nineteenth century, and led to an attempt to study history by pure documentation and the scientific accumulation of facts; yet even the biologist permits himself theories in order to explain the facts, and even men who think they have answered the question of the origin of life by saying that we come from the sperm of the sea, cannot refrain from asking the question 'Whither?' and to this pure biology has no answer: the question 'To what end?' implies a meaning, and a meaning requires a moral.

Thus the idea of evolution takes on a moral significance and we are, we are told, evolving towards something better. We must let the ape and tiger die, as Tennyson says; and then we may perhaps be rewarded by seeing freedom slowly broadening down from precedent to precedent until all is for the best in the best of all possible worlds. We are so far from this liberal humanitarian optimism that there is not much to be said except that we cannot believe in it.

The Marxian view partakes of something of both of the

last two: it has the scientific, or pseudo-scientific, attitude of the biologist and the millenarianism of liberalism, and also the view that the millennium will be established on this earth.

The ancient world, it is hardly necessary to remind the reader, took a quite different view of history. Almost all, if not all, the Ancients held not that they were moving toward the perfect State but that they were moving away from it. The Garden of Eden lay in the past; some time long ago there had been a Golden Age. Later, the doctrine of the Fall took a narrow theological form which obscured its very profound meaning. But for the moment we are more concerned with the idea which runs parallel with it, the idea of a direct descent from the gods. Perhaps we shall not find it strange in a world which is still inhabited by Germans (and English) if each race of the ancient world seems to have imagined that it alone enjoyed this advantage. Even the wise Chinese, even the subtle Greeks, were not exempt from this parochialism, and with the Hebrews it became such a burning conviction that even their enemies call them to this day 'The Chosen People'. It is a view which at least has the merit of simplifying history. History is the story of the Chosen People, its struggle against its enemies and its ultimate triumph; but unfortunately the progress of the Chosen People meets with some unaccountable setbacks – unaccountable, that is, unless we conclude that the Chosen People, still far from perfect, is being subjected to a series of trials and chastisements which God visits upon it in order to make it worthy of the kingdom which it shall one day inherit. This is a moral idea of the utmost magnitude and, in a transmuted form, is an abiding element in all spiritual religion.

The early Christian being essentially international – neither Jew nor Greek – no longer felt himself a member of the national community but of a community of a different kind. 'The poet saith, "Dear city of Cecrops." Shall not I say, "Dear city of God"?' The nation in fact had become a church and it is as members of a church that men are visited by trials and temptations. Some seemed to have abolished even this sense of the community and to have made the individual evolution, or growth in grace, the sole reason for the apparently incomprehensible trials which befell. We may call one of these attitudes Catholic and one Protestant.

Both doctrines amount to a belief in the strict irrelevance of history: history is something outside. It can be a nuisance, a torment, even a martyrdom, but it is no longer something we do: it is something that is done to us – an earthquake, or a Roman persecution. Such things may kill us but they are not, strictly speaking, our affair. 'Come out from among them and be ye separate,' said the Lord. History is meaningless, or rather it would be meaningless unless it had, like an otherwise incomprehensible tale, a dénouement – a dénouement in which villainy is punished and innocence rewarded as completely and as satisfactorily as in any transpontine melodrama.

Now whatever we may think of the Last Judgement, it certainly gives a meaning to history. Whether we think of it through the perhaps excessively legalistic mind of the Romans as a kind of ultimate Assize, or whether we conceive of it as the final resolution of opposites by re-absorption in the Godhead, it lends a meaning to human life and fulfils aspirations which can never perhaps be satisfied even by the most perfect of Communist States.

Apropos of the Last Judgement, it is difficult to refrain from mentioning another prophet, in his way as remarkable as Nostradamus – the Irish St Malachy. Malachy, who lived from 1094 to 1148, was Bishop of Armagh. In 1139 he went to Rome for the Lateran Council under Innocent II, and while there wrote and, such is the story, deposited in the archives of the Vatican a series of Latin devices all of which were supposed to refer in their correct order to the future occupants of St Peter's Chair, not necessarily to their own characters but to the most striking events of their pontificates or even to their coat-of-arms. Malachy died at Clairvaux on his way home and his prophecies, long forgotten in the Vatican archives, were rediscovered at the end of the sixteenth century. And if it is impossible to believe that, then it is necessary to believe that someone forged them about that period and published them in 1595 [1]; and that the forger also had the gift of prophecy. For these Latin devices, most of them consisting of two words only, are astonishingly accurate. It is true that many of them are non-committal, but some of them have an exactitude which it is difficult to explain by mere coincidence.

Pius VI was the Pope who was chased from his realms by the French Revolution and spent the rest of his life a wandering fugitive. He had previously, in 1785, made a useless journey to Vienna in the hope of placating Joseph II. No other pope had left Italy since Clement VII went to Marseilles. Malachy's motto for him is 'Peregrinus Apostolicus.' His successor, Pius VII, was Napoleon's captive and was only released from his confinement at Fontainebleau by the tyrant's abdication. His motto is 'Aquila Rapax.' Most curious of all in its particularity is the motto attached to Gregory XVI (1831-46). This Pope belonged to a religious order whose mother house was situated in Etruria, and he founded the Etruscan Museum in the Vatican. Malachy, or the sixteenth-century forger, remarked of him: 'De Balneis Etruriae,' and one can only ask oneself in astonishment what an Irish Bishop of the twelfth century (or even what an Italian forger of the sixteenth century) knew about Etruscan antiquities. Pio Nono is 'Crux de Cruce', the Cross persecuted by the Cross, the second cross, of course, being that of the House of Savoy. Leo XIII is 'Lumen in Coelo': not only was he indeed, by his intellect, a 'light in Heaven', but his crest was a comet. The author of a book on the subject written in the early years of the twentieth century falls to wondering what can be meant by the motto of Pius X, which is 'Ignis Ardens'. He wonders if it meant some great fire in the Vatican. We know that it implied a conflagration which embraced half the world.

1. They were published at Venice in the *Lignum Vitae*, a two-volume work by the Benedictine Arnold de Wion; born at Douai, May 13th, 1554.

For the mountain-climbing Pius XI, 'Fides Intrepida' is singularly happy. Pius XII, as the newspapers duly announced at the time of his election, was 'Pastor Angelicus'. He was succeeded by John XXIII, formerly Cardinal Angelo Giuseppe Roncalli, patriarch of Venice, and Malachy's motto for him is 'Pastor et Nauta'. The Oecumenical Council which opened in Rome in 1962 was one of the great achievements of his short reign, and evidence of his burning desire to set the Church on to a different course. Then follow four more Popes, then a fifth, and to the fifth Malachy gives not a little Latin Motto of two words but a whole sentence whose magnificent oratorical rotundity concerns him who shall be Pope at the end of the world: 'In persecutione extrema sanctae Romanae Ecclesiae sedebit Petrus Romanus qui pascet oves in multis tribulationibus; quibus transactis, civitas septicollis diruetur, et Judex tremendus judicabit populum.'

In extreme persecution of the Roman Church shall sit (in the Chair of the first Peter) Peter the Roman who will feed his flock amid many tribulations; which things being finished, the City of the Seven Hills will be removed and the Great Judge will judge the people.

Now the curious thing is that between the present Pope and Peter II who shall be Pope at the End of the World, Malachy places three others[1], and this, if we calculate the average period of pontificates, would bring us roughly to the end of the twentieth century. So that Nostradamus with his 1999 and seven months, agrees with the other Prophet. He may, of course, have been aware of the Prophecy of Malachy, but if not, the coincidence shows that both men were reflecting a universal tradition.

Pure superstition, or a mystical truth that escapes our rationalizings? The older among us may never know; the younger can only be counselled to wait and see.

1. De Medietate Lunae, De Labore Solis, De Gloria Olivae.

Epilogue

THE reader who has followed the argument thus far is probably convinced that there is *something* in Nostradamus. If he were not he would have flung the book away long ago. Now, therefore, casting aside the mask of 'the present author' and the impersonal manner which I have tried to maintain throughout the narrative, I hope to set down to the best of my ability the personal lines on which I have tried to solve the baffling problem provided by the *Centuries*.

First, however, it is necessary to clear away a few objections. Is it not possible, we shall be asked, that the whole thing is a forgery, like the works of so many so-called prophets? The answer is plain. A glance at the list of early editions of Nostradamus at the end of the volume will show that here is no question of manuscript copies alleged to have been taken by persons since dead of books now no longer in existence. We rest on the firm ground of bibliographical certainty. The early editions, the genuineness of which is admitted by all bibliographers, are in public collections and may be readily consulted. That Nostradamus was known as a prophet in his own day we have ample contemporary evidence. The stream of comment, criticism and interpretation begins in the sixteenth century and by the end of the seventeenth it would have been possible to collect an extensive library of Nostradamiana. We know that Pascal had a copy of the *Centuries* in his library; the English seventeenth-century gossip John Aubrey declares that in his time the book was common. There is therefore no escape in this direction.

The second objection takes a somewhat different form. Granted, we are told, that the greater part of the *Centuries* has existed in print since 1555 and the complete text, including the *Présages* and the *Sixains*, from 1605, yet we can still believe that the references to later events which commentators have found in them are nothing but a trick of interpretation, a tortuous ingenuity fitting *tant bien que mal* the words of the Prophet to the facts of history.

That commentators have been over-ingenious will hardly be denied; that some of the quatrains are so obscure and ambiguous that they might be, and have been, forced to do duty for different events, cannot be disputed. Yet there remain, in my opinion at least, a sufficient number which it is impossible to explain away in this fashion. Even hostile critics have been constrained to admit that Nostradamus did seem to know a great deal about the French Revolution, and this, after all, was no mean feat for a man who lived and died under the Valois Kings.

The third objection falls back upon a theory of probabilities. We are told that a monkey, playing with a fount of type, and having infinite time at his disposal will, *in the end*, and purely by hazard, arrange the letters in the correct order of those in *Paradise Lost*. Nostradamus (such is the theory) wrote so many quatrains peppered with names straightforward and obscure, and linked them with so many vague menaces of calamity, that something was bound to turn up trumps. Pure chance may include in one quatrain an Elected Capet in flight and the word 'Varennes', mere coincidence may give us an old Cardinal who is also 'Liqueduct', a simple calculation of probabilities will produce a line like:

Senat de Londres mettront à mort leur Roy.

In order to make such 'probabilities' probable Nostradamus ought to have written not a thousand quatrains but a million. For my part I find the theory utterly untenable, and this road of escape therefore also barred.

I find it impossible to avoid the conviction that Nostradamus *could* sometimes foresee the future and foresee it with an astonishing particularity of detail. Most of the commentators, of course, go much further than this. They believe that the whole scroll of future history was, by a privilege accorded to no other mortal man, unrolled before his eyes, and that the admitted obscurity of his message is deliberate.

This is to take the authorship of the *Centuries* from Nostradamus and to give it to the Deity Himself.

When Nostradamus claimed in his Epistle to Henri II that he could easily have given each quatrain a date if he had wished, I think he was simply mistaken. Nor can I believe that all the anagrams are deliberate, although some of them like 'Rapis' for Paris or 'Eiovas' for Savoie are obviously so. I think that most of them were simply a part of the conditions under which his inspiration happened.

That Nostradamus did not obtain his results by purely astrological calculations may be inferred, not only from his own statement, but by the facts of the case. Whether Astrology be a genuine science or not it has never claimed to foresee the fate of people still unborn, still less to give their names. In fact there is no astrological calculation which can give a name at all, and the *Centuries* positively bristle with names.

Chavigny, perhaps quoting a phrase which he had heard from the lips of the Prophet himself, describes his condition of mind while composing his works: *'plein d'un enthousiasme & comme ravi d'une fureur toute nouvelle, il se mit à écrire se Centuries'*. The prophecies were received by Nostradamus while in a state of ecstasy, or in other words they were not entirely the work of the conscious mind.

Of course what has come down to us is something quite different. We have a series of quatrains in French verse, but their curious syntax and construction leads us to suppose that they must previously have existed in Latin, either in the shape of verse or of mere jottings. I am inclined to believe that Nostradamus, either by automatic writing, or by making notes immediately on emerging from his trance, wrote down a series of Latin sentences or phrases, and afterwards worked them up on the analogy of the verse-oracles of Delphi.

Perhaps I am begging the question in using the word 'trance'. Yet it is certain that something in the nature of trance is necessary for the reception of any 'messages' other than those transmitted between conscious minds by the ordinary methods of speech, writing, etc. Those who have experimented with telepathy know that the first requirement is to put the mind into a condition which is very difficult to describe in words but which is easily induced after a little practice.

Every one at some period of his life has paid a visit to a fortune-teller, even if it was only on a fair-ground or at a church-bazaar. Such fortune-tellers, whether they call themselves palmists, or phrenologists, or tea-leaf readers, or crystal-gazers, fall into two categories: they are either mere frauds or they are trance-mediums. With the latter the process is always the same. At first they gaze intently into the glass ball or at the lines of the hand and utter a certain amount of non-committal jargon – the 'journey over the sea' and the 'dark woman' of whom we must beware. Then suddenly they begin to breathe deeply, their eyes turn upward or close, and from the depths of their own unconscious they fish out some fact which could not possibly be known to their conscious intelligence.

A palmist at Dymchurch once described the route I took to reach my office. She said that I entered a very large building through a high doorway, turned to the left, ascended a flight of marble stairs, turned again, passed down a corridor in which there were many clothes and so on. She certainly did not know that I was an official of the Victoria and Albert Museum in London and that the route she had described did in fact take me to my own department.

But this is mere telepathy! Quite so. But if the reader accepts 'mere telepathy' he has already taken an important step towards the understanding of Nostradamus. I am myself convinced that telepathy is a fact.

There is now in existence a very considerable body of literature dealing with telepathic experiments, and the reader in search of further enlightenment may be referred to two of the most remarkable books on the subject, one by the well-known American writer Upton Sinclair and one by the

French *savant* René Warcollier.[1] It is not my purpose here to investigate the nature of telepathic communications, but we may note in passing the curious similarity between the kind of message received by telepathic 'recipients' and by Nostradamus. In both there is the same vagueness of general outline and the same strange particularity of detail.

In one of the experiments described by Upton Sinclair, it was arranged that Mrs Sinclair's brother-in-law, Robert L. Irwin, a young American business man priding himself on having no 'crank' ideas, should, in his house at Pasadena, at a certain hour each day, take pencil and paper and make a drawing of an object and then sit and concentrate his mind upon the drawing. Mrs Sinclair at Long Beach, forty miles away, put herself at the same hour in a state of receptivity and drew whatever came into her head. The very first attempt was a success. Robert L. Irwin drew a chair which was before him and Mrs Sinclair also drew a chair. She then drew a star, and it was afterwards found that the chair which Irwin had drawn had a carved star upon it although he had not indicated it in his drawing and had not consciously noted it at the time.

This is in line with the results obtained in the very interesting series of tests conducted by René Warcollier. Warcollier found that some unimportant detail was often transmitted with almost photographic accuracy even when the main object was received imperfectly or not at all. In one experiment the transmitter gazed at a picture postcard of an early airship entering its hangar, and drew part of the balloon body. The recipient drew a ball, which the end of the airship resembled, but also drew what she thought was a ladder leaning against a wall. This, in position and shape, was exactly similar to one of the ladder-like struts of the hangar which had been neither drawn nor (consciously) noticed by the transmitter.

The 'messages' obtained by Nostradamus were, in my

1. Upton Sinclair, *Mental Radio – Does it Work, and How?* London, 1930. René Warcollier, *Experiments in Telepathy*, translated by Josephine B. Gridley, London, 1939.

view, of a similar nature, both in their obscurity and in their particularity, and he obtained them by a similar semi-suspension of the consciousness. But whereas Mrs Sinclair and other modern experimenters attained this by merely sitting in a chair and allowing their attention to relax to the point where sleep had almost intervened, Nostradamus went about the matter in a much more elaborate and traditional way. In a word he practised Magic.

What is Magic? To the rationalist it is a mere superstition, to the Catholic it is a terrible reality, a forbidden commerce with real devils, to the modern occultist it is a profound and complex philosophy, the reality behind all religions, the Eternal Orthodoxy of which they are but the successive transmutations. Like Religion it has its ritual, but only the superficial mistake the ritual for the reality which it expresses. A ritual is a means to an end, and it need not be ineffective because, to the outsider, it seems absurd or revolting or both.

We are only beginning to re-discover, after the Age of Scepticism, the real power of symbolic gestures and evocative words. Whatever Magic may be or not be, it must be admitted that by its practices you can, at least, do something to your own mind, you can draw upon the hidden contents of your own unconscious, you can attain, artificially, to that condition of auto-hypnosis which is so similar on the one hand to the 'receptivity' of the telepathists and on the other to the ecstasy of the prophets.

I suggested half-way through the present book that Magic was a technique for going into a trance. Dim lights, monotonously iterated words, certain perfumes, known drugs, fixity of gaze, deep and rhythmic breathing – these are the accepted methods of Indian fakirs, Polynesian kahunas and African witch-doctors just as they were of the sorcerers of the ancient and mediaeval world. By such means you can induce what the modern psychologists call 'dissociation of the personality' and more credulous ages called 'possession'.

By such methods you can 'lull the conscious mind asleep' or rather you can balance it on the razor-edge which divides sleeping from waking. In full consciousness the phantoms of the unconscious are invisible; from complete unconsciousness they are not recoverable by the waking mind. The problem is to let everything go but the will which cries 'Remember'. Can we doubt that the practices of Nostradamus had this end in view?

Well, we have now got both Mrs Sinclair and Nostradamus in the same kind of trance but while one is merely conducting a series of experiments in telepathy, the other is prophesying the French Revolution two hundred years before it happened. What is the connexion between them? More than would, at first sight, be apparent.

In the course of her experiments Mrs Sinclair found that her results could not always be explained by mere telepathy. She obtained an astonishingly high percentage of successes even when the drawings were made a dozen at a time, put into a sealed envelope and shuffled. We are here leaving the realm of telepathy proper and entering that of clairvoyance. But clairvoyance is very much more difficult to believe in, for it implies that material objects send out radiations which can be picked up and interpreted by the human mind. It is at least incredible to any kind of rationalism that such radiations, if they exist, could possibly register the difference between a drawing of (say) a bulldog and a drawing of a rose.

There is however another possibility. Mrs Sinclair was not clairvoyant, but she *foresaw what she was going to see*. If this is so, we have at once an acceptable explanation of all feats of so-called clairvoyance and something which may help us to understand the possibility of prophecy.

In the year 1927 appeared a book which created a tremendous impression not only among professional philosophers but on the general educated public. *An Experiment with Time*, by J. W. Dunne, opened with an account of some of the author's experiences with dreams and went on to expound a mathematical theory of the nature of Time quite revolutionary in its implications. Most readers, it is perhaps fair to say, were more interested in the author's dreams than

EPILOGUE 249

in his theories, and the dreams were remarkable enough. While in South Africa in 1902 he dreamed of the volcano disaster in Martinique some days before the newspapers containing the news arrived. From certain minor details it was plain that he had not had clairvoyance of the actual event but had foreseen his own reading of a paragraph in the *Daily Telegraph*. In the same way he foresaw a disastrous fire in a rubber factory in Paris. He dreamed, before it occurred, of the great Silvertown explosion of 1917. But it was not only great events which stirred this faculty, if faculty it was. The merest trivialities were also foreseen, such as the details of a combination lock or the hour at which his watch had stopped. Dunne found, in short, that of the images which floated through his dreams (and which he trained himself by a special technique to recapture and remember) some belonged to the past and an equal number belonged to the future. He seemed to be able to range as easily in one direction as the other.

He also found that this capacity was not confined to sleep, but was equally manifest in that intermediate condition when we are half asleep and half awake but still retain control of our faculties. He was able, in this condition, to read the time by his watch without looking at it, in other words, to *foresee what he would see* when he did look.

This bald account does little justice to the charm of the author's manner and the convincing character of his corroborative detail. For these the reader can only be referred to the book itself. But this discovery of Dunne's has very far-reaching implications, and the method adopted may perhaps help us to understand the procedure of Nostradamus.

Most of Dunne's foreseeings were of events in the very immediate future. He quotes one, however, where the gap between vision and fulfilment was as long as twenty years. If twenty years why not two hundred years? Because, it will be answered, a man cannot (on the theory we have been discussing) foresee what he will not live to see. But can we limit the possibility of prophecy in this way? May not the occultists be right in claiming that there is something which they call the Akasha Record, a Scroll of the World not bounded by the limitations of individuality? Then if it is possible to foresee the events of twenty years hence it is equally possible for the events of 1793 to be foreseen in 1555; and if the Prophet of Salon foresaw them with the distortions of a telepathic message and the ambiguity of a dream that is no argument against the validity of his vision. It might even lead us to give it more credence. But how can prophecy be possible at all?

It is not my purpose, or within my capacity, in a work of this description, to attempt a detailed analysis of J. W. Dunne's conclusions. His argument is a mathematical one, based on the theory of 'Serialism'. There must be a 'Time behind Time', for this is the legitimate consequence of the universally accepted hypothesis of a *movement* through Time's length. Motion in Time must be timeable, for if the moving element is everywhere along the Time length at once it is not moving. But the time which times that movement is another Time. And the 'passage' of that Time must be timeable by a third Time, and so *ad infinitum*.

For an observer in Time 2, Time 1 is akin to a dimension of 'ordinary' space, and Dunne postulates the first law governing his series in the following terms:

'Every Time-travelling field of presentation is contained within a field one dimension larger, travelling in another dimension of Time, the larger field covering events which are "past" and "future", as well as "present", to the smaller field.'

The author of *An Experiment with Time* does not think that this involves an acceptance of absolute determinism. He thinks there is still room for minor variations in possible conduct, and it will be admitted that all that most of us are capable of is minor variations. Our actions are largely determined by our circumstances and our own characters. Perhaps it is idle to say that a little more determination on the part of Louis XVI would have got his carriage safely through Varennes and changed the course of history. A little more determination was precisely what was lacking in

EPILOGUE 251

the character of Louis. Yet how many generations of men called Sauce had to beget children and refrain from leaving Varennes in order that a man of that name should be present on the fatal night in 1792. The slightest variation, one feels, in the conduct of any of them and the *procureur* of the *commune* would have borne some quite different name, and the Nostradamian prophecy would have been incomprehensible. Does the phrase that 'Character *is* Destiny' entirely satisfy us here?

Perhaps our free-will is a delusion. The analogy of the railway train has often been proposed. When we travel in a train it seems to us that the houses and the fields fly past us. But it is we who move. Do we move through Time in like fashion, future Time being merely the country we have not yet reached, with all its hills reared, its valleys carved and its cities established? Is it already Present in the Collective Unconscious or the Mind of God. Is World-history a drama already written, and does the wind from the wings occasionally flutter the pages of the prompt-book so that sharp eyes can catch a glimpse of their contents? Such images may help us to envisage the problem; they do not help us to solve it.

The whole notion of the Collective Unconscious is a proof how far we have travelled from the sceptical individualism of nineteenth-century thought. Between one conscious mind and another there is no communication except through some mechanical means. In Jung's phrase the conscious mind is 'capsulated'. But the ego is not the whole of us, and Jung is driven back on a theory of the 'Collective Unconscious'. According to this the deeper we descend into ourselves the less of self we find. The Collective Unconscious contains a number of patterns which are common to the whole of humanity. 'The unconscious is anything but a capsulated personal system; it is the wide world, and objectively as open as the world ... a boundless expanse full of unprecedented uncertainty, with apparently no inside and no outside, no above and no below, no here and no there, no mine and no thine, no good and no bad. It is the world of water, where everything living floats in suspension; where the kingdom of the sympathetic system, of the soul of everything living begins, where I am inseparably this and that, and this and that are I; where I experience the other person in myself, and the other, as myself, experiences me.'[1] The language of modern psychology here approaches the old mystical notion of the Anima Mundi, the Soul of the World.

In this World-Soul or Collective Unconscious there is certainly all the Past, and if there is anything in Nostradamus or in the theories of J. W. Dunne, there is all the Future also, and both Future and Past are but one Eternal Present.

The mind grows dizzy at the edge of this abyss. We cling to our pathetic individualities and would have them continue for ever, not knowing that the phrase has no meaning and that the Ego is not the essential part of ourselves. We are already absorbed into the fullness of God, and even if this absorption were still to come it would not be annihilation, for the Ocean into which we are absorbed is not an Ocean of Matter but an Ocean of Mind. But Mind is a unity and to be part of it is to be all of it. Physically we are animals, but psychically and spiritually we are trees, or rather we are One Tree and its name is the Banyan Tree. We are members one of another and Time is merely one of our dimensions.

But I am exceeding my brief. My purpose was only to indicate the lines on which I have striven to explain the (to me) inescapable fact that Nostradamus was a true Prophet.

1. Carl G. Jung, *The Integration of the Personality*. Translated by Stanley M. Dell. London, 1940, p. 70.

APPENDIX

The Prophecy of Olivarius and the 'Prophétie d'Orval'

EUGÉNE BARESTE, in an article in *Le Capitole*, October 21st, 1839, under the pseudonym of 'Un Ancien Sénateur,' declares that when Napoleon was one evening at Malmaison with the Empress Josephine they were talking of superstition and prophecy and the Emperor, producing from his pocket an old manuscript volume composed in 1542, handed it to his wife and asked her to read it aloud.

Josephine read the title: *The Predictions of Master Noël Olivarius*.

'Well?' she asked.

'They say it concerns me,' replied the Emperor.

'What! in a book written in 1542?'

'Read it and see.'

The Empress tried to do so, but as the style was in old French and the letters badly formed, she paused for a moment, casting her eyes over the three pages of this chapter, then, with a confident voice, she began as follows:

'Italian Gaul shall see born not far from her bosom a supernatural being; this man will emerge while quite young from the sea and will come to learn the language and the ways of the Celtic Gauls. While still quite young he will open for himself, over a thousand obstacles, a road among the soldiers and will become their chief. This winding way will cause him many pains; he will make war near his native land for a lustre and more.

'Overseas he shall be seen making way with much glory and valour, and he will make war again in the Roman world.

'He will give laws to the Germans; pacify troubles and terrors among the Celtic Gauls, and he will thus be named not King, but a little afterwards Imperator by the great enthusiasm of the people.

'He will battle everywhere throughout the Empire; he will unthrone princes, lords and kings for two lustres and more. Then he will raise new princes and lords to life and speaking from his chair will cry: *O sidera, O sacra!*

'He shall be seen with an army of forty-nine times twenty-thousand armed men, carrying arms and trumpets of iron. He will have seven times seven times seven thousand horses mounted by men carrying a great sword or lance and wearing a cuirass. He will have seven times seven times two thousand men who will work terrible machines vomiting sulphur and fire and death. The total computation of his army will be forty-nine times twenty thousand men.

'He will carry in his right hand an eagle, sign of his victory in battle.

'He will give many lands to the nations, and to each peace.

'He will come to the great city, commanding many great things: buildings, bridges, ports, aqueducts, canals; he will do with his own power and riches as much as a Roman and that in all the dominions of the Gauls.

'He will have wives twain. . . .' Josephine stopped, but the Emperor bade her continue, 'and an only son. He will go, making war, to the place where cross the lines of longitude and latitude, fifty-five months. There his enemies will burn the great city with fire, and he will enter it and depart with his men over ashes and ruins; and his men, having no more bread or water, by great cold which will be so unfortunate for them, two-thirds of his army will perish, and half the rest will be no more under his domination.

'Then the great man, abandoned, betrayed by his own friends, pursued in his turn by great loss even to his own city by great European population. In his place shall be placed the Kings of the old blood of the Capets.

'He, constrained to exile in the sea from which he came so young and near to his native place, staying there for eleven moons with some of his true friends and soldiers, not being more than seven times seven times seven times two in number. Then when the eleven moons are accomplished, he and his friends will take ship and set foot on the territory of Celtic Gaul.

'And he will make his way towards the great city in which is seated the King of the old blood of the Capets, who rises, flies, carrying with him the crown jewels; takes up his old rule, gives to the peoples many admirable laws.

'Then, unthroned once more by a trinity of the European population, after three moons and the third of a moon is put back in his place the King of the old blood of the Capets. And he will be thought dead by his warlike people who, in these times, will long keep against their heart the *penates* (*sic*).

'The Celts and the Gauls like tigers and wolves will fight among themselves. The blood of the old King of the Capetan line will be the plaything of black treasons. The contentious will be deceived, and by sword and fire slain; the lily will be upheld; but the last branches of the old blood will be once more menaced.

'Thus they will fight amongst themselves.

'Then a young warrior will make his way to the great city; he will bear the lion and the cock on his arms. Also the lance will be given to him by a great prince of the Orient.

'He will be marvellously supported by the warlike people of Belgian Gaul who will unite with the Parisians to put an end to troubles, to gather soldiers and to cover them with branches of the olive tree.

'Fighting yet with much glory for seven times seven moons so that the trinity of the European population with great fear and cries and tears offer their sons as hostages and accept the yoke of wholesome and just laws, loved by all.

'Thus peace will last twenty-five moons.

'In Lutetia (Paris) the Seine reddened with blood will overflow with ruin and death. There will be new seditions of the contentious.

'Thus they will be driven from the palace of the kings by the man of valour, and afterwards great Gaul will be declared by all the nations great and mother of nations. And he, saving the remains of the old blood of the Capets, regulates the destinies of the world, makes himself the sovereign counsellor of all nations, plants a tree without end and dies.'

The reader will no doubt have been conscious of growing scepticism as he pursues this strange document to its close. It is so exact up to the fall of Napoleon and so vague and apocalyptic afterwards, and it is therefore not surprising that we find it first in the *Mémoires* of Josephine by Madame Lenormand, her favourite fortune-teller.

Bareste, writing in 1840, stoutly maintains its authenticity. The story he tells is as follows: At the Revolution large numbers of libraries in private houses, palaces and monasteries were pillaged and their contents turned over to the authorities. A vast mass of books and manuscripts was thus collected and a certain François de Metz was entrusted with the task of going through them, preserving such as seemed of interest and destroying the rest. While engaged on this he came across a number of magical books, probably coming from the Library of St Geneviève in Paris known to be rich in such works, and among these he found a small duodecimo volume, the *Livre des Prophéties* composed by Philippe Dieudonné Noël Olivarius, doctor in medecine, surgeon and astrologer. It was dated 1542.

François de Metz was so struck with its contents, in spite of never having heard of Napoleon, that he copied them out, and this copy Bareste claims to have found among his papers. The copy itself was dated 1793. Bareste himself may have been perfectly honest (his edition of Nostradamus is, on the whole, a scholarly and reassuring work) but what proof is there that the copy was actually made in 1793 or that the book ever existed?

The internal evidence leads one to the exactly opposite conclusion. The 'prophecy' is the work of a Bonapartist writing *after* the fall of Napoleon and indulging, for the second part of his prophecy, in a vague Messianic hope. The same hope distorts the vision and falsifies the judgement of many of the later commentators on Nostradamus. Bareste professes to be reproducing the style exactly and to have merely modernized the spelling. But the style bears only a slight resemblance, in spite of its wilful archaisms, to the style of the sixteenth century. No sixteenth century writer could possibly have written '*appelé Imperator par grand enthousiasme populaire*'. We must abandon the whole picturesque tale. The 'Prophecy of Master Olivarius' is a forgery composed about 1820, and the question of its being (as some writers have contended) the work of Nostradamus need not therefore arise.

There is another work which some of the commentators are even more insistent on attributing to the Prophet of Salon. This is the so-called *Prophétie d'Orval*, which he is said to have composed while staying in the abbey during his wanderings.

The story of its discovery is curiously (and suspiciously) similar to that of the finding of the prophecy of Master Olivarius. Once more the fatal date is 1793. In May of that year, runs the account,[1] several distinguished exiles, including the Bishop of Saint Claude and the Baron de Manonville, found themselves at the Abbey of Orval situated in a secluded glen of the forest of Chiny, in the Ardennes. Louis XVI was to have stayed there if he had not been arrested at Varennes, and it had sheltered General Bouillé and his staff on the occasion of the ill-starred royal flight. The conversation naturally turned on these events and one of the monks declared that they were no surprise to him, for they had all been prophesied beforehand. He then produced a little book from the dusty archives and read the relevant passages. Every one present was struck with astonishment, and five copies are said to have been taken. But the copyists did not copy the portions concerned with the fate of Louis XVI, but only the passages referring to the future. Josserand declares that 'M. Rossigneux, professor at the College of Autun, had read this prophecy in a little book printed in 1800'. No trace

1. See *Deux prophéties célèbres; Prophétie d'Orval; Prophétie de Blois*, P. H. Josserand, Lyon, 1870, and *The Prophecy of Orval* ... translated from the French by H. D. Langdon. London, *Catholic Opinion* Office, 1871.

of this publication has ever been found nor (it is perhaps needless to remark) is any copy known of the original work alleged to have been published in 1544. The Abbey of Orval was reduced to ruins in June, 1793, a month after the copies are said to have been made, and perhaps the sole example of the book perished with it.

Bareste speaks of a copy made in 1823 from an edition printed at Luxemburg in 1544, but he confesses in a footnote that he had never been able to find the original book. The prophecy is however not without interest, in view of its frequent attribution to Nostradamus. It runs as follows:

'In those times a young man, come from over the sea into the land of Celtic Gaul, will manifest himself by force of arms; but the offended great ones will send him to make war in the island of captivity. Victory will bring him back to the first country. The sons of Brutus shall be struck with stupor at his approach: for he will overcome them and take the name Emperor.

'Many high and mighty kings are in a state of fear, for the eagle will carry off many sceptres and many crowns. Footmen and cavaliers carrying bloodstained eagles speed with him like flies through the air; and all Europe is much astonished and bleeding, for he will be so strong that God will seem to fight with him.

'The Church of God consoles itself a little seeing its temples open once more to the strayed sheep, and God is blessed.

'But it is finished, the moons are passed. The Old Man of Sion cries to God from his heart afflicted with sharp pain, and behold the mighty one is blinded by sin and crimes. He leaves the great city with an army so beautiful that the like was never seen. But hardly a warrior will hold firm before the force of the times, and behold the third part of his army and again a third has perished by the cold of the Lord. But two lustres are passed after the century of desolation as I have spoken in its place. The widows and the orphans have cried aloud and, behold God is not deaf.

'The Great Ones bowed down regain power and make a league to overcome so feared a man. Behold comes with them the old blood of the centuries which regains its place in the great city: meanwhile the man much abashed goes to the country beyond the sea from which he came.

'God alone is great; the eleventh moon has not yet shone, and the bloody whip of the Lord returns in the great city: and the old blood leaves the great city.

'God alone is great; he loves his people and hates blood; the fifth moon has shone again on many warriors from the East; Gaul is covered with men and machines of war; all is finished for the man of the sea. Behold again coming the old blood of the Capets.

'God's will is peace and that his holy name be blessed. Then, great and flowering peace shall be in the land of the Gaul. The white flower is in great honour; the Name of God chants many psalms; nevertheless God is still much displeased by reason of his elect and because the holy day is much profaned. Nevertheless there will be a return to God in eight times twelve moons.

'God alone is great; he purges his people with many tribulations; but the wicked will always have an end.

'Behold therefore, a great conspiracy against the white flower grows in the shadow in view of the accursed company; and the poor old blood of the Capets leaves the great city, and there is much rejoicing among the sons of Brutus. Hear how the servants of God cry aloud to God and how God cannot hear through the noise of the arrows which he tempers in his wrath to plunge them into the breast of the wicked.

'Woe to holy Gaul! the cock will efface the white flower, and a great one will call himself King of the People. There will be great commotion among the people and the crown will be placed [on his head] by the hands of workmen who have fought in the great city.

'God alone is great; the reign of the wicked will increase; but let them make haste. Behold the thoughts of holy Gaul are confused and in understanding there is great division.

The King of the People is weak and against him go many of the wicked. He is not well seated and behold God throws him down.

'Cry aloud, sons of Brutus, call upon the beasts who will devour you. Great God! what a noise of arms. It is not yet a full number of moons and behold, come many warriors.

'It is finished: the mountain of God is desolate and cries to God; the sons of Judah have cried to God from the foreign land, and behold God is no more deaf. What fire goes with his arrows! Ten times six moons and then again six times ten moons have nourished his anger. Woe to thee, great city! Behold the kings armed by the Lord; but already the fire has levelled thee to the earth. Yet thy just ones shall not perish, for God has heard them. The place of crime is purged by fire; the great stream, all red with blood, has sent its waters to the sea; and Gaul, which seems ruined, is re-united.

'God loves peace. Come young prince; leave the island of captivity; join together the lion and the white flower.

'That which is foreseen is the will of God; the old blood of the centuries will end once more the long divisions. Then a single shepherd will be seen in holy Gaul. The man strong in God will be firmly established; many wise laws will bring peace. God will be believed, so wise and prudent shall be the scion of the Capets.

'Thanks to the Father of Mercy, holy Sion sings again in her temples to the one great God. Many strayed sheep come to drink in the living stream: three princes and kings put off the mantle of error and hear clearly in the faith of God.

'In those times a great people of the sea will recover, for two parts out of three of their number, the true belief. God is yet blessed during fourteen times six moons and six times thirteen moons. God is weary of his mercies, and yet he wishes for the sake of the good to prolong peace for yet ten times twelve moons.

'God alone is great. The good things are finished; the saints must suffer. The evil man comes of two bloods, and begins to grow. The white flower is observed for ten times six moons and six times twenty moons, then vanishes to appear no more.

'Many evils war against the good in those times; many cities are devoured by fire. Return then, Israel, to the Lord.

'Evil and faithful sects are divided clearly. But it is finished; God alone shall be believed, and the third part of Gaul and again the third part and a half shall be without faith.

'Also shall it be the same with other peoples.

'And behold! already six times three moons and four times five moons and all is divided and the final century has begun.

'After an incomplete number of moons God fights by his two just men and the evil man is overcome. But it is finished. The Most High God sets up a wall of fire which obscures my understanding and I see no more. May He be blessed for evermore.'

Such is the celebrated Prophecy of Orval, and it is obvious that it is not a work of the sixteenth century any more than was the Prophecy of Olivarius. It would seem, even, to be a later work than that, and one is inclined to reject Bareste's date of 1823 and to conclude that it must have been composed in an anti-Orleanist intention some time after the Revolution of 1830. The reference to the Great One who calls himself the King of the People obviously points at Louis-Philippe. It is true that it also prophesies his downfall which did not take place until 1848, whereas it must have been composed before 1840, for that is the date of Bareste's book in which the text is given. It would perhaps not be too rash to assume that this tendenciousness reveals the whole motive of its composition, and it therefore takes its place alongside the forged quatrains against Mazarin as an example of pseudo-prophecy directed to political ends.

From these quagmires of forgery, falsified dates and alleged manuscript copies from non-existent books it is a relief to return to Nostradamus and to tread once more the solid ground of bibliographical certainty.

Bibliography

Principal Early Editions of the Centuries of Nostradamus

Les Prophéties de Me. Michel Nostradamus. Lyon, chez MACÉ BONHOMME. MDLV.

This is the first edition and contains: The Preface of Michel Nostradamus to his prophecies, the Epistle to César, his son, dated March 1st, 1555, and the three first *Centuries* complete and fifty-three quatrains of the fourth. It is excessively rare. Bareste had handled a copy and has left bibliographical details, but the volume he saw, which was then in a private collection, seems to have vanished.

Les Prophéties de M. Michel Nostradamus. Dont il y en a trois cens qui n'ont encore iamais esté imprimees. . . . A Lyon, chez PIERRE RIGAUD [1558 and 1566].

This, the Editio Princeps, a copy of which is in the *Bibliothéque de Paris*, appears to be made up of two fascicules, one, printed in 1558, containing the Preface of Nostradamus, Ad Caesarem Nostradamum filium, and the seven first *Centuries*, of which the last, incomplete, stops at Quatrain 42; the other, printed in 1566, containing the Epistle to '*Henry Roy de France second*', and *Centuries* VIII, IX and X.

Les Prophéties de M. Michel Nostradamus. . . . A Lyon, par BENOIST RIGAUD, 1568.

This contains the same text as the edition of Pierre Rigaud, but with some variants and corrections.

Les Prophéties de M. Michel Nostradamus. Reveuës et corrigées sur la coppie imprimée à Lyon par BENOIST RIGAUD, MDCV.

This edition, which has no name of printer or place of origin, contains, in addition to the above, a dedicatory Epistle to Henri IV and fifty-eight sixains, said to have been found among the papers of Nostradamus and collected by Vincent Sève of Beaucaire.

Other editions appeared at Troyes, 1611; Paris, 1649 (Edition falsely dated 1568 and containing the two forged quatrains against Mazarin); Marseilles, 1643; Paris, 1650; Leyden, 1650; Amsterdam, 1668; Paris, 1668; Paris, 1669; Rouen, 1689; Cologne, 1689;

Lyons, 1697; Lyons, 1698; Riom and Clermont, 1792; Antwerp, 1792; Paris, 1816; Avignon, 1839. In addition some of the commentators such as Bareste and Le Pelletier print the text in full.

Principal Commentators on Nostradamus

LAURENS VIDEL. *Déclaration des abus, ignorances et séditions de Michel Nostradamus.* Avignon, 1558.

ANTOINE COUILLARD. *Les Contredits du seigneur du Pavillon aux fausses et abusives prophéties de Nostradamus*, 1560.

JEAN AIMÉ DE CHAVIGNY. Janus Gallicus. Lyons, 1594.

PLEIADES, DU S[IEUR] DE CHAVIGNY. Lyons, 1609.

ETIENNE JAUBERT. *Eclaircissement des véritables quatrains de maistre Michel Nostradamus*, 1656.

THEOPHILUS GARENCIÈRES. *The True Prophecies or Prognostications of Michael Nostradamus.* London, 1672.

CHEVALIER DE JANT. *Prédictions tirées des Centuries de Nostradamus.* Paris, 1673.

B. GUYNAUD. *La Concordance des Prophéties de Nostradamus.* Paris, 1709.

JEAN DE ROUX (l'Anonyme de Louvicamp). *La Clef de Nostradamus.* Paris, 1710.

D. D. *The Prophecies of Nostradamus concerning ... the Kings and Queens of Great Britain*, 1715.

PIERRE JOSEPH DE HAITZE. *Vie et Testament de Nostradamus.* 1789.

THÉODORE BOUYS. *Nouvelles Considerations ... sur les Oracles ... et particulièrement sur Nostradamus.* Paris, 1806.

DR BELLAND. *Napoléon, premier Empereur des Français, prédit par Nostradamus.* Paris, 1806.

EUGÈNE BARESTE. *Nostradamus.* Paris, 1840.

H. TORNÉ-CHAVIGNY. *L'Histoire prédite et jugée par Nostradamus.* 3 vols. Bordeaux, 1860–2.

ANATOLE LE PELLETIER. *Les Oracles de Michel de Nostredame.* 2 vols. Paris, 1867.

H. TORNÉ-CHAVIGNY. *Nostradamus éclairi*, 1874.

H. TORNÉ-CHAVIGNY. *Influence de Nostradamus dans le Gouvernement de la France*, 1878.

CHARLES A. WARD. *Oracles of Nostradamus*, London [1891].

ELISÉE DU VIGNOIS. *Notre histoire racontée à l'avance par Nostradamus.* Paris, 1910.

CHARLES NICOULLAUD. *Nostradamus, ses prophéties.* Paris, 1914.

P. V. PIOBB. *Le Secret de Nostradamus.* Paris, 1927.

JEAN MOURA ET PAUL LOUVET. *La Vie de Nostradamus.* Paris, 1930.

JACQUES BOULENGER. *Nostradamus (Les Grands Illuminés).* Paris, 1933.

P. V. PIOBB. *Les Vrayes Centuries et Prophéties de Maistre Michel Nostradamus.* Introd. Paris [1936].

M. J. DE MERICOURT. *Gesta Dei Per Francos.* Paris, 1937.

E. RUIR. *Le grand carnage d'après les prophéties de Nostradamus de 1938 à 1947.* Paris, 1938.

E. RUIR. *L'Écroulement de l'Europe, d'après les prophéties de Nostradamus.* Paris, 1939.

E. FONTBRUNE. *Les Prophéties de Maistre Michel Nostradamus.* (2nd Ed.). Sarlat, 1939.

H. I. WOOLF. *Nostradamus.* London, 1944.

E. RUIR. *Nostradamus, ses prophéties 1948–2023.* Paris, 1947.

R. BUSQUET. *Nostradamus, sa famille, son secret.* Paris, 1950.

Other Works Consulted

JOHN AUBREY. *Miscellanies.* 2nd Edition, 1721.

BRANTÔME. *Vie des hommes illustres.*

A. CABANÈS. *Cabinet secret de l'histoire.* Paris, 1897.

CATHERINE DE' MEDICI. *Lettres* (1533–88). 1880–1905.

EUGÈNE DEFRANCE. *Cathérine de Médicis, ses astrologues et ses magiciens-envoûteurs,* Paris, 1911.

G. B. DEPPING. *Les Juifs dans le Moyen-Age.* 1834.

J. W. DUNNE. *An experiment with Time.* London, 1927.

PIERRE ESTIENNE (attrib. to) *Discours merveilleux de la vie de Catherine de Médicis,* 1575.

J. F. C. FULLER. *The Secret Wisdom of the Qabalah.* London [1937].

J. GARINET. *Histoire de la Magie en France.* 1818.

ERNEST HART. *Hypnotism, Mesmerism and the New Witchcraft.* London, 1893.

BERNARD HOLLANDER. *Hypnosis and Self-Hypnosis.* London, 1928.

P. L. JACOB (P. Lacroix). *Curiosités des sciences occultes.* Paris, 1862.

CARL G. JUNG. *The Integration of the Personality.* Translated by S. M. DELL. London, 1940.

ELIPHAS LÉVI. *The History of Magic.* Translated by A. E. WAITE. 2nd Ed. London, 1922.

JEAN MARQUÈS-RIVIÈRE. *Amulettes, Talismans et Pentacles dans des Traditions Orientales et Occidentales.* Paris, 1938.

L. F. A. MAURY. *La Magie et l'astrologie*. Paris, 1860.
CÉSAR NOSTRADAMUS. *L'Histoire et Chronique de Provence*. Lyons, 1614.
BARON DE NOVAYE. *Demain...?* Paris, 1905.
T. K. OESTERREICH. *Possession, Demoniacal and Other*. London, 1930.
PAPUS. *The Tarot of the Bohemians*. Translated by A. P. Morton. London, 1892.
PAPUS. *Traité elémentaire de science occulte*. Paris, 1903.
J. B. RHINE. *New Frontiers of the Mind*. London, 1938.
UPTON SINCLAIR. *Mental Radio*. London, 1930.
JOSEPH SINEL. *The Sixth Sense*. London, 1927.
LYNN THORNDIKE. *A History of Magic and Experimental Science*. 2 vols. London, 1923.
A. E. WAITE. *The Book of Ceremonial Magic*. London, 1911.
MILTON WALDMAN. *Biography of a Family*. London, 1936.
RENÉ WARCOLLIER. *Experiment in Telepathy*. London, 1939.